**UNIVERSITY OF GLAMORGAN
LEARNING RESOURCES CENTRE**

Pontypridd, Mid Glamorgan, CF37 1DL
Telephone: Pontypridd (01443) 482626

Books are to be returned on or before the last date below

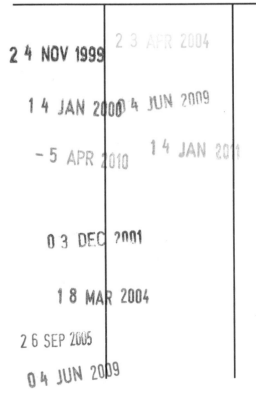

QUANGOS, ACCOUNTABILITY AND REFORM

Quangos, Accountability and Reform

The Politics of Quasi-Government

Edited by

Matthew V. Flinders
Political Economy Research Centre
University of Sheffield

and

Martin J. Smith
Political Economy Research Centre
University of Sheffield

Foreword by David Marquand

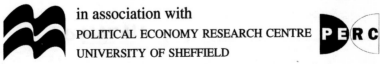

in association with
POLITICAL ECONOMY RESEARCH CENTRE
UNIVERSITY OF SHEFFIELD

First published in Great Britain 1999 by
MACMILLAN PRESS LTD
Houndmills, Basingstoke, Hampshire RG21 6XS and London
Companies and representatives throughout the world

A catalogue record for this book is available from the British Library.

ISBN 0–333–72488–7

First published in the United States of America 1999 by
ST. MARTIN'S PRESS, INC.,
Scholarly and Reference Division,
175 Fifth Avenue, New York, N.Y. 10010

ISBN 0–312–21644–0

Library of Congress Cataloging-in-Publication Data
Quangos, accountability and reform : the politics of quasi-government
/ edited by Matthew V. Flinders and Martin J. Smith.
    p.   cm.
"St. Martin's Press in association with Political Economy Research
Centre, University of Sheffield."
Includes bibliographical references and index.
ISBN 0–312–21644–0 (cloth)
1. Administrative agencies—Great Britain—State supervision.
2. Executive advisory bodies—Great Britain—State supervision.
3. Administrative agencies—State supervision.   4. Executive
advisory bodies—State supervision. 5. Civil society.
I. Flinders, Martin V.   II. Smith, Martin J. (Martin John), 1961–
.
JN409.Q94   1998
352.2'6'0941—dc21   98–28244
                                                          CIP

This book is printed on paper suitable for recycling and made from fully managed and
sustained forest sources.

11676140

10   9   8   7   6   5   4   3   2   1
08   07   06   05   04   03   02   01   00   99

Printed and bound in Great Britain by
Antony Rowe Ltd, Chippenham, Wiltshire

Contents

Foreword by David Marquand   vii

Preface   ix

Notes on Contributors   xi

Part I   History, Perspectives and Debate   1

1   Setting the Scene: Quangos in Context
Matthew V. Flinders   3

2   Diversity and Complexity: the Quango-Continuum
Matthew V. Flinders and Hugh McConnel   17

3   Quangos: Why Do Governments Love Them?
Matthew V. Flinders   26

4   Quangos and Local Democracy
Gerry Stoker   40

Part II   An International Perspective   55

5   Quangos in Germany?
Jürgen Fiedler   57

6   Quangocratization in the Netherlands
Frans L. Leeuw and Sandra van Thiel   72

7   Quangos in New Zealand
Enid Wistrich   84

8   Quangos in Denmark and Scandinavia:
Trends, Problems and Perspectives
Carsten Greve   93

Part III   The Insider's View   109

9   The Housing Corporation:
Multiple Lines of Accountability
*Anthony Mayer (Chief Executive, The Housing
Corporation)*   111

10 Of Ministers, Mandarins and Managers
    Brian Landers (Ex-Director of Finance,
    HM Prison Service)   120

11 Local Government and the Unelected State
    Andrew Purssell (London Borough of Barnet)   132

12 Quango Watch – a Local Authority Perspective
    Andrew Peet (Councillor, Tameside Metropolitan Council)   144

13 A National Health Service in Quangoland
    Sir Peter Baldwin, KCB (Ex-Chief Executive, South East
    Thames Regional Health Authority)   152

14 The Accountability of Training and Enterprise Councils
    Alistair Graham (Ex-Chief Executive, Leeds TEC)   162

15 Balancing the Scales – the Growth, Role and
    Future of the Regulators
    Alan Booker (Ex-Deputy Director General, OFWAT)   180

16 Reforming the Patronage State
    Tony Wright, MP   191

Conclusion   199

17 Realizing the Democratic Potential of Quangos
    Matthew V. Flinders and Martin J. Smith   201

Index   211

Foreword

If quangos did not exist, they would have to be invented. That, of course, is why they do exist – and in such profusion. For quangos are a ubiquitous feature of modern governance, not only in Britain but throughout the developed world and on the supranational as well as the national level. The European Commission is a quango of sorts. So are the IMF and the World Bank. In a world without quangos there would be no World Trade Organization, no European Monetary Institute, no BBC, no Bank of England, no Arts Council and no Sports Council. None of the multifarious agencies created to regulate utilities, police the safety of food and drugs and ensure compliance with anti-discrimination legislation could exist. On the sub-national level, there would be no Training and Enterprise Councils, urban development corporations or housing associations.

Despite (or perhaps because of) their ubiquity, however, debate about the role of quangos in the modern state has been bedevilled by ignorance, special pleading, nostalgia for a largely imaginary past and hope for an unrealizable future. Before the 1997 election, denunciations of the 'quango state' were *de rigueur* among many on the Left – mirroring the situation that existed on the Right before the election of 1979. Implicit in these denunciations were the assumptions that quangos were, by definition, incompatible with democratic accountability, and that accountability could be restored only by returning to a lost golden age when the norms of ministerial and local government responsibility were fully observed.

The quango project of the Political Economy Research Centre at Sheffield University was launched against that background, with three concerns in mind. One was the belief – fully justified by subsequent events – that, irrespective of the rights and wrongs of the case, a change of government would not, in practice, make quangos any less ubiquitous. Quangos, we thought, were here to stay: the question was not how to get rid of them, but what to do with and about them. Our second concern was that, given the virtual certainty that quangos were not about to disappear, the question of how to square them with the basic principles of democratic accountability, transparency and participation was of central importance. Our third concern was a strong suspicion that the alleged golden age of ministerial and local government responsibility had not, in reality, been all that golden in any case since the mechanisms that were supposed to ensure accountability, transparency and participation were defective.

This book marks the latest stage in the PERC quango project and takes the debate on quangos a stage further. Three features of it seem to me particularly valuable. In the first place, it has much to say about foreign experience – a crucial aspect of the whole question, which is all too often forgotten in this parochial country. Second, it contains a series of chapters by practitioners, ranging from the Chief Executives of a Housing Corporation and a Training and Enterprise Council to the parliamentary private secretary to the current Lord Chancellor. These throw invaluable light on the issues of practice and principle involved. Last, but by no means least, the editors, Matthew Flinders and Martin Smith, rightly insist that quangos should – and could – become agents of accountability, strengthening civil society and widening the circle of participation in public affairs. For a government set on democratizing the British state, that message is particularly pertinent.

David Marquand
Principal, Mansfield College,
Oxford

Preface

This book originates from the Political Economy Research Centre's 'Quango Project' which ran between October 1995 and March 1997. The project was directed by Professors David Marquand and Ian Harden, with Hugh McConnel as the Project Officer. The project was generously sponsored by the Joseph Rowntree and Esmee Fairbairn Charitable Trusts and had one defining question: *'Quangos: Why do we have them and what should we do about them?'*

Over the 18 months, a series of high-level workshops were held in London which brought together a mix of politicians, academics, senior civil servants, practitioners, thinktank representatives and members of the media to explore and elucidate the issues surrounding quasi-government. The aim of the project was to design a realistic reform agenda which would tie quangos down with democratic credentials – without impairing economic efficiency. Our involvement in this project not only fuelled our interest in the topic but also allowed us to meet a range of individuals whose energy, enthusiasm and ideas convinced us of the need to collect their opinions and viewpoints in one collection.

It is no accident that this book has been written and published at this particular time. The new Labour government, elected on a platform of high political morality and constitutional reform, offers the opportunity for a reappraisal of the quango debate and the introduction of positive reforms. It is also fitting that this collection is being published by Macmillan who also published the three volumes arising from the 1975 Carnegie Corporation's Anglo-American project on accountability and Anthony Barker's seminal collection *Quangos in Britain* in 1982.

Owing to the contemporary nature of this debate this book has been put together in a very short time. The editors would like to thank all the contributors for delivering their chapters in good time and embracing this project with such enthusiasm. A special debt of thanks is due to Tony Payne, Andrew Gamble, Gavin Kelly, Dominic Kelly, Claire Annesley and the indefatigable Sylvia McColm for all their help and encouragement. The support and friendship offered by Phil, Jane and Susanna Crowson was a key factor in the success of the project. Finally, we would like to thank all the anonymous officials, from a range of organizations and government departments, who have been a constant source of inspiration and information.

Matthew V. Flinders
Martin J. Smith

Notes on Contributors

Sir Peter Baldwin, KCB, Chairman of the Charities Aid Foundation, served in the Cabinet office and for 22 years in HM Treasury, rising to Deputy Secretary, and then became Permanent Secretary of the Department of Transport in 1976. From 1983 to 1991 he was Chairman of the South East Thames Regional Health Authority.

Alan Booker retired from the post of Deputy Director General of Water Services (OFWAT) in February 1988. He is now a consultant to the World Bank on private sector participation, institutional reform and regulation. He is a civil engineer by profession with wide experience in environmental management.

Jürgen Fiedler is Sub-Director in the German Federal Ministry of Finance, Bonn. He is currently working mainly in the areas of administrative organization and personnel in the ministry. For several years his work in the German financial administration has focused on questions of financial federalism.

Matthew V. Flinders is a research officer at the Political Economy Research Centre, the University of Sheffield. His research interests focus on bureaucratic reform and quasi-government and he was a research assistant on the original PERC Quango Project. He is currently working on the ESRC Whitehall Programme.

Alistair Graham is Chairman of the Northern Ireland Parades Commission. Prior to this he was chief executive at The Leeds TEC, the Calderdale and Kirklees TEC, Director of The Industrial Society and General Secretary of the Civic and Public Services Association.

Carsten Greve is an assistant professor in public administration at the University of Copenhagen, Denmark.

Brian Landers was the first Finance Director of the Prison Service from 1993 to 1996. Prior to that he held senior private sector appointments in the UK and overseas. After a successful period with W.H. Smith Retail he is now chief executive of Waterstone's.

Frans L. Leeuw is professor and director of the Department of Humanities, Netherlands Open University, and a part-time professor at the Department of Sociology, University of Utrecht, the Netherlands.

Anthony Mayer is chief executive of the Housing Corporation. Between 1965 and 1985 he served as a senior civil servant which included a period in the Central Policy Review Staff (1974–6) and as the Principal Private Secretary to the Secretary of State for Transport (1980–2). After a successful period in the private sector he joined the Housing Corporation in 1991.

Hugh McConnel was the PERC Quango project officer and comes from a background in public sector management, specializing in management information. He is now Deputy Director of Information for an NHS Trust.

Andrew Peet is a councillor for Tameside metropolitan borough council with a special responsibility for 'Quango Watch'. Working with a colleague, Cllr June Evans, he has produced a register of quangos that have an impact on the borough.

Andrew Purssell is currently employed as Environmental Policy Officer by the London Borough of Barnet. Between 1989 and 1997 he worked for the Association of District Councils, latterly dealing with constitutional and contractual issues. He is a graduate of London and Kent Universities.

Martin J. Smith is a Reader in politics at the University of Sheffield. He is currently researching the changing role of central government departments under the ESRC Whitehall programme. His publications include *Contemporary British Conservatism* (co-editor) and *The Core Executive in Britain*.

Gerry Stoker is Professor of Politics at the University of Strathclyde and Programme Director of the ESRC Local Governance Research Programme. He has lectured at a number of other universities and was visiting professor, CULMA, at Wayne State University, 1990–1. He is the author or editor of more than ten books and was a member of the Commission for Local Democracy.

Sandra van Thiel is a research fellow at the inter-university Centre for Social Science Theory and Methodology (ICS), Department of Sociology, University of Utrecht, the Netherlands.

Enid Wistrich is research co-ordinator in the School of History and Politics at Middlesex University, where she was formerly Reader in Politics and Public Administration, and was a visiting lecturer at Waikato University, New Zealand. She has been a local councillor and a governing member of numerous quangos.

Tony Wright is the Member of Parliament for Cannock Chase. A former member of the Public Service Select Committee in the Commons, he is the author of *Citizens and Subjects* (Routledge, 1993) and many other books and articles.

Part I

History, Perspectives and Debate

1 Setting the Scene: Quangos in Context

Matthew V. Flinders

The Keynesian post-war bureaucracy has been the subject of a prolonged attack. Whether one views this as 'reinventing government', a new global paradigm or even the abandoning of government is disputable. However, what is beyond challenge is that the structure and working of the public sector have changed dramatically in recent years. The traditional bureaucratic structures which formed the backbone of the state have crumbled at both the central and local levels. While this is not an exclusively British phenomenon, recent reforms have brought with them a fundamental questioning of the role of the state and a concomitant blurring of the lines between the public and the private spheres. Just as liberal democracy is said to have triumphed over socialism, the private sector has been seen to triumph over the public sector as the private sector's procedures, practices and beliefs are increasingly imposed on the public.

INTRODUCTION

Today's society is an uncertain one. British politics is struggling to offer the public security and confidence at a time when the pressures of globalization demand flexibility, short-termism and increased geographic mobility. It is a time when politicians must find new and innovative solutions to new and increasingly pressing problems. The role, size and structure of the public sector have been at the forefront of this debate for some time. The need to cut public spending, increase efficiency and exercise fiscal restraint has forced, and will continue to force, politicians to move away from traditional public sector organizations and towards more efficient, but democratically questionable semi-autonomous organizations: in a word, quangos.

The demise of the classic public/private dichotomy has created a new tier of governance in British politics. This is made up of a range of bodies which are neither public nor private, but are a hybrid. They are organizations that utilize private sector methods to achieve public aims in the most efficient manner possible. They are 'quasi' in every respect: quasi-independent, quasi-public, quasi-private, quasi-legitimate and

quasi-accountable. We are no longer governed by politicians alone but by a
'new magistracy' of unknowable, and often untouchable, individuals.

Defining what is meant by the term 'quango' is a difficult task in any
one country and it is all but impossible to produce an international definition which is valid over a number of different constitutions and approaches
to government. What is more, the trend in government to which I have
already alluded means that there is little benefit in seeking to label one
body a quango and another not. The world of quangos should be seen as a
continuum from Next Steps[1] agencies to TECs and beyond into the world
of contracting out and privatization: a huge range of diverse bodies, but
each in its own way posing questions of independence, legitimacy and
accountability. This book's working definition is therefore necessarily
woolly: 'Any body that spends public money to fulfil a public task but
with some degree of independence from elected representatives.'

Employing this rather loose and 'catch-all' definition, which allowed
each author a degree of flexibility, was a reluctant but necessary decision.
The number and range of bodies commonly referred to under the acronym
'quango' is already so wide as to render the term both priceless and
worthless, or as Anthony Barker once wrote, 'as useless as it is inelegant'
(1982: 220). The term 'quango' represents no firm, tangible or clear organization, but instead provides a continuum on which a diverse range of
bodies can be placed.

This lack of definitional clarity has obviously hampered serious discussion and constructive research. The last Conservative government, for
obvious reasons, employed a limited definition, which included only Non-
Departmental Public Bodies (NDPBs). These are bodies that exist at the
national level and 'have a role in the processes of national government but
which are not government departments or parts of one, and which accordingly operate to a greater or lesser extent at arm's length from ministers
although ministers remain accountable to Parliament for their performance' (Cm 3179: 6).

There are four types of NDPB: advisory bodies, which consist of groups
of specialists set up by ministers to advise them and their departments on
matters within their spheres of interest, for example the Expert Advisory
Committee on AIDS, Advisory Committee on Pesticides and the Advisory

---

[1]Much to the annoyance of senior civil servants the authors have always classed
Next Steps agencies as quangos. While they are officially still parts of departments,
their arm's length relationship with ministers raises questions of accountability,
legitimacy and control, which mirror any of the wider bodies. Agencies should be
classed as the first step on the quango continuum, maybe even quasi-quangos!

Committee on Conscientious Objectors; tribunals fulfil a quasi-judicial function in that they, independently of the executive, decide the rights and obligations of citizens between each other or between individuals and the state, for example the Industrial Tribunals and the Social Security Appeals Tribunals; Boards of Visitors oversee the penal establishments in Great Britain; and finally, executive NDPBs are usually set up under statute and enjoy both financial and managerial independence, for example the Legal Aid Board, Housing Corporation or the regulators. The number of different types of NDPB varies greatly from department to department (see Table 1.1).

For the Conservative government, concentrating on NDPBs was politically convenient as statistically their numbers had fallen by 45 per cent, a drop of 973 bodies (from 2,197 to 1,194) between 1979 and 1996 (see Table 1.2).

Among the quangos that were abolished, privatized or declassified between 1995 and 1996 were the National Breastfeeding Working Group, the Polar Medal Groups and several of the New Town Development Corporations; while those created included the Environment Agency, the Scottish Salmon Task Force and the Pensions Ombudsman (see Johnson, 1996; Wolmar, 1996).

Despite the fact that, using the Conservative government's definition, the number of quangos would have appeared to have fallen, this measure is an unreliable indicator of their activity or power. More reliable is the amount of public money channelled into these bodies. Here lies the paradox: despite a reduction of 45 per cent in the number of executive NDPBs, the amount they spend has increased in the same period by over 300 per cent, from £6 billion in 1979 to £21.4 billion in 1996.

The definition of what bodies are included in the government's figures and reports is highly controversial. Despite the fact that appointed quasi-autonomous bodies have burgeoned in the health and education sectors, the government does not include the 429 NHS Trusts or the 108 health authorities, because these are defined as 'local bodies' with no national interest. Nor does it include the 123 Next Steps agencies that have been created since 1988, which, despite their formal position as parts of their parent departments, are designed to be semi-independent and have been the focus of concerns about their control, accountability and future within the public sector.

The lack of an agreed definition, and the employment of both mini-malist and maximalist perspectives, has undermined academic research and led to a heated debate as differing definitions produce widely varying indicators of quango numbers and activity (Hogwood, 1995). Compare and contrast, for example, the government's own figures with those of

Matthew V. Flinders

Table 1.1: Selected Departmental Breakdown of NDPBs

Dept.	Executive NDPBs			Advisory bodies	Tribunals	Boards	Total NDPBs
	No. 1 April 1996	Staff 1 April 1996	Total expenditure (millions)				
MAFF	36	1,900	£130	38	4	—	78
MOD	7	300	£13	16	—	—	23
DfEE	15	13,900	£8,760	64	2	—	81
DOE	32	19,100	£3,350	15	3	—	50
HO	9	2,200	£120	12	11	132	164
SO	41	8,900	£2,100	97	3	—	141
DTI	28	14,400	£1,870	25	7	—	60
DoT	4	900	£68	2	1	—	7
WO	25	2,100	£880	26	5	—	56
Total (all depts)	309	107,000	£21,420	674	75	136	1,194

Notes: For ease of interpretation, expenditure over £100 million has been rounded to the nearest £10 million; staff numbers over 1,000 have been rounded to the nearest 100. Therefore totals may not be exact. (a) Figures include civil sevants at the Advisory, Conciliation and Arbitration Service, and the Health and Safety Commission and Executive. (b) Excludes those bodies which in Northern Ireland fulfil functions carried out by local government in Great Britain.

Source: Public Bodies 1996 (at http:/www.open.gov.uk/co/publicbo.htm).

Table 1.2: The Number of NDPBs in 1979 and then annually from 1982 to 1995

Year	Executive NDPBs				Total NDPBs
	Number	Staff	Total expenditure (millions)	Expenditure by Depts in support of all NDPBs (millions)	
1979	492	217,000	£6,150	£70	2,167
1982	450	205,500	£8,330	£87	1,810
1983	431	196,700	£9,940	£94	1,691
1984	402	141,200	£7,280	£111	1,681
1985	399	138,300	£7,770	£116	1,654
1986	406	146,300	£8,240	£116	1,658
1987	396	148,700	£9,100	£112	1,643
1988	390	134,600	£9,450	£118	1,648
1989	395	118,300	£9,410	£142	1,555
1990	374	117,500	£11,870	£114	1,539
1991	375	116,400	£13,080	£106	1,444
1992	369	114,400	£13,750	£150	1,412
1993	358	111,300	£15,410	£170	1,389
1994	325	110,200	£18,330	£170	1,345
1995	320	109,200	£20,840	£190	1,227
1996	309	107,000	£21,420	£190	1,194

Notes: (a) Figures include civil servants at the Advisory, Conciliation and Arbitration Service, and the Health and Safety Commission and Executive. (b) Current prices. (c) Staff and expenditure figures exclude the English and Welsh Water Authorities which were reclassified as nationalized industries. Staff numbers in 1983 were approximately 58,000, expenditure was approximately £2,600 million.
Source: Public Bodies 1996 (at http:/www.open.gov.uk/co/publicbo.htm).

Weir and Hall (1994). The government's quango count includes only national NDPBs, whereas Weir and Hall's includes local and regional bodies, e.g. housing associations, NHS Trusts, police authorities, grant maintained schools, Training and Enterprise Councils (TECs). The government's minimalist quango definition gives a figure of 309 bodies (ENDPBs) with an annual expenditure of around £18 billion, whereas Weir and Hall's wider definition produces a total of 5,573 bodies spending £46.6 billion – nearly a third of total government expenditure (Weir, 1995).

8   *Matthew V. Flinders*

The construction of a definition is in itself a political decision. The Conservative government, by focusing on NDPBs, could claim that they had reduced the number of quangos as the number of NDPBs was falling due to structural reorganizations (see Gay, 1994). But at the same time the financial power of these NDPBs was increasing threefold, and the number of local and regional quasi-autonomous organizations, which were governed from Whitehall but not included in the government's own definition, was growing rapidly.

This lack of definitional and structural clarity severely impedes progress. A solution to this problem would be to develop a sub-sectional map of the quango topography which would accept the diversity inherent in the quango debate while allowing for increased clarity and focused research into specific areas of this continuum (see Chapter 3). No statement or proposal for reform will fit every type of quango, but proposals can be drawn up to fit specific sub-sections, such as Next Steps agencies or TECs. Plotting the position of various bodies on such a continuum also allows the process of 'quango drift'[2] to be followed and analysed.

HISTORY AND DEBATE

Quangos have been readily used and created by both Labour and Conservative governments, despite the disparaging cries of both parties when in opposition and token cullings when in power. They have existed in their present from since the Second World War, and semi-independent public bodies have been part of British governance for hundreds of years. In many ways the quango state mirrors the British constitution itself. It is flexible, executive-centric and ill-defined, has evolved in a piecemeal and incremental fashion and, for the most part, relies on the 'good chaps' theory of governance, which has, until recently, lacked formal rules and regulations (Doig, 1996).

Although the reasoning behind the increased creation and use of quangos over and instead of traditional bureaucratic structures will be

---

[2]Quango drift refers to the tendency for the degree of independence enjoyed by an organization to increase gradually, and its position to move along the arm's-length axis, as long as the body enjoys public confidence and there are no major incidents. For example, the movement of sections of departments into agencies and then into contracted-out tasks and then complete privatization. The gradually increasing autonomy and independence of the Bank of England would make an interesting case in point.

explored later (see Chapter 2) it is worth briefly mentioning some of the key factors at this early stage. From a managerial perspective the allocation of a task to a semi-independent organization does offer positive benefits. The creation of a new, single-purpose organization allows the introduction of private sector management techniques and focused policy-making. This, theoretically, should deliver increased efficiency and value for money (VFM). The creation of new bodies also opens up the opportunity for increasing the role of experts and specialists. There are also obvious benefits of removing many executive areas from the day-to-day rigours of partisan party politics. It is also true that scientific and medical advances have laid new issues at the door of politics – genetic engineering, for example. Overloaded politicians are neither capable nor willing to take on the responsibility for these issues and the result is often a new quango: in this case, the Human Fertilization and Embryology Authority.

It is easy to disguise subtly the reasons behind the creation of new quangos in neutral-sounding managerial rhetoric such as VFM, increased efficiency and the need for specialist control, but this would provide only half the truth. Without doubt one of the key driving forces behind the quango explosion of recent years was pure and simple politics. Although parties might employ anti-quango rhetoric when in opposition, the attraction of these bodies becomes apparent on gaining office and it will be interesting to see whether the new Labour government can resist the temptation of the quango. As the Labour Party knows well, they can be used to circumnavigate the democratic process and undermine troublesome local authorities; they offer a tool which can be used to conceal the true size of the bureaucracy; and they provide a plethora of prizes to reward the party faithful. The creation of a new quango is also a convenient way for ministers to delegate a political hot potato, the creation of the Commission for Racial Equality in 1976 being a classic example. They are also a way of rebuilding public confidence when the public has lost faith in the established political structures. Contemporary British politics provides us with a host of examples of this – the recent creation of the Food Safety Council to take over functions previously conducted by the Ministry of Agriculture Fisheries and Food in light of the BSE scandal and the creation of the Criminal Cases Review Commission in light of the series of recent miscarriages of justice are two recent cases. An older example is the creation of the Committee for the Safety of Medicines (CSM), which was formed in direct response to the public outcry following the Thalidomide disaster of 1959–61.

In Britain, quangos have a very poor public image. They are portrayed in the media as illegitimate, corrupt, sleazy, unaccountable and fundamentally undemocratic. No doubt many of these accusations contain an element of truth, but it should not be forgotten that quangos also have a positive side. Indeed, Dr David Clark, Chancellor of the Duchy of Lancaster, recently requested that the quango debate be approached in a 'non-hysterical way' which accepted both the positive and negative aspects of quangos (*The Stakeholder*, Vol. 1, No. 3, 1997).

On the positive side a number of attributes can be listed: quangos do place sensitive issues away from the vagaries of party politics; they allow the introduction of the most suitable management techniques; they attract experts, who would not otherwise have become involved, into politics and the policy-making process; they are an efficient, cost-effective and quick way of getting information; and they involve a large number of people in the public sector on a voluntary basis – the vast majority of individuals serving on quango boards are not remunerated but are volunteers, who give their time for expenses only. Potential reforms should be careful not to throw out the baby with the bath water.

Take, for example, the regulators. These executive NDPBs now play a central role in protecting the public from privatized utilities providers. In recent years they have often been more outspoken and aggressive than opposition frontbenchers. Surveys indicate that the public places a high degree of trust in these regulatory offices created since the privatization of gas, water, the railways and, more recently, the National Lottery. Their independence is taken for granted but if the last 18 years are taken into account, their creation, power and willingness to take on the private sector on behalf of the public are remarkable. Thatcher detested and aimed to abolish or reduce both bureaucracy and regulation wherever she found it, but here we have a new breed of powerful regulatory bureaucrats who enjoy both high public confidence and a large element of discretion. Mr Spottiswoode in gas, Mr Byatt in water and Professor Littlechild in electricity have become the public's protectors against the monopolistic providers of sensitive public services.

But from a democratic perspective what right do these individuals have to fulfil this role? They are appointed, only notionally accountable to Parliament, they have only to produce an annual report and are subject to the most cosmetic and sporadic parliamentary scrutiny. Nevertheless, the regulators command public confidence thanks to their aggressive style and the inability of the respective industry to 'capture' the regulator. For example, Mr Cruikshank, Chief Executive of OFTEL, is currently protecting Britain's digital telecommunications network from Rupert Murdoch, and Mr Swift, of the Office for Rail Regulation, has played a key role in highlighting Railtrack's under-investment in the railways and also demanding the release of publicly sensitive information on franchises which would otherwise have been withheld.

Quasi-government is fundamental to any analysis of British politics, as it is now a critical layer of governance which, despite rhetoric to the contrary, is unlikely to be dismantled under any government. There is a growing concern that these reforms have focused too heavily on efficiency and effectiveness to the detriment of democratic principles, such as legitimacy and accountability. Although the issues of accountability and legitimacy will be strands running throughout this book, the aim is not to focus exclusively on these issues but to attempt to engender a fresh and original reappraisal of this debate which is born in the acceptance that, despite their suspicious democratic credentials, quangos are here to stay. Consequently, this book seeks to reinvigorate the currently insipid academic literature by avoiding the voluminous anti-quango polemics, and instead aims to construct a realistic range of reforms which will confer an element of democratic legitimacy on these bodies without reducing their independence or efficiency.

Although the literature on British quangos is substantial, this book offers two particularly illuminating and revealing perspectives.

The second element the book offers is a comparative analysis of quangos. Although much of the literature on New Public Management (NPM) stresses the global nature of the reforms, on the whole the British quango debate has suffered from a severe lack of comparative analysis (Greve, Flinders and Thiel, forthcoming). By examining countries as diverse as The Netherlands, Denmark, New Zealand and Germany it is clear that quangos are by no means a British phenomenon and have a long and distinguished history in many countries. Despite clear differences in institutional structure and political culture there is much to be learnt from the trends and experiences of other countries.

Part III, 'An Insider's View', brings together a collection of essays written by individuals who are closely involved in the central issues of the quango debate due to the nature of the posts they hold. These include a local government official, a councillor, a former senior civil servant, the Chief Executive of one of the largest executive NDPBs, the Chief Executive of a TEC, a former Chief Executive of a Regional Health Authority and the chairman of the all-party parliamentary committee on constitutional affairs. In these chapters the authors highlight the growth of quangos, suggest ways in which their work could be improved and tentatively plot the future of the quango state.

It is interesting to compare and contrast these with the official government view and also academic opinions. It is apparent from the various chapters that the roles and relationships between quangos and local and central government are by no means clear. It is this confusion over respective roles and responsibilities which gives the quangos flexibility, but it is also at the root of many of the problems over accountability and independence. Moreover, the Chief Executives of quangos harbour concerns about their own lack of accountability and legitimacy and actively seek ways to break down the 'them and us' mentality that exists currently between local government and quangos. Indeed, one of the main aims of this book was, for the first time, to bring together the views of politicians, academics, policymakers, civil servants, local government officials and practitioners in the belief that it was only through an inclusive and constructive dialogue that progress could be made.

THE FUTURE

The British constitutional settlement is currently being rewritten by a new Labour government. The importance of this cannot be overstated and many of the plans will have a major effect on the quango state. The Labour government is currently launching the process through which Britain's first Freedom of Information Act will be drafted and implemented. The lack of a clear public/private divide is hampering the construction of a Freedom of Information Act (FIA). Where does the public sector end and the private begin? Should the Act apply to private companies that provide a public service or spend public money? How can the right to public information be meaningfully combined with commercial confidentiality? All these questions need to be answered through a long and exhaustive consultation process, but once answered the existence of a strong and coherent FIA would place the quango debate in a new environment in which the public once again become citizens instead of consumers and are empowered with legal rights to information and access.

Labour's plans for devolution to a Scottish Parliament, Welsh Assembly and ten English Regional Assemblies provide a new constitutional infrastructure to oversee and shadow the quango state. For example, the government White Paper, *A Voice for Wales*, on Welsh devolution outlines significant plans for Welsh quangos. The White Paper indicates that the number of quangos will be reduced from 45 to 36, with a further review of all the existing bodies (see *Guardian*, 22 July 1997). The nine to be abolished include two health authorities, two TECs, the Cardiff Bay Development Corporation, the Development Board for Rural Wales and the Land Authority for Wales. They have a combined budget of

£70 million and the savings will go towards funding the new Welsh Assembly.

As Chapter 2 highlights, quangos tend to have an element of immortality; abolition is rarely what it seems. Often quango culls transpire to be clever structural reorganizations which usually revolve around the amalgamation of several smaller bodies into one larger one. This is the case in the plans for Welsh devolution. Several of the quangos which are to be abolished, including the Development Board for Rural Wales, Land Authority for Wales and the Welsh Development Agency, are actually to be amalgamated into one 'super-quango', to be called the Economic Development Agency (*A Voice for Wales*, paras 2.5–2.12).

But despite claims by some backbench Labour MPs that the promised bonfire of quangos has not gone far enough, the government has clearly indicated its willingness to grasp the quango nettle. Under the devolution plans published in the White Paper on Welsh devolution, ministers would take immediate steps to reform the Welsh quango state even before the new Assembly is created. Although disappointed with the narrow yes vote in the Welsh referendum, Ron Davies, the Welsh Secretary, has announced that substantive legislation will be passed by the government to abolish the nine bodies already mentioned as soon as time can be found in the legislative time table. The new Welsh Assembly will meet for the first time on 6 May 1999 and its 60 elected members will have the powers to review, reform and abolish the remaining appointed bodies as they see fit. The White Paper also outlines some significant proposals for increasing accountability and local representation. For example, the new government will change the criteria for TEC membership to make specific provision for elected local authority members, with all other board vacancies being openly advertised (para. 2.18).

Devolution also offers the opportunity to forge a new relationship between local and central government based on partnership instead of friction. It offers local government, which has been 'hollowed out' in terms of both functions and funding over the last 18 years, the opportunity to build a new co-operative relationship with appointed public bodies. For example, the plans for Welsh devolution offer Wales's 22 unitary councils a guarantee that they will not suffer any reduction in powers with the establishment of an Assembly and may even gain from the redistribution of quango functions.

Although quangos surfaced as a significant issue during the publication of the plans for Welsh devolution, it is interesting to contrast the complete absence of any debate on the topic when the government's White Paper on Scottish devolution was published. This does not represent a lack of quangos in Scotland nor the lack of any mention of them in the White Paper. On the contrary, *Scotland's Parliament* is replete with constructive sentences on the issue. For example: 'It [the new Parliament] will receive reports and will be able to investigate and monitor their activities; and it will be able to alter their structure or wind up existing bodies and create new ones' (para. 2.9).

Labour's plans for the creation of nine regional assemblies in England may have attracted little media attention, but they need to be considered in the context of the quango debate. Indeed, in opposition the creation of directly elected regional assemblies was highlighted as a possible panacea to the problems of quasi-government. It is an interesting reflection of the new government's commitments and priorities that in their first Queen's Speech, plans were announced to create a new breed of powerful quangos in the form of nine Regional Development Agencies (RDAs) but at the same time plans to create regional assemblies to shadow these new bodies, which had been championed in opposition, were sidelined (see particularly the Millan Report, 1996: 33–6; Parker and Tighe, 1997: 1).

The role of the RDAs will be to: promote inward investment; help and encourage small business; and co-ordinate regional economic development. Few would dispute the need to foster economic regeneration at a regional level, but the establishment of these bodies should be mirrored by the concomitant creation of a new tier of democratically elected regional government to oversee both these RDAs and other quasi-autonomous bodies (see *The Financial Times*, 4 August 1997: 7).

Although it is envisaged that the RDAs will work closely with a variety of bodies and organizations, such as regional government offices and TECs, it is disappointing that the boards and directors of RDAs will be appointed by ministers and their accountability is only secured through the tenuous line of ministerial accountability to Parliament. The need for regional economic growth is not doubted, but should not be achieved at the cost of democratic principles, such as acountability and control. Regional assemblies, appointed in the first instance and directly elected within two years, would not detract from the RDAs' economic potential but improve the quality of both co-ordination and coherent policy-making, while at the same time ensuring accountability and transparency at the regional level.

Given the utility of ministerial accountability to Parliament in recent years, and in the absence of formal regional assemblies, the existing regional structures appear to be the only mechanism capable of securing any true accountability. Although informal regional assemblies already exist, such as the Yorkshire and Humberside regional assembly, their structure is far from comprehensive or complete and it is doubtful whether they would be able to fill the constitutional lacunae of policing a new breed of regional quangos. Even the establishment of regional assemblies in the future is far from certain. Should the Welsh referendum produce a negative result the future of devolution in England would become much more uncertain while the creation and future of RDAs is already secure.

In 1982 Anthony Barker optimistically hoped that the term quango would 'have only a brief life, dying out with the political campaign against governmental bodies when that has run its course, probably during 1980' (p. 220). His optimism was misplaced, but we are now on the verge of a crucial period for the future of this large layer of governance. The new Labour government has a clear choice. It can either maintain the status quo and replace the Tory placement with Labour sympathizers, or it can embark on a search for a new constitutional equilibrium in which these bodies still exist but are subject to a range of democratic controls and safeguards.

In many ways the first path is much easier for the new government to follow as it is straight and clear and offers immediate political rewards and advantages. It is to the credit of the government that they have embarked upon the first steps along the second path which is strewn with constitutional hurdles and party political pot-holes. This book provides no map to the second path, nor does it guarantee a safe journey, but the editors feel that by taking into account the wide range of views and opinions expressed in this volume, and the lessons to be learnt from the comparative analysis, the new government might avoid just one or two of the many obstacles they will encounter on their way to creating a new, more open, accountable and inclusive public sector.

REFERENCES

Cm 3179 (1996) *Spending Public Money: Governance and Audit Issues* (London: HMSO).

Doig, A. (1996) 'From Lynskey to Nolan: the Corruption of British Politics and Public Service?', *Journal of Law and Society*, Vol. 23, No. 1, pp. 36–56.

Flinders, M. V. and Thiel, S. van (1997) 'Going Dutch – Quangos in Holland', *The Stakeholder*, Vol. 1, No. 4.

Gay, O. (1994) *Quangos and Non-Departmental Public Bodies*. Research paper 94/67. Home Affairs Section, House of Commons Library.

Greve, C. Flinders, M. and Thiel, S. van (1998) 'Quangos – What's in a Name?' (forthcoming).

Hogwood, B. (1995) 'The Growth of Quangos: Evidence and Explanations', in F. Ridley and D. Wilson, *The Quango Debate* (Oxford: Oxford University Press).

Hood, C. (1995) 'Contemporary Public Management: a New Global Paradigm', *Public Policy & Administration*, Vol. 10, No. 2, pp. 104–17.

Johnson, P. (1996) 'Quangos Dwindle but Spend More than Ever', *Daily Telegraph*, 11 December.

Local Government Association (1997) *Regional Development Agencies*, Circular, 19 June.

Osborne, D. and Gaebler, T. (1992) *Reinventing Government* (London: Plume).

Painter, C. (1994) 'Public Service Reform: Re-Inventing or Abandoning Government?', *Political Quarterly* July/Sept, pp. 242–63.

Parker, G and Tighe, C. (1997) 'Labour puts English Assemblies Plan on Hold', *The Financial Times*, 22 August, p. 1.

Pike, A. (1997) 'Plans for Agencies Sparks Accountability Fear', *The Financial Times*, 4 August p. 7.

Pike, A. (1997) 'Mixed Feelings on Diversity in the Regions' *The Financial Times*, 4 August p. 7.

Report of the Regional Policy Commission (1996) 'Renewing the Regions: Strategies for Regional Economic Development' (Sheffield Hallam University: PAVIC Publications) (The Millan Report).

Ridley, F. (1995) 'Re-Inventing British Government', *Parliamentary Affairs*, Vol. 48, No. 3, pp. 375–401.

Weir, S. and Hall, W. (1994) EGO *Trip: Extra-Governmental Organisations in the UK and their Accountability*, The Democratic Audit of the UK (University of Essex: Democractic Audit/Scarman Trust).

Wolmar, C. (1996) 'Quangos Fall to the Cull but their Costs just Rise and Rise', *The Independent*, 11 December, p. 13.

2 Diversity and Complexity: The Quango-Continuum

Matthew V. Flinders and Hugh McConnel

This chapter explores the 'What is a quango?' question. In theory it would be convenient if we could offer a narrow, clear and widely accepted definition of a quango. The debate about the minimalist and maximalist definitions in Chapter 1 highlights the impossibility of creating such a definition. Nevertheless common characteristics do exist amongst certain species of quango, but there are no single solutions to accountability which can imposed across the whole sphere of quasi-government. A quango continuum is offered as a methodological tool on which to place the range of bodies commonly referred to as quangos. This allows similarities and differences to be highlighted and the phenomenon of 'quango drift' to be followed. The chapter concludes with a general discussion about accountability in theory and the accountability of these bodies. Specific reform proposals will be the topic of the final chapter.

MAPPING OUT THE TERRITORY

The word 'quango' has permeated society. The term is found in daily papers; it ricochets around the airwaves; it is even found lurking in the lyrics of songs by popular bands. Everyone knows what a quango is – except those of us who have tried to define them! Looking back 20 years or more, a definition might be: 'A body fulfilling a public function and spending public money, but with some independence from directly elected politicians.' Such a definition includes the Arts Council as well as bodies first appearing in the 1970s such as the Equal Opportunities Commission. Today such a definition includes Next Steps Agencies and the regulators of the privatized utilities, through NDPBs to TECs.

So what should our present definition be? Our first inclination is to seek a narrower wording, to get back to NDPBs such as the Housing Corporation. Yet isn't that to miss the point? Public concern is centred on fears about the accountability of bodies with independence from politicians. (It also centres on distrust of politicians, which is a point we will return to.) The degree of independence varies, but we now have a wide range of bodies raising issues of independence and accountability. There is a trend in Britain, and in many other European countries as well as Australia and New Zealand, towards the greater use of bodies with some independence from politicians. Pliatzky (1992) is right to point out that Next Steps agencies are constitutionally still part of their departments, but recent incidents have shown that they too raise issues of independence, control and accountability. TECs largely perform public functions and their private law basis does not relieve them of the need for accountability within a democracy. How do quasi-independent regulators fit into ministerial accountability?

We do not suggest that there is a single solution to concerns about the accountability of this huge range of bodies. Common characteristics do exist within a particular species of quango. such as TECs, but any attempt to compare between species ends up with too many exceptions to allow a single way forward. Yet similar issues arise in different species; common lessons can be learned. So it seems essential to view the whole range of bodies rather than to attempt an artificial boundary. Call them what you will, the bodies we are examining come within that original definition of 'fulfilling a public function and spending public money, but with some independence from directly elected politicians'. We do not consider tribunals, for they are governed by quasi-judicial processes which are not currently a matter of public concern. Advisory bodies are harder to pass over. The official view is that they only offer advice to ministers, yet by virtue of their specialist knowledge some advisory bodies produce recommendations which effectively determine ministers' decisions.

Consequently, it is difficult to provide a definition with clear boundaries. Anyone doubting that should consider the bodies listed in Figure 2.1. Where would you place them with respect to central government, and why? (For simplicity, we have restricted the figure to central government, but quangos have relationships with local and EU levels, and now there is regional government and devolution in the wings. Chapter 3 clearly illustrates that quangos have been a means of moving power from local to central government.)

The vertical axis of Figure 2.1 picks up on a question inherent in our definition, what is 'public'? Partnerships are being developed between public and private provision. Indeed there is no agreed line on where 'public' ends. Public services do not have to be publicly supplied, but they will still be publicly driven. How was the body created? Who sanctions its continuation? Who appoints its board members? What is the source of its funding? To whom is it accountable?

Some bodies, although private in origin, may have *de facto* public power. The courts have recognized this in allowing judicial review of

Figure 2.1 *Central Government Control*

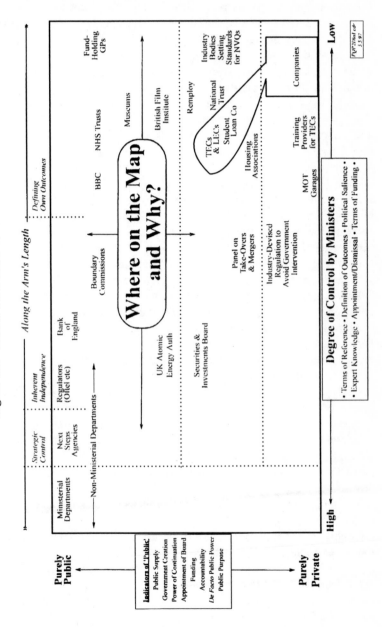

the actions of bodies such as the Panel on Take-Overs and Mergers and the Advertising Standards Authority. Finally, some functions, such as imprisonment, are generally accepted as having a public purpose, irrespective of how they are provided. It should be clear from these points that legal constitution is not a reliable guide to what is public.

Let us turn now to the horizontal axis. Certain quangos were set up to be at arm's length from ministers, sometimes to protect the body from party politics, sometimes to distance the minister from particularly sensitive issues, and often in response to new scientific and technological advances. The Arts Council, Commission for Racial Equality and the Human Fertilization and Embryology Authority are examples. New Public Management has promoted further reasons for 'moving down the arm': to introduce private sector management techniques and 'shake up' the public sector in the hope of delivering efficiency savings in a time of fiscal restraint. Some bodies, such as Next Steps agencies, are controlled at a strategic level; others through regulation of a market, whether competitive, monopolistic or internal. Bodies such as the regulators of the privatized utilities have a degree of inherent independence. Such limits can be summarized as belonging to the terms of reference of the body.

Discussions of strategic control have made much of the split between policy-making and implementation, yet this distinction does not bear close examination. Policy has to be made at every level of management. A clue lies in the degree to which a body defines its own outcomes rather than just its processes: 'What is it there for?' rather than merely the 'How?'.

That's the theory. However, in a constitution based on parliamentary sovereignty, which has effectively created an executive hegemony, the degree of autonomy enjoyed by a body will depend on a number of dynamic factors, not least political saliency (Dudley, 1994): politicians will intervene if they see a political need to do so. Independence can be affected by the degree of expert knowledge of the body (Committee on the Safety of Medicines, for example), the power of appointment and dismissal and control of the funding.

The terms covered in the previous paragraphs indicate where a body might lie on the map. Lines do have to be drawn – no one is calling for public board meetings of MOT garages – yet the figure seeks to show that boundaries cannot be easily placed. The Panel on Take-Overs and Mergers is one of the Stock Exchange's self-regulating bodies, yet the High Court deemed it to be performing a public duty, so making it subject to judicial review (*ex parte Datafin*). The Press Complaints Commission was devised by the industry to avoid the creation of a public body and external regulation. Does it perform a public function? Companies such as

the Student Loan Co. and the TECs and LECs have significant public roles
and must be subject to some form of public accountability. Quango drift
may well move some bodies across the map over time: the Bank of
England's relationship with the government being a case in point (Brittan,
1997: 22). In short, legal standing is a poor guide to what has a public role.

ACCOUNTABILITY ISSUES

In its very broadest sense, the concept of accountability is often used as
a benchmark against which systems of government can be judged.
Accountable government is deemed to be good government, and carries
with it connotations of advanced democracy. (Pyper, 1996)

The bodies we are considering lie at the heart of a paradox: public administration needs to be insulated from the cut and thrust of party politics, yet
the exercise of independent powers by unelected bodies is contrary to the
basic principles of representative democracy. For example, the Arts
Council exists to ensure that arts grants are not used as electoral sweeten-
ers, but how then is the Council accountable? The public may distrust
unelected quangos, but it certainly distrusts politicians, especially in central government. The Next Steps process has occasionally demonstrated
another twist in the paradox: greater independence from ministerial control can sometimes lead to greater transparency.

This is certainly not to suggest that quangos are sufficiently accountable. Stuart Weir and Wendy Hall have clearly shown that the mechanisms
in place are sketchy and inconsistent. Including organizations such as
TECs and housing associations in their definition *extra governmental
organizations (EGOs)*, they found that only 14 per cent of these bodies
came under the remit of the relevant ombudsman and only 33 per cent
were subject to public audit (1995: 313). Furthermore only 2 per cent of
the bodies surveyed were operating the government's new Code on Access
to government information. The public's right to attend meetings, examine
minutes and obtain annual reports and accounts varied widely.

So much for whether there is accountability, but we must also consider:
to whom? Accountability need not always be upwards to central or local
government. It can be downwards directly to members of the public,
or horizontally to peers such as the BMA. It can be exercised through the
courts or through published business plans or framework documents. A
number of functions once carried out by local government have been put in
the hands of appointed bodies whose tenuous line of accountability is
through a minister to Parliament (Flinders, 1997). This move from territorial

to functional decentralization has led to the creation of a 'new magistracy in the sense that a non-elected elite are assuming responsibility for a large part of local governance' (Stewart, 1992).

Whether we are considering the locus of accountability or the means of achieving it, different functions require different answers. A body may have several *constituencies* to whom it should be accountable for different reasons. TECs, for instance, are formally accountable to the minister, but have three other constituencies: local business, the local authority and the local community. Accountability in the accountant's sense – whether the money was spent legally and efficiently – is mostly routed upwards to the department and the minister. The other constituencies need to be involved in decisions on priorities and the allocation of resources. Who should decide the manner in which the tasks are carried out (equality of access, employment conditions, environmental issues)? Only when such questions have been answered can effectiveness (achieving what you are meant to be achieving) be defined, let alone monitored.

Defining effectiveness is indeed a key issue. Much monitoring of effectiveness is carried out using an audit model which shows its accountancy parentage. In theory financial audit can be seen as testing practice against agreed rules. It is doubtful if that is really true, even of financial systems. It certainly misses the mark for effectiveness, where questions of purpose and priorities are political in the sense that different people may legitimately have different answers. Public determination of the '*why*' questions should be a significant part of audit. Ironically, quangos such as the former National Curriculum Council have been one of the mechanisms for stimulating public in this way.

Another route to greater public involvement has been to give the consumer of public services more power through charters and the development of choice. It has been argued by William Waldegrave among others that this greater consumer-responsiveness has increased accountability (Waldegrave, 1993). This is true to a degree, but it has also had the reverse effect of reducing the power of traditional methods of political accountability. Public policy must be about provision for the community as a whole and should not be reduced to individual choice. While there have been benefits from greater consumer-responsiveness in public service, consumerism cannot be an adequate substitute for public accountability. The Charters cover only what Jim Bulpitt (1983) has called 'low politics' and offer the individual no opportunity to question the 'high politics' of policy and resource allocation.

Equally, the answer does not lie in a retrenchment into British political tradition, which has always been centred on accountability through ministers and local councillors. Would the reintegration of the Prison Service agency into the Home Office, as Jack Straw mooted before the 1997 general election really have cured the problems of accountability or simply provided the façade of ministerial responsibility for everyone to hide behind? These political models of accountability were designed in times when the state was much smaller and simpler and the executive lacked the stranglehold it now has on Parliament. Ministerial responsibility has increasingly been shown to be a shield for the executive rather than a weapon with which parliament can demand a true and full account. Meanwhile, local government had lost legitimacy because of a lack of public responsiveness, leaving the way open for the removal of many of its powers, which have often been passed to quangos.

Local government has rethought its approach and now central government is beginning to do so. As the final chapter argues, reforms to central and local government are crucial to any attempt to tackle our current problems. These two political channels must remain powerful forces in public accountability. Yet, much as the authors reject the notion of charterism as a substitute for the political process. we welcome the recognition that we must look for new channels of accountability.

One approach could be to elect board members of some quangos. However, while the right to vote is the *sine qua non* of democracy, it does not of itself ensure accountability. It would be a mistake to think that elected members are more conscious of the need for subsequent channels of accountability than those appointed. A recent study comparing elected and non-elected members of various public bodies discovered that while the appointed held concerns about their lack of democratic legitimacy and forcefully sought innovative ways to account to the public and user groups, elected members assumed that their electoral mandate, no matter how limited, absolved them of the need to worry about such matters (Wright, 1996: 16).

Furthermore, election will not rid us of our paradox. It would still be necessary to find ways of nominating candidates without losing the distance from party politics. There are, however, methods of creating contestability short of election, such as the power to vote out a board in certain circumstances. We need to be more innovative if we are to find a solution to our paradox. We must get away from the notion of electoral accountability as the sole solution. Nor should we look for any other single solution. We must deepen our democracy by introducing direct forms of popular involvement, not as a substitute for elections, the courts, audit, managerial structures and transparency, but as part of a variety of different approaches, each contributing in different ways to the overall mix. Can we achieve that?

The main problem is that we live in a 'parliamentary state' with executive control of the legislature and no coherent framework of administrative law (Judge, 1993). The problems of accountability are therefore twofold: it is not sufficient just to think of good ideas, we also need to find ways of getting these ideas implemented and working. In Peter Hennessy's words, 'we sit here and devise these improvements... but in the end it is really rather like expecting ministers not to behave like politicians' (1996: 17, Q.68). This book is written in the hope that we are at a unique historical juncture in which a reform-minded government is willing to decline the opportunity to use the obvious benefits of the constitutional infrastructure and instead reform the system for the benefit of society as a whole. Maybe this faith will prove to be misplaced. We hope not.

REFERENCES

Cmnd. 7797 (1980), *Report on Non-Departmental Public Bodies* (London: HMSO).

Brittan, S. (1997) 'Bank Held to Account', *The Financial Times*, 25 September, p. 22.

Bulpitt, J. (1983) *Territory and Power in the UK* (Manchester: Manchester University Press).

Cantle, E. (1996) *Quangos and the Government – Future Relationships: The Proposal 'Duty of Partnership'* (Office of the Chief Executive, City of Nottingham: Paper presented to an ADC conference, 27 March).

Clarke, C. (1996) *Quangos and the Future of Local Government* (Paper presented at an ADC workshop, 27 March).

Coote, A. and Lenaghan, J. (1997) *Citizens' Juries: Theory into Practice* (London: IPPR).

Dudley, G. (1994) 'The Next Steps Agencies, Political Salience and the Arm's Length Principle', *Public Administration*, Vol. 72, pp. 219–40.

Flinders, M. V. (1997) 'Quangos: Why Do Governments Love Them?' in M. Flinders, I. Harden and D. Marquand, *How to Make Quangos Democratic* (London: Charter 88).

Gray, C. (1994) *Government beyond the Centre: Sub-National Politics in Britain* (Basingstoke: Macmillan).

Harden, I. (1994) *The Changing Constitutional Role of the Public Sector Audit* (Sheffield: PERC/Dept. of Law).

Hirst, P. (1995) 'Quangos and Democratic Government', *Parliamentary Affairs* Vol. 48, No. 2, pp. 341–60.

Hennessy, P. (1996/7) Evidence to the Public Service Select Committee Inquiry, *Ministerial Accountability and Ministerial Responsibility*, Vol. III (London: HMSO).

Johnson, N. (1974) 'Defining Accountability', *Public Administration Bulletin*, No. 17, pp. 3–14.

Johnson, N. (1982) 'Accountability, Control and Complexity: Moving beyond Ministerial Responsibility', in A. Barker (ed.), *Quangos in Britain* (London: Macmillan).

Judge, D. (1993) *The Parliamentary State* (London: Sage).

Kelly, G., Kelly, D. and Gamble, A. (1997) *Stakeholder Capitalism* (London: Macmillan).

Lawton, A. and Rose, A. (1994) *Organisation and Management in the Public Sector* (London: Pitman).

Lewis, N. and Longley, D. (1996) 'Ministerial Responsibility: The next Steps', *Public Law*, pp. 490–508.

Mulgan, G. (1994) 'Democratic Dismissal, Competition and Contestability among the Quangos', *Oxford Review of Economic Policy*, Vol. 10, No. 3, pp. 51–60.

O'Donnell, A. (1996) 'Legal and Quasi-Legal Accountability', in R. Pyper (1996) *Aspects of Accountability in the British System of Government* (Eastham: Tudor).

Oliver, D. and Drewry, D. (1996) *Public Service Reforms: Issues of Accountability and Public Law* (London: Pinter).

Pliatzky, L. (1992) 'Quangos and Agencies', *Public Administration*, Vol. 70, pp. 555–63.

Power, M. (1994) *The Audit Explosion* (London: Demos).

Public Service Select Committee (1996) *Ministerial Responsibility and Accountability* HC313–I/II/III (London: HMSO).

Pyper, R. (1996) *Aspects of Accountability in the British System of Government* (Eastham: Tudor).

Rhodes, R. (1994) 'The Hollowing out of the State: the Changing Nature of the Public Service in Britain', *Political Quarterly*, Vol. 65, No. 2, pp. 138–51.

Stewart, J. (1992) *The Rebuilding of Local Accountability* (London: European Policy Forum).

Stone, B. (1995) 'Administrative Accountability in the Westminster Democracies: Towards a New Conceptual Framework', *Governance*, Vol. 8, No. 1, pp. 505–25.

Waldegrave, W. (1993) *The Reality of Reform and Accountability in Today's Public Service* (London: CIPFA).

Weir, S. and Hall, W. (1994) *Ego Trip: Extra-Governmental Organisations in the United Kingdom and Their Accountability* (University of Essex: Democratic Audit/Scarman Trust).

Weir, S. and Hall, W. (1995) *Behind Closed Doors: Advisory Quangos in the Corridors of Power* (London: Channel Four TV).

Weir, S. and Hall, W. (1996) *The Untouchables: Power and Accountability in the Quango State* (Democratic Audit Paper No. 8, Human Rights Centre, University of Essex).

Woodhouse, D. (1993) *Ministers and Parliament: Accountability in Theory and Practice* (Oxford: Clarendon Press).

Wall, T. (1996) 'Mine, Yours or Theirs? Accountability in the New NHS', *Policy and Politics* Vol. 24, No. 1, pp. 73–85.

Wright, T. (1996) 'Reinventing Democracy', in P. Hirst and S. Khilnani, *Reinventing Democracy* (Oxford: Basil Blackwell).

3 Quangos: Why Do Governments Love Them?
Matthew V. Flinders

This chapter analyses the underlying dynamics that have led to the growth of quasi-government in the UK. The term 'quango' is employed loosely to indicate the broad variety of bodies that now exist to conduct a public service using public funds but have a degree of distance from politics. This raises questions of control, legitimacy and accountability. The chapter is divided into three sections. The first provides a history of this new layer of governance. The second section elucidates some of the key factors which have both forced and attracted successive governments to create these new bodies. The final section looks to the future and highlights some of the possible approaches a new government could take to quasi-government. The chapter concludes that for all its problems quasi-government is here to stay.

A BRIEF HISTORY

The recent 'reinvention' of government has led to major structural reforms in the British state. Quasi-government is fundamental to any analysis of British politics as it is now an integral layer of governance which, despite rhetoric to the contrary, is unlikely to be dismantled under any future government. Indeed, the growth in, and use of, quangos is evident at all levels of governance from local quangos such as HATs and RHAs, to central government and agencies and finally at the European level, where new bodies have been created which reflect similar problems of accountability and legitimacy – the European Monetary Institute, for example. At an international level there has been a concomitant growth in the use of non-governmental organizations (NGOs) instead of traditional official bodies (see Brookes, 1996).

This book employs a wide-ranging definition of the word quango which captures a broad range of bodies. In many ways the vague and nebulous nature of the term made this essential. So why have we witnessed the post-war development of a large and diverse range of bodies which have confused the once clear demarcation between public and private? What do they have to offer governments? Why have similar bodies emerged in many other advanced countries around the world?

Not surprisingly, as with any issue concerning quangos, the answers are neither definite nor simple. Nor does one answer apply to all forms of quasi-government. In reality there is a complex plethora of factors which, taken together, explain and provide the background to the creation of quangos. These include economic, social, historical and political factors. But before these factors are examined it is necessary to push the debate back even further than the chapter's central question: *Why do governments love quangos*? Namely, how were successive governments able to embark on such fundamental bureaucratic reforms, which question the basic nature of the public sector, without informed dialogue between themselves and the wider society?

The answer would seem to stem from our political system's lack of constitutional backbone. For example, in Britain local government exists by the grace of central government which explains how central government can usurp its functions so easily. At a central level the Next Steps reforms have no legal foundation and therefore Parliament was not involved in their creation, nor in the construction of framework documents, and has no influence over the appointment of their chief executives.

This fact links in with the question: *Why do governments love them*? British governments have the ability to construct new bodies or embark on bureaucratic reforms with an element of freedom denied to the governments of many other West European countries. Britain does not have a written constitution or a system of constitutional law which is superior to ordinary legislation. In Britain the executive has a dominance over the legislature that is unparalleled in Western Europe. Indeed British bureaucratic reform has been conducted under Crown prerogative rather than through legislation. Elsewhere similar reforms would have necessitated major legislation (Dunleavy, 1994; Lewis, 1995; Ridley, 1996). Therefore, the creation of quasi-government has been a much easier option for successive British governments than it has been in other countries as there was very little law needed and no strong tier of local or regional government to battle against. By contrast, in Germany the constitution states that the civil service must be organized according to traditional principles and there is a strong and legally protected layer of regional *Länder* government; and in France, the *Conseil d'État*, comprised of civil servants, scrutinizes all draft laws.

Historically, quangos are not new. Semi-independent bodies have been a part of British governance for 200 years or more. The Board of Trade is the last existing example of the boards set up in the seventeenth and eighteenth centuries to carry out activities which were seen at the time as not fully in the domain of government. Ironically, concerns about the accountability and legitimacy of these boards led to their being absorbed into ministerial departments. Despite this, bodies with some element of independence continued to be created, such as the Arts Council before the Second World War.

Quangos certainly seem to have an element of immortality. Some die naturally, either because the reason for which they were created is achieved or the environment in which they were born changes significantly. Obvious examples include the Colonial Empire Marketing Board and the Decimal Currency Board. A more recent example is the Millennium Commission as it is understandably expected that this body's natural life will end with the passing of the millennium. There is also evidence to suggest that quangos may die only to be reincarnated at a later date: examples include the Physical Training and Recreation Council and the Council for the Encouragement of Music and the Arts of the 1940s. These bodies passed away some time ago in one sense, but have been reincarnated in another sense in the Sports Council and the Arts Council. Amalgamation is another method through which seemingly abolished quangos can survive. For example, the Labour government has announced plans to abolish the Development Board for Rural Wales, the Land Authority for Wales and the Welsh Development Agency but in reality their death certificates have been turned into new birth certificates as they are to be amalgamated into one 'super-quango' called the Economic Development Agency.

With the advent of post-war social democracy and construction of the welfare state the use of quasi-autonomous public bodies exploded. They were seen in many forms including the boards of the nationalized industries, the new regulatory bodies such as the IBA, CAA, Health & Safety Commission, Equal Opportunities Commission, NEDC and the Commission for Racial Equality which were all created in the 1970s.

Whilst attacks by opposition parties are common, quangos have been created by both Labour and Conservative governments. Despite threats to 'cull the quangos' when in opposition, and the commissioning of the Pliatzky Report on taking office, Margaret Thatcher immediately set about creating new quangos, the early approval of Michael Hesletine's Docklands Development Corporation being one example. Thatcher was surprisingly complimentary about the Pliatzky Report, which did not recommend an all-out cull. Sir Leo Pliatzky commented, 'That such undogmatic findings should have been accepted, against the background of the dogmatic anti-quango campaign ... seemed to me, in a small way, a satisfactory result'

(Pliatzky, 1992: 557). The Conservative government continued this now well-established political tradition by creating new and increasingly innovative forms of quasi-government. This is clear to see as the British polity now bears witness to a range of regulators: Next Steps agencies, UDCs, RHAs, HATs and NHS Trusts to name but a few.

1979 is a crucial year in any analysis of why governments, not just in the UK, have consistently moved from traditional bureaucratic state forms to new forms of quasi-government. At the end of the 1970s quangos were vulnerable to assault as in hard times the government would have been expected to reverse the trend in government growth on a 'last in, first out' basis of retrenchment (Hood, 1981), the expectation being that quangos, rather than the central bureaucracy, would have borne the brunt of reforms. When the Conservative policy commitment to cutting back these bodies is added one would have expected that quangos would have faced an uncertain future. History shows that the expected 'quangocide' never happened. Rather, after largely cosmetic cutbacks, the growth of these bodies exploded and is testament to the immortal qualities of quangos.

WHY CREATE QUANGOS?

While a chronological account of the development of quangos is relatively straightforward it avoids the more difficult motive behind this chapter: Why were these new bodies created? The Pliatzky Report (1980) provides a sound starting point outlining four reasons for the creation of these bodies:

> Because the work is of an executive character which does not require ministers to take responsibility for its day to day management; because the work is more effectively carried out by a single purpose organisation rather than by a government department with a wide range of functions; in order to involve people from outside of government in the direction of the organisation; in order to place the performance of a function outside the party political arena (p. 557).

While the above explanations have undoubtedly been key factors, in line with contemporary civil service ethics, they provide only half the truth. The true motives are infinitely more complex and political. Historically, as the post-war state grew unchecked, there was an increasing sense of ungovernability and that the state was overloaded. The creation of quangos was one way of reducing the size and scope of the state. The political institutions were simply not designed and not able adequately to oversee and control the burgeoning bureaucracy. By the 1970s the British state had become 'a massive machine hooked up to a two-stroke engine' (Kemp, 1996). Indeed, the creation of Next Steps agencies at the central level was designed to reduce 'ministerial overload' (Ibbs, 1987).

The expansion of the state, which led to the backlash against post-war British statism, had created a bureaucracy which had been grafted on to a structure that was simply inappropriate to big government. The government found itself doing things it was not good at. As one ex-senior civil servant pointed out: 'elected representatives may well be good for democracy, but they are not necessarily good managers.' Governments liked quangos because they recognized that government could not carry out all functions well. It also allowed specialist or sensitive functions to be delegated to experts who could make long-term decisions at a distance from the adversarial nature of British party politics. Delegating 'hot potatoes' to specific bodies also had obvious benefits to politicians as well: the Commission for Racial Equality, for example.

Another related issue concerns the growth of the state and the 'politicization of the previously non-political'. Whole sections of societal affairs suddenly came under the remit of the state (see Beck, 1992). This had snowballed from the development of the post-war welfare state and also evolved out of technological advances. If there was any problem in society, the public now looked to the government to correct it, while advances in science put new issues and concerns at the door of politics.

But at this same historical juncture public apathy towards politics was at an all-time high. When politicians were being asked to do more than ever before, they, and the institutions they worked through, were, seen to be bankrupt. This led to what Brian Hogwood (1995) has termed 'institutionalitis' in which the panacea was seen in quasi-autonomous non-governmental organizations. They allowed control and regulation by new bodies of experts or appointed individuals who worked with an element of independence from traditional politics and therefore were not tainted by conventional politics. In many ways the government created quangos because the public wanted them. The public did not want, or trust, politicians to regulate areas that were previously unregulated, nor did they want new areas of concern, such as medical ethics, to be governed by party politics. Hence the creation of the Human Fertilization and Embryology Authority.

Because of the lack of confidence in traditional politics, the degree of independence given to quangos gave them a legitimacy in the eyes of the public that traditional institutions had lost. Quangos served a new role for a public that wanted control and regulation, but did not trust politicians. Ironically, it is this attempt at de-politicization through independence which gave these bodies an element of legitimacy which is now at the centre of the concerns over accountability and control. This has led to recent calls for re-politicization through traditional channels, either ministers or councillors.

Historic and societal explanations are a major contribution to any explanation of the development of quasi-government, but often overlooked are the economic factors which also played a significant role. Macroeconomics and the government's responsibility for the economy arrived only after 1945. Once central government took on this responsibility it became concerned about all public expenditure, including that at a local level. Central government quickly discovered that of all expenditure, local expenditure was the most difficult to control and predict, for obvious reasons. Central government's concerns over local expenditure pre-date the 1976 débâcle with the IMF.

The 'hollowing out' of local government was in many ways a response to this problem as the creation of quangos to conduct tasks previously under the remit of local government allowed central government to control local expenditure (Rhodes, 1994). It represented a fundamental shift from 'government to governance' in which ministers 'steered but did not row themselves', once again reflecting the desire to unburden the political process. It also allowed for the introduction of private sector management techniques and efficiency gains. As one senior representative from a TEC commented in conversation recently: 'the government was able to deliver the programmes which it deemed to be its business ... to the same number of individuals, to an increased quality, for half the cost.'

In the area of industrial relations economic and historical factors converged, leading to the creation of a range of new bodies. The history of post-war industrial relations has been concerned with the complex interaction between the voluntarist tradition and the growing pressures from the state for regulation in the public interest (Taylor, 1996). In post-war Britain the government found itself responsible for the economy, but in industrial relations there was an entrenched voluntaristic tradition. This 'collective laissez-faire' approach to industrial relations allowed individual trade unions to negotiate their own pay settlements with employers without regulation. While this caused few problems in the immediate post-war years, by the 1960s creeping wage demands convinced politicians of all parties that some form of government regulation was needed. The unions were committed to their voluntarist tradition and saw no need for government intervention. Against this opposition Barbara Castle's efforts to reform industrial relations collapsed, as did Edward Heath's ambitious Industrial Relations Act 1971.

It was clear that direct government intervention was not going to be successful, but the government needed some way of curbing increased wage demands. The answer was found in the creation of new semi-autonomous bodies with some degree of autonomy from the government. These would semi-regulate industrial relations in a voluntarist manner. For example, in 1973 the Manpower Services Commission was formed as a public agency designed to take over the administration of employment and training services directly from the Department of Employment. The body offered a solution to all sides of a dispute. The unions warmed to these new bodies as they were not legally imposed and continued the voluntarist tradition. The government and employers favoured them as they created a structure of semi-regulation and the opportunity for trade union leaders and employers to sit down, with independent nominees, and negotiate issues. In the following years these bodies grew as the government recognized that they were the best way to temper the traditional voluntarism with regulation. In 1974 the Health and Safety at Work Commission was established, along with Advisory, Conciliation and Arbitration Service. The example of industrial relations shows that many bodies exercising some degree of autonomy were not created because governments loved creating quangos, but because in some policy areas they were the only option when direct intervention and regulation had failed.

While economic considerations may well have played a key role in the move from territorial decentralization, based on local government, to functional decentralization based on centrally appointed quangos, it would be naive to omit the overtly political considerations. Governments find creating quangos an attractive choice as they provide the option of increasing or decreasing control. But whether quangos are used to distance a function from central government or tighten central government's control, the power of appointment provides the trump card in the power relationship. Just as the creation of quangos provided a convenient way to decrease central government's control over sensitive areas, it also offered the opportunity of increasing central government's dominance over areas deemed out of control – local government, for example.

Margaret Thatcher's disdain for local government was well known. She viewed it as both inefficient and irresponsible. The Thatcher government loved quangos because they enabled functions to be removed from local government and placed in the hands of appointed 'can-doers', who would implement centrally imposed policies (Jenkins, 1996). Where functions could not be removed completely a wave of new laws, such as CCT, has increasingly forced local government to contract out its services to the lowest private sector bidders. This has led to what Harden (1992) has termed the 'Contracting State'.

As Hogwood (1995) notes, while the post-1979 creation of quangos was ideologically motivated to undermine Labour-controlled local authorities, it also fits into an historical process in which governments of both parties have removed functions such as gas, electricity, water, health care, etc., from local government. From the late 1980s central government embraced quangocratization. These new bodies were democratically questionable. Their only legitimacy was to central government, through the tenuous line of ministerial responsibility; they were controlled by central government, and the chief executives and board members are appointed by central government. Also the resurrection of the policy/operations dichotomy through the arm's length relationship offers ministers the opportunity of control without responsibility as incidents can be defined as operational and placed on the shoulders of the chief executive rather than the minister (Barker, 1996).

Politically, government created quangos for several reasons: they allowed local government to be circumnavigated and placed the implementation of polices in the hands of bodies headed by individuals, the vast majority of whom were, unsurprisingly, Conservatives (Hall and Weir, 1995); they allowed the introduction of new management techniques; concealed the true size of the bureaucracy and allowed politicians committed to shrinking the state to appear triumphant; they provided a buffer-zone between ministers and politically salient areas of government; and they theoretically reduced ministerial overload and relieved ministers from the minutiae of government.

The historical, economic and political factors all converged in the late 1980s, culminating in a reappraisal of the role of the state and the role of the individual within the state. Historically, post-war Keynesianism and collectivism had been replaced by the New Right and rampant individualism. Economically, it was a period of fiscal retrenchment. Politically, Thatcher had won a third term and was embarking on her most radical period in office. Politicians were trapped by a public who demanded increased and improved services without tax increases. This led to politicians following what Osborne and Gaebler term 'the third option': fundamentally reforming the public sector with the aim of increased productivity without increasing costs – 'getting more bang from each buck' – as witnessed in the advent of New Public Management (NPM).

In recent years the growth of quangos has been directly related to politicians' faith in NPM. As Hood (1991) points out, 'Its rise is linked to four megatrends, namely; attempts to slow down government growth in terms of spending; the shift towards privatization and quasi-privatization and away from the core government institutions; the development of IT; and the development of an international agenda.' This is reflected in the drive towards disaggregation in the public sector.

The transfer of functions from traditional bodies, such as government departments or local government into quangos – from Next Steps agencies at a central level, to TECs at a local level, to parent boards in schools or practice trusts in medicine – enabled the introduction of NPM and innovative new management practices largely derived from the private sector. It also broke down the old public/private distinction and allowed a wider and more diverse range of individuals and organizations to be involved in conducting public tasks. For example, TECs were created to transcend the classical public/private dichotomy, building links with local businesses and ensuring that local training suited the needs of the local economy. The creation of the Millennium Commission is a classic example of a quango being set up to perform a public service. The aims of the Commission required a specialist and innovative body comprised of members of the public and private sectors to foster links with businesses and voluntary organizations. It has an element of distance from politics which reduces the ministerial burden and also builds confidence in the eyes of the private sector as it is at one remove from party politics.

The rise of NPM in the late 1980s reinforces Hood's (1981) proposition that the creation of quangos follows an historical pendulum and can therefore be described as a fashion. 'Hiving off' functions first came into fashion in the 1960s, most notably with the Fulton Report (1968), which led to the creation of an assortment of bodies. In the late 1970s the pendulum swung and an anti-quango environment developed. The mid-1980s heralded a repositioning of the pendulum and the rapid growth in quangos, though due to Mrs Thatcher's original anti-quango election campaign many of the quangos were disguised under the subtle veil of agencification. One could argue that the current anti-quango sentiment is simply the next swing of the pendulum.

This theory would seem to fit into an historical analysis. Despite this it is probably nearer to the truth to state that quangos of varying forms have been created continuously and in different forms since 1960s. 'Quango-bashing' has also been a popular opposition sport, along with promises to cull which have been promptly reneged upon once in office as the benefits of quangos become apparent. The much vaunted quango cull promised by Edward Heath in 1974 and Margaret Thatcher in 1979 both proved to be modest affairs.

In recent years there has been another downturn in the public perception of politics and its institutions. This has once again culminated in the creation of a deluge of bodies that gain their legitimacy in the eyes of the public due to their independence from government. Camelot is a private company conducting a public task which needed to be seen to be independent of the government. The National Audit Office, due to its role in scrutinizing the governments accounts, obviously gained legitimacy from autonomy. The Nolan Committee is one of the most important constitutional creations in British political history and looks like developing into a standing committee. Yet the Nolan Committee is also a quango in that it provides a public service yet works at one remove from government. In many ways Nolan had to be a quango, as any body without the arm's length relationship and autonomy from politics, which the Committee has, would never have achieved legitimacy in the eyes of the public.

Nolan is a particularly interesting body as it inverts popular perceptions about quango/government relations. Quangos are appointed and are therefore unaccountable and illegitimate, whereas governments are elected and are therefore accountable and legitimate. But in this case we have an appointed body with a high level of public legitimacy, and the elected chamber needs to follow the recommendations of this appointed body to regain legitimacy in the eyes of the public. So once again the government chose to work through a quango, rather than attempt to reform Parliament or public life itself, because setting up a body offered two things which the government could not achieve through traditional mechanisms: specialism and legitimacy in the eyes of the public.

FUTURE TRENDS

Although there are some general trends, such as cuts in public spending and the introduction of New Public Management, this chapter has verified the opening statement that no one explanation can account for why governments love quangos. If anything, it has reinforced the need to adopt a pluralistic approach to any analysis of quasi-government. If indisputable answers were sought, the only practical research agenda would be to examine each species of quango independently, case by case. There are no macro-political explanations.

Despite this fact common trends emerge which allow the future of quangos to be tentatively predicted. Quangos are here to stay. In reality regardless of the problems associated with them, quangos will continue to be an important part of British governance. Economically the demand for increased efficiency in the face of fiscal restraint, popular resentment towards tax increases and social change, and not least the ageing population, will continue to exert a pressure on any government to keep and further extend quasi-government, as will technological and scientific advances.

Politically, a new stalemate has developed which demands urgent attention. A factor behind the development of quangos is that the public no longer trusts conventional politics; new bodies gain legitimacy from their arm's length relationship. Politicians now face an informed public that has lost faith in politics and its institutions to an extent never before seen, yet the public is also aware of the explosion of quangos and the issues and controversies that surround them. The aim of politicians, policy-makers and academics should be to abandon anti-quango polemics and admit that quangos are here to stay. It is therefore necessary to design methods that can impose a democratic 'ball and chain' on these bodies, which will maintain their freedom and flexibility while anchoring them firmly to the democratic process. The answer is not to sweep all quangos under the carpet of local government, nor to pull back the executive agencies into their parent departments. That would create more problems than it solved.

Whether Labour understands the complexity of quasi-government or has a coherent reform agenda is debatable, although the plans for devolution, moves towards abolishing certain quangos (while also launching a review of the remaining bodies) and embarking on drawing up a Freedom of Information Act are brave and encouraging. Realistically, Labour has a number of options to consider. These can be termed: refreshment; cosmetic reform; and stricter control.

Refreshment refers to patronage and whether a new government can resist the temptation simply to appoint their own party faithful to quango directorships and boards. Indeed, one benefit that such bodies bring to a government is the wide range of positions it can offer to loyal servants of their party. Refreshment, as a political option, has the benefit of not demanding abolition or structural reforms – though would leave the problems of quangos unaddressed. This has been done in the past by both Labour and Conservative governments. When Labour took office in 1974 it influenced the Price Commission, set up under the Conservatives in 1972, by appointing to its board a number of Labour Party sympathizers. Similar tactics were employed by the Conservatives in 1979 as they, despite attacking party political patronage when in opposition, proceeded to replace the chairman and board members of several quangos, not least the Scottish Development Agency, British National Oil Corporation and the National Enterprise Board (Hood, 1981).

Following such a course would have an obvious attraction for any government yet a new Labour government would be wise to avoid this option. Instead, it should build on the work of Sir Len Peach, by introducing a new meritocratic and open process in which quango heads are appointed through open competition and are subject to 'advice and consent procedures'. This would involve new appointments being subject to the scrutiny and acceptance of the relevant local authority or select committee.

Such a move would deliver a political reward for Labour that would be far larger than patronage alone in the form of increased public confidence in politics as they realize that they might have voted into office a government which won't promise one thing and then do opposite. Such a move would also help increase the legitimacy of quangos while giving local government a role to play, so breaking down the current 'them and us' mentality.

If the attraction of patronage is too tempting, a new government may well embark on some pruning or cosmetic surgery. This is an easy option. Quangos are so hard to define that there are many opportunities to introduce impressive-sounding reductions in their numbers by drawing selected bodies back into departments, dismantling functionally or historically marginal bodies, or by amalgamating several bodies into one to achieve an apparent reduction. In reality such an exercise is worthless. Though several governments have tried it in the past, academic centres, not least the Political Economy Research Centre and the Democratic Audit, and investigative journalists invariably examine the sacrificial lambs and highlight the shallow and cosmetic nature of such a tactic. Indeeed, as Hood (1981) points out, this happened in 1979 when Michael Heseltine triumphantly declared victory in his war against quangos by declaring that he had abolished over 50 bodies in the Department of the Environment. This was quickly seized on by the press and several Tory backbenchers, who revelled in undermining his victory by pointing out that these bodies represented less that 1 per cent of the Department's spending on quangos and less than 0.5 per cent of the department's paid appointments (*The Times*, 17 January 1980).

A final option would be to introduce a system of stricter control over these bodies to allay fears of lack of accountability and legitimacy. The obvious problem with such a move is that the introduction of stricter and tighter reporting, oversight and quango-shadowing procedures would demand increased central bureaucracy and counteract many of the advantages of setting up these bodies in the first place.

The reasons for the creation of quangos are both varied and dynamic. They have been created for a number of economic, societal and political reasons. Technological and scientific advances, the need for economic efficiency and the desire of politicians to distance themselves from politically salient issues will ensure their place in British politics for the foreseeable future. If one had to pinpoint the single most important factor, the core strand of quasi-government DNA, it would have to be that these new bodies are not tainted by the cynical popular perception of conventional politics and therefore have an element of public legitimacy which traditional institutions have lost. The creation of these bodies is often an attempt to win back public faith in the old political institutions. For example, the recently created Food Safety Council (FSC) which will be independent of the Ministry of Agriculture, made up of experts and free to criticise government policy (Hornsby, 1997).

REFERENCES

Barker, A. (1982) *Quangos in Britain* (London: Macmillan).
Barker, A. (1996) *Myth versus Management: Individual Ministerial Responsiblity in the New Whitehall*. Essex Papers in Politics and Government No. 105.
Beck, U. (1992) *Risk Society* (London: Sage).
Brookes, B. (1996) *Accounts and Accountability: UK Parliamentary Funding and Scrutiny of the World Bank and IMF* (London: Christian Aid).
Cmnd. 7797 (The Pliatzky Report) (1980) *Report on Non-Departmental Public Bodies* (London: HMSO).
Dunleavy, P. (1994) 'The Globalization of Public Services Production: Can Government be "Best in the World"?', *Public Policy & Administration*, Vol. 9, No. 2, pp. 36–64.
Efficiency Unit (1988) *Improving Management in Government the Next Steps* (London: HMSO).
Hall, W. and Weir, S. (1995) *Ego Trip: Extra-Governmental Organisation in the UK and their Accountability* (University of Essex: Democratic Audit/Scarman Trust).
Harden, I. (1992) *The Contracting State* (Milton Keynes: Open University Press).
Hirst, P. (1995) 'Quangos and Democratic Government', *Parliamentary Affairs*, Vol. 48, No. 2, pp. 341–60.
Hogwood, B. (1995) 'The "Growth" of Quangos: Evidence and Explanations', in E. Ridley and D. Wilson, *The Quango Debate* (Oxford: Oxford University Press) pp. 207–24.
Hood, C. (1991) 'A Public Management for all Seasons?', *Public Administration*, Vol. 69, pp. 3–19.
Hood, C. (1981) 'Axeperson, Spare that Quango...' in C. Hood and M. Wright (eds) *Big Government in Hard Times* (London: Martin Robertson).
Hornsby, M. (1997) 'New Food Watchdog Will be Given Teeth, Promises Hogg', *The Times*, 31 January, p. 5.
Jenkins, S. (1995) *Accountable to None: the Tory Nationalisation of Britain* (London: Hamish Hamilton).

Kemp, P. (1996) *Delivering Public Services*. Annual Lecture to the Centre for Socio-Legal Studies, Sheffield University, 12 November.

Lewis, N. (1994) 'Reviewing Change in Government: New Public Management and the Next Steps', *Public Law*, pp. 105–13.

Lewis, N. (1995) 'Responsibility in Government: the Strange Case of the United Kingdom', *European Public Law*, Vol. 1, Issue 3, pp. 371–94.

Marquand, D. and Seldon, A. (1996) *The Ideas that Shaped Post-War Britain* (London: Fontana Press).

Marr, A. (1995) *Ruling Britannia: The Failure and Future of British Democracy* (London: Michael Joseph).

Osborne, D. and Gaebler, T. (1992) *Reinventing Government* (London: Penguin).

Pliatzky, L. (1992) 'Quangos and Agencies', *Public Administration*, Vol. 70, pp. 555–63.

Rhodes, R. (1995) *The New Governance: Governing Without Government*. Lecture delivered as part of the 'State of the Nation Series', 24 January.

Rhodes, R. (1994) 'The Hollowing out of the State: the Changing Nature of the Public Service in Britain', *Political Quarterly*, Vol. 65, No. 2, pp. 138–51.

Ridley, F. (1996) 'The New Public Management in Europe: Comparative Perspectives', *Public Policy & Administration*, Vol. 11, No.1, pp. 16–29.

Taylor, R. (1996) 'Industrial Relations: Regulation against Voluntarism', in D. Marquand and A. Seldon, *The Ideas that Shaped Post-War Britain* (London: Fontana).

Weir, S. (1995) 'Quangos: Questions of Democratic Legitimacy', *Parliamentary Affairs*, Vol. 48, No. 2, pp. 306–23.

4 Quangos and Local Democracy
Gerry Stoker

This chapter starts by recognizing that a range of appointed bodies and quangos play a substantial role in the governance of local communities. The strengths and weaknesses of such a position are then briefly reviewed. As a result three areas of possible reform are identified and examined: procedural reforms to ensure openness and fairness in the conduct of the affairs of these publicly funded organizations; institutional changes and developments in policy processes to tackle the problems of fragmentation and co-ordination raised by the rise and spread of quangos; and democratic reforms to facilitate the political accountability of these non-elected institutions.

THE EMERGENCE OF A SYSTEM OF LOCAL GOVERNANCE

The institutional map of local government has been transformed since 1979. Local authorities initially in metropolitan areas and then elsewhere have been reformed. In the most urbanized areas of England there is a system of single-tier local government, although in other areas a multi-tier system has survived. In Wales and Scotland single-tier local government has been established. A majority of the population live in so-called unitary systems of local government. The unitary system established in many areas is claimed by the Conservatives to have simplified government. A clear line of accountability, it is argued, is provided to a local authority and complex tasks of service integration are made easier by the arrival of unitary single local government.

However the claims of streamlined accountability and better co-ordination have a somewhat hollow ring because alongside the reorganized local authorities a range of other institutional changes have occurred. First, as a side-effect of local authority reorganization, a range of joint boards and committees have been established to run services such as fire and transport in metropolitan areas. Second, a number of services have been moved out of the sphere of elected local government. In England and Wales water authorities, which in 1979 had a majority of their management board members appointed by local authorities, are in 1997 privatized companies. In Scotland responsibility for water has shifted from local authorities to boards appointed by central government. Police authorities have, in a similar way, been removed from the sphere of direct local authority influence.

Third, a distrust of local authorities by central government has led to the establishment of a range of local agencies funded from the centre. The arrival of Urban Development Corporations (UDCs), Housing Action Trusts (HATs) and the provision of a greater role for housing associations reflects this trend, as too does the launch of new institutions of higher and further education and the establishment of grant-maintained schools.

A fourth factor in institutional fragmentation has been the desire to bring new 'non-political' actors into decision-making. Training and Enterprise Councils, City Technology Colleges and many of the boards set up to manage City Challenge or other regeneration schemes reflect a concern to incorporate, in particular, business people in local decision-making, with funding and overall control in the hands of central government.

A fifth factor in the growth of local non-elected agencies has been the rise of a managerialist and consumerist perspective on government, sometimes referred to as the 'New Public Management'. Public service organizations, so the argument goes, have tended to become dominated by producer interests and as a result are neither efficient in terms of saving public money nor in being responsive to consumer needs. The fragmentation of existing 'monopolistic' bureaucratic structures, the establishment of a purchaser–provider divide and the introduction of performance targets and measures are seen as solutions to the problem of producer domination by creating on an organizational 'home' for the client/consumer voice within the system and enabling consumers and their surrogate purchasers to allocate resources to competing providers whose performance and achievements they are able to measure. This managerialist and consumerist logic has been used by Conservative ministers to justify the rise of non-elected bodies and in particular the reforms in the health sector. Health authorities in the past had some minority local authority representation in their management structures split into purchaser and provider camps, neither with any local authority nominees.

The overall effect of these changes can be summarized as a shift from a system of local government to a system of local governance. Local authorities now share to a greater extent than before 1979 service provision and strategic decision-making responsibilities with other agencies. As Table 4.1 makes clear, some of these local quangos are appointed directly by central government, others are self-governing in the sense that they

Table 4.1:   The Centrally Sponsored Local Quango State – Key Bodies
(Expenditure £bn)

Functional area	Government appointed bodies	Self-governing bodies
Education	City Technology Colleges (0.05)	Grant Maintained Schools (1.7) Higher Education Corporations (7.56) Further Education Corporations (3.2)
Housing	Housing Action Trusts (0.09)	Housing Associations (1.5)
Urban Development and Training	Urban Development Corporations (0.5)	Training and Enterprise Councils (1.4) Local Enterprise Companies (0.5)
Health	District Health Authorities (12.9) Family Health Services Authorities (6.8) Health Trusts (6.0)	

Note: Figures for expenditure taken from Nolan (1996: 10) and Greer and Hoggett (1995: 24, Table 2).

appoint their own boards. The agencies listed in Table 4.1 are significant actors in local communities. They are responsible for over £40 billion of public funds, a figure not far from the spending responsibilities of local authorities.

IF THERE IS A PROBLEM, WHAT IS IT?

The shift to a system of governance has been marked since 1979, but appointed bodies, quangos and joint arrangements were a feature of the local political scene before that date. What is different is how such quasi-governmental agencies have moved from the periphery of the policy process to become major agents of new policies and approaches. From the perspective of central government such agencies have a number of attractions. They provide:

- a mechanism for giving a greater push or profile to an area of activity;
- a capacity for concentrated and effective effort with respect to a particular issue;

- a tool for involving non-partisans in decision-making on the basis of their expertise, or their involvement in relevant private or voluntary sector activity;
- an expression of an 'above politics' or bipartisan approach to decision-making in certain areas.

These qualities of quasi-governmental agencies ensure that they will have attractions to central government regardless of the outcome of the last election.

The rise of local governance, however, is not entirely unproblematic. Criticisms come under three broad headings. First, there is a raft of concerns about standards of such agencies in the conduct of their business. People are appointed to the boards of quangos, not on the basis of merit or as a reflection of their expertise but because of political sympathies, it is claimed. In some instances having failed to win public office by election, people are appointed by the 'back door' to public positions. The management and decision-making of many quangos, it is argued, are shrouded in secrecy and there is a lack of openness in the conduct of their affairs compared to that of elected local authorities. A further criticism is that appropriate standards in declaring interests or ensuring probity in the management of public finances have not always been in place or observed. Second, there is a view that although quangos may be effective in their narrow area of operation the existence of a diverse and complex range of such agencies exacerbates the problem of corporate governance – the bringing of the parts together.

The increasing differentiation, along with the weakening of the relative position of local authorities, represents a fragmentation within the overall system. Differentiation has the strength of specialization and focus. Organizations have a clear, if bounded, task and bring relevant expertise to that task. But a system of governance has to have a capacity for integration as well as differentiation. The relative weakening of the position of local authorities in the system reduced the capacity for integration through a multipurpose if not an all-purpose authority.

Many of the new agencies of local governance are subject to direct influence from central government through the appointment of their controlling boards or by way of their funding coming directly or indirectly from the centre. Central government, however, cannot readily provide integrative mechanisms at the local level. The integrative mechanisms of central government, which have themselves often been criticized, focus on the central government departments, the Cabinet and its committees, and processes of consultation. They do not, however, provide the necessary integrative mechanisms at the local level.

The third batch of criticisms about quangos is focused on the issue of accountability. Quangos are subject to strict financial and managerial accountability in many instances, but what they lack, it is argued, is political accountability. The key point is that these other forms of accountability cannot replace the need for collective accountability for the policy and resource allocations of these bodies. The requirements of further and more general accountability are not met by the framework of democratic control through Parliament. The effective control that can be exercised over so complex a machinery of bodies through this central route is inherently limited. Moreover, the issue is whether in any event public accountability at national level is appropriate for appointed bodies at local level. If there are local choices to be made by appointed bodies about priorities or the setting of policy, even though these choices may take place within a framework of national policy and funding for such agencies, the argument is where there is local choice there should be an opportunity for local voice.

SOLVING THE ISSUE OF STANDARDS: PROCEDURAL REFORM

Since the early 1990s when the debate about the operation of quangos began to gain prominence, a number of government-inspired and quango-initiated schemes have been launched to set out what are appropriate standards in the conduct of these public bodies. The issues have been dealt with in a comprehensive manner by the Nolan Committee, whose First Report made a series of recommendations to ensure probity and openness in public life. In a Second Report dealing specifically with local spending bodies, the essential need for appropriate standards to be put into practice – proportional to the size and nature of individual bodies – is emphasized.

The Nolan recommendations cover four areas (See Table 4.2). First, they argue that the process of appointment to quangos should be open and subject to proper procedures. Nominations should be encouraged from a wide range of people. Selection should be made on the basis of clear criteria. Reappointment should not be automatic. Second, in the management of their business appointed boards should be as open as possible, argues Nolan. Agendas and minutes should be widely available, as too should audit and annual reports. Efforts should be made to develop user-friendly ways to communicate with and consult the public and important interested parties.

Third, a code of conduct should guide the action of members of appointed bodies. The codes would state the aims and purposes of the

Table 4.2: The Seven Principles of Public Life

SELFLESSNESS: Holders of public office should take decisions solely in terms of the public interest. They should not do so in order to gain financial or other material benefits for themselves, their family, or their friends.

INTEGRITY: Holders of public office should not place themselves under any financial or other obligation to outside individuals or organizations that might influence them in the performance of their official duties.

OBJECTIVITY: In carrying out public business, including making public appointments, awarding contracts, or recommending individuals for rewards and benefits, holders of public office should make choices on merit.

ACCOUNTABILITY: Holders of public office are accountable for their decisions and actions to the public and must submit themselves to whatever scrutiny is appropriate to their office.

OPENNESS: Holders of public office should be as open as possible about all the decisions and actions that they take. They should give reasons for their decisions and restrict information only when the wider public interest clearly demands.

HONESTY: Holders of public office have a duty to declare any private interests relating to their public duties and to take steps to resolve any conflicts arising in a way that protects the public interest.

LEADERSHIP: Holders of public office should promote and support these principles by leadership and example.

Elements of Best Practice
Best practice, subject always to proportionality for smaller organizations, includes:

APPOINTMENTS
- a publicly available written appointments process;
- job descriptions and person specification;
- the use of advertisement and/or consultation with interested bodies and other forms of canvassing;
- the encouragement of nominations (including self-nominations);
- the sifting of candidates by a nominations committee;
- defined terms of appointment after which reappointment should not be automatic.

OPENNESS
- making the agendas and minutes of governing body meetings widely available, together with board papers where this will not inhibit frankness and clarity;
- publicizing forthcoming meetings and summarising decisions in a newsletter or through some other user-friendly method;
- holding an open annual meeting at which board members can be questioned by the public and press;
- setting up more specialized consultation bodies for important interest groups;

Table 4.2:   (*Continued*)

- publishing an annual report which includes information on the role and remit of the body, its plans or strategy; the membership of the board; and where further information can be obtained;
- publishing audit reports;
- making publications available as widely as possible, for example by sending them to interested parties and putting them in local public libraries.

CODES OF CONDUCT
- a statement of the aims and values of the body;
- statements of the obligations of the body towards its customers, staff, community, and other interested parties;
- information about the body's approach to openness and arrangements for acquiring information about its activities;
- procedures for handling inquiries and complaints;
- procedures for raising complaints with an independent body.

WHISTLEBLOWING
- a clear statement that malpractice is taken seriously in the organization and an indication of the sorts of matters regarded as malpractice;
- respect for the confidentiality of staff raising concerns if they wish, and the opportunity to raise concerns outside the line management structure;
- penalties for making false and malicious allegations;
- an indication of the proper way in which concerns may be raised outside the organization if necessary.

Source: Second Report of the Committee on Standards on Public Life. May 1996. *Local Public Spending Bodies*, Vol. 1, Cm 3270.

organization. Statements about the obligations of the body to its staff, customers and the community would be presented. Procedures for handling complaints would be outlined. Finally, Nolan recommends that appointed bodies make a clear statement about how 'whistleblowing' activities are to be managed. The aim should be to balance opportunities for genuine examples of malpractice to be brought to life and the need to avoid making false or malicious allegations.

There is little doubt that if the recommendations of the Nolan Committee were followed in practice, then most of the issues raised by critics about the conduct of public affairs by local quangos would be resolved. The issue is whether the good practice outlined by Nolan will become the norm. Some argue that to rely on voluntary codes of conduct is not enough and that a new statutory code for public governance stipulating the standards for all public spending bodies is required.

MEETING THE CHALLENGE OF COMMUNITY GOVERNANCE

In the light of complex social and economic challenges and an increasingly differentiated polity there is a clear need to establish effective integrative mechanisms at a community level. In broad terms there are at least three types of formal integrative mechanisms available:

- giving a leading role to a local elected body;
- developing binding agreements between relevant organizations;
- providing an overarching responsibility to a regional office of central government.

It is the first option which is commended here. There are attractions in arrangements such as the *'Contrat de Ville'* developed in France in which the leading public sector players in a locality commit themselves to a formal agreement about priorities and policy. The Government Offices of the Region in England and the respective territorial ministries elsewhere in the UK have a substantial role in providing a focus for integrated decision-making and co-ordination which has a local–regional focus. However, giving a leading role to a local elected body provides not only a base for co-ordination, but also the starting point for a form of local accountability.

A leading role for a local authority in ensuring effective integration is an attractive option in many respects. Local authorities have local knowledge. They have experience of co-ordinating and networking in their areas. They can offer civic leadership and their legitimacy as elected and accountable bodies. The potential role for local authorities as conductors of community activity and leaders in community governance is considerable. It is a role that could be shared with any newly created regional tier of government. Yet it is important to recognize that local authorities have not always proved themselves adept at strategic thinking and community leadership.

To fulfil the potential of community leadership, local authorities will have to develop further new ways of working and reaching out to their communities. Painter (1996) argues that local authorities need to develop a targeted approach. Given the range of appointed bodies it is vital for local authorities to develop a focus on those agencies 'that most directly impinge on the local authority's objectives and where influence can realistically be exercised'. Beyond developing a strategic approach local authorities will need to release and mobilize the resources of influence at its disposal: legal, regulatory, financial, physical, staff skills and expertise and information. Releasing resources to take on the wider role of community leadership may in turn require changes in internal organizational and decision-making structures. Time and organizational space for both officers and councillors will have to be created so that local authorities can pursue concerns beyond their immediate service delivery responsibilities.

Above all local authorities will need to extend and enrich the legitimacy they have as elected bodies by demonstrating a capacity to develop new ways of engaging with local communities and developing the local democratic discourse. There are a considerable range of options for democratic innovation within existing legislative arrangements (open forums, scrutiny committees, citizens' juries, market research, etc.). Local authorities might be able to utilize existing planning responsibilities to provide the umbrella for drawing together the different elements in a number of policy areas (transport, community care, economic development, land-use, etc.).

There would also be a need for central government to encourage or even instruct the appointed bodies to co-operate with local authorities in the development of community co-ordination. Ted Cantle, Chief Executive of Nottingham, suggests that quangos should be placed under a 'duty of partnership'. They would have to consult the local authority(ies) in the area they operated. They would have to reconcile their plans with those of the local authority as far as possible. They would be expected to co-operate with specific partnership projects in their local area.

There have been some suggestions that local authorities might need some statutory backing for a more developed community leadership ole. A range of observers have argued that legislation should be passed to facilitate initiatives in new forms of internal management and civic leadership.

The suggestion for a separately elected executive mayor is the most high-profile of these proposals. The Labour Party (1995) has proposed giving local authorities a new duty 'to promote the social, economic and environmental well-being of the communities they serve' (p. 5) and a new power of community initiative to give 'them greater freedom to respond to local needs, providing what they did was not unlawful and did not wholly duplicate the functions of other statutory bodies' (p. 13). Both the duty and the power are seen as mechanisms to encourage and facilitate local authorities taking on a wider community leadership role.

DEVELOPING MECHANISMS OF
LOCAL POLITICAL ACCOUNTABILITY

The attraction of local authorities being given a leading role in integrating the work of a range of appointed bodies to ensure that community needs are addressed is that, as well as tackling governance issues, it also makes considerable strides with respect to political accountability. The process of co-ordination would help ensure that appointed bodies were made accountable to local needs and concerns to a degree.

Accountability has a number of different meanings. It should not be reduced to a matter of democracy or election. Nor should it be seen as simply a legal or contractual concept. Accountability is about the construction of an agreed language or discourse about the assessment of conduct and performance (Klein and Day, 1987). Accountability is best seen as a multi-layered concept. It is closely related to the concept of responsibility. In the context of governmental arrangements recent work as part of the ESRC's Whitehall programme reveals a spectrum of understandings of accountability (Hogwood and McVicar, 1996). These include minimalist to maximalist positions:

- the keeping and verification of a correct record;
- the requirement to provide information;
- a formal recognition that a person or persons are 'in charge';
- a recognition that those 'in charge' have substantial ownership of their function and should be required to explain or justify its action/ non-action;
- accepting responsibility if things go wrong to take appropriate action;
- accepting blame or praise;
- facing reward or punishment;
- suffering revocability of a mandate, losing office.

The governance mechanisms discussed in the previous section would potentially facilitate all the elements of accountability except the last one: losing office. Winning or losing office as a result of election by the public is at the heart of the debate about the political accountability of quangos.

There are a number of options to be considered with respect to establishing electoral accountability to the public.

- giving responsibility for quango functions to local authorities;
- supervising quango functions through an elected tier of regional government;
- providing for direct and separate elections for particular quango functions.

One option for achieving political accountability is to pass quango responsibilities back to elected local authorities. Stewart (1996: 4) treats 'the
issue of ensuring local accountability through democratic control as one to
be resolved through the relationship with local authorities'. However, for
accountability to be based in local authorities does not necessarily mean
that the full responsibility for a function be given to local authorities or
that they discharge that responsibility through the traditional committee
and departmental structure. It may be desirable to have direct control exercised through the authority's own structure. Another possibility is indirect
control leaving a separate agency in place but ensuring it pursues policies
approved by the authority through giving the authority the roles of budget
approval, policy setting and appointment (or some combination of these
institutional devices).

The Association of Metropolitan Authorities (AMA, 1995) has put
forward a series of proposals in relation to specific appointed bodies. The
health commissioning role of DHAs and FHSAs should be given to
local authorities and controlled within the authority, and health trust
providers should have their boards opened to local authority nominees.
UDCs and HATs should be wound up and the steering and funding of
housing associations should be a shared responsibility of local authorities
with government regional offices. TECs should be required to work in a
policy framework laid down by the local authority and the appointments
process ultimately controlled by local authorities, with other partners
being brought in as appropriate. Grant maintained schools and CTCs
should be returned to direct local authority control.

The arguments for greater local authority involvement have considerable potential strength. Local authorities as elected agencies can provide
a direct accountability in relation to the functions covered by these
currently unelected agencies. Moreover they can organize the integration
of services. Health, housing and education, as already argued, have a
cross-cutting impact on one another. The local authority could bring the
fragments together. Even where much of the funding for such services
would come from national sources there is still scope for local priorities
to be set.

The doubts about whether bringing local government back in is the
appropriate response reflect uncertainty about the democratic and managerial capacity of local authorities. Do local authorities with the low turn-
out in their elections and the low-key nature of their political leadership
have the ability to provide a focus for democratic control over the major
functions currently provided by non-elected agencies? Given the over-
burdened position of councillors, is it realistic to imagine they would have

the space and time to take on wider responsibilities? Do local authorities, or can they, demonstrate in practice a real capacity to integrate services? Finally, is it anything other than a phoney form of control if local authorities are given control of quangos but not the capacity to raise additional resources?

Not all observers are convinced by arguments that accountability is best restored by bringing elected local government back in. In part such arguments express uncertainty about the quality and strength of democratic and management processes in local government and in part they express a positive commitment to other forms of democratic involvement. Hirst (1995) makes a case for quango reform strategy resting on regional government, a more functionally based system of supervision by self-governing voluntary associations and democratization through direct election.

> Regional governments could take over the responsibility for rendering key quangos like UDCs and TECs more accountable. If local democracy is to be restored, the chances are that regional government are a better bet than existing local authorities. If they acquire major functions of central government, then they are more likely to attract the attention of voters; because they are bigger and more diverse, they are less likely to become single party 'rotten boroughs' (especially if they are elected by proportional representation); and as they will be of some consequence, they are more likely to attract high-quality politicians than existing local authorities. (p. 179)

Hirst suggests that alongside this broader territorial base for democracy the scope for a functional base for democracy should also exist. Here one option is to devolve functions to self-governing voluntary associations. Another is to

> Directly democratize many quangos, like NHS Trusts, higher education corporations, locally managed schools, and HATS, involving both their personnel and their consumers in their boards of management. This would return institutions to those involved in them rather than having them controlled by nominees who often do not use the services in question or know little about them. (p. 180)

Hirst's proposal for a comprehensive and radical restructuring is not widely shared among those most likely to be the policy-makers of the future, but some of the thinking and options Hirst has identified are, on a more piecemeal basis, part of the current agenda.

A potential role for regional government in relation to quangos has been canvassed by the Labour Party. The option of direct election to some quangos was floated by the Commission for Local Democracy (1995). Health authorities (DHSs and FHSAs) in particular are seen by some as viable institutions for direct election (Whitehead, 1995). In the case of TECs the Association of British Chambers of Commerce offers a business-led solution to accountability by arguing that restyled local Chambers of Commerce should take over the control and running of TECs and LECs. These reshaped Chambers would also have a wider role in providing the business voice on other quangos (for a discussion see Jones, 1996).

The argument for introducing new institutions of accountability rests on a number of claims. In the case of regional government it is the scale and capacity of a tier at that level which is seen as attractive. Health, training, further and higher education, economic and regeneration strategies could be better planned at such a level. A new regional institution would attract public attention and high quality political leadership. Direct elections for some bodies would enable particular groups and interests to find a clear focus to express their concerns. It might attract a wider range of participants into the representative process.

The doubts about a reform strategy based on a combination of regional government and direct elections are considerable. Again the potential worthiness of the proposed reforms can be conceded but the issue is what will be achieved in practice. Is regional government an option that carries democratic legitimacy in all parts of the country? Could a series of direct elections be sustained in terms of public interest and willingness to vote? How would integration be achieved in the system? Would the separately elected agencies simply come into conflict all the time and engage in political posturing?

It is difficult to be certain which of the options for providing electoral accountability is likely to be most appropriate for particular functions and quangos. In the light of such considerations there is a strong case for a period of experiment. Some local authorities might be provided with the health commissioning role. Direct election to police authorities in some areas might be encouraged. Regional supervision, as the appropriate institutions develop, might be initiated in some areas.

ACKNOWLEDGEMENT

This chapter draws on work undertaken as Director of the ESRC's Local Governance Programme.

REFERENCES

Association of Metropolitan Authorities (1995) *Changing the Face of Quangos* (London: AMA).

Commission for Local Democracy (1995) *Taking Charge: The Rebirth of Local Democracy* (London: CLD).

Greer, A. and Hoggett, P. (1995) 'Non-Elected Bodies and Local Governance', in J. Stewart, A. Greer and P. Hoggett, *The Quango State: An Alternative Approach*, CLD Research Report No. 10 (London: Commission for Local Democracy).

Hirst, P. (1995) 'Quangos and Democratic Government', in F. Ridley and D. Wilson (eds) *The Quango Debate* (Oxford: Oxford University Press) pp. 163–82.

Hogwood, B. and McVicar, M. (1996) 'Agencies and Accountability'. Paper presented to ESRC Conference, 22–23 March.

Jones, M. (1996) *TECs and Local Accountability: Options for Reform* (London: Local Government Information Unit).

Klein, R. and Day, D. (1987) *Accountabilities in Five Public Services* (London: Tavistock).

Labour Party (1995) *Renewing Democracy, Rebuilding Communities* (London: Labour Party).

CM 3270–1 (1996) Second Report of the Committee on Standards in Public Life (Nolan Report). *Local Public Spending Bodies Volume 1: Report* (London: HMSO).

Stewart, J. (1996) *Reforming the Local Appointed Boards* (London: Local Government Information Unit).

Whitehead, A. (1995) *Holding Quangos to Account* (London: Local Government Information Unit).

Part II

An International Perspective

5 Quangos in Germany?
Jürgen Fiedler

INTRODUCTION

In Germany as in Britain 'lean management' in public administration, 'lean government' and the privatization of state activity have been widely debated subjects. Nevertheless, because of the differences between the British and German legal, constitutional and political systems the debate in Germany takes a somewhat different direction from that in Britain. The differences in the system account for why it is difficult to find the exact equivalent of a quango in Germany. The definition of quangos as 'part of direct public administration but with some independence from ministerial control' would in the German context cover a very wide range of bodies including both the traditional public law structure of administration and the newly developed or rather particular type of public administration in the shape of a private law institution.

Surveying the structure of public administration in Germany, it appears that the equivalent of the British quango debate in Germany would be the discussion concerning the use of private law institutions to fulfil tasks of public administration. But apart from certain spectacular cases of privatization, such as the privatization of the *Post* and *Bundesbahn*, the reform of the various tiers of government in Germany took place gradually on a case-by-case basis. It was not the result of a major reform programme by the federal or *Länder* governments. For example, privatization was a pragmatic response to both the cost of unification and the problems of the economy in Eastern Europe.

This chapter is divided into two sections. The first examines:

- the basic administrative structure of the Federation, the *Länder* and the communes in Germany;
- the traditional public law structures of administrative bodies with some independence from the various tiers of government;
- the private law structures for the organization of public administration; and
- some aspects from the German viewpoint of which state activity could be completely privatized.

The second section offers an insight into the current debate in Germany about the use of private law structures for public administration in describing:

- the legal frame for the choice of the organizational structure for public administration; and
- some of the main arguments and counter-arguments for the choice of private law structures.

DO QUANGOS EXIST IN GERMANY?

The Basic Administrative Structure of the Federation, the *Länder* and the Communes

Germany is a federal state. Its administrative apparatus has three levels: federal, *Land* (state) and local. The federal and *Land* administrative authorities are considered institutions of direct state administration; by contrast, the administrations of the communes, which from a legal point of view form independent self-government bodies (so-called local self-government), are considered institutions of indirect state administration. Local self-government falls into two categories: communes (*Gemeinden*) on the one hand, which may be organized as unitary communes (*Einheitsgemeinden*) or as a kind of association of communes (*Ämter, Verbandsgemeinden, Verwaltungsgemeinschaften*) and, on the other hand, the district counties (*Landkreise*) consisting of the communes which form part of the county territory. Bigger towns may be non-district municipalities and therefore independent of a county (*kreisfrei*) and thus combine the two levels of local self-government. Both levels carry out public administrative functions, with the counties and the non-district municipalities (*kreisfreie Städte*) being lower administrative authorities of the state in parts of their administration. As, according to the Basic Law, the execution of even federal laws is a competence of the *Länder*, there is no need for federal representation at the *Land* level.

Most *Länder* have a three-level administrative structure: higher, intermediate and lower level. Higher-level authorities fulfil administrative functions for the entire *Land* from one central location. These authorities are subordinate to the ministries and do not have any administrative substructure. Intermediate-level authorities fulfil functions for an administrative district within the *Land*. Staff working for these administrations are civil servants and employees of the *Länder*. Some *Länder* do not have intermediate-level authorities. Lower-level authorities are either *Land* authorities or local authorities acting on behalf of the *Land*.

From a legal and political point of view, the Federal *Länder* and the communes perform their tasks within the framework laid down by federal or *Länder* statutes and by the constitution independently and on their own responsibility. From a constitutional point of view, the *Länder* generally execute federal statutes independently. The Federation merely exercises supervision to ensure that the *Länder* execute the statutes in accordance with applicable law. In the case of specific federal statutes referred to in the Basic Law, which the *Länder* have to perform as agents of the Federation, federal supervision also covers the lawfulness and appropriateness of execution. Where local authorities perform their designated tasks, legal supervision is exercised by the *Land*; where they perform tasks which are not part of the free self-government tasks, the *Land*, within the framework set by statute, also exercises supervision regarding the lawfulness and appropriateness of execution. The office of the head of the county government, as the lower public supervisory body, executes public supervisory functions *vis-à-vis* the towns and communes forming part of a county. The local authorities are subject to direct instructions where they execute Federal or *Land* statutes as agents of the Federation or the *Länder*. Furthermore, the administrative courts may verify the lawfulness of local authority administrative action.

Traditional Public Law Structures of Semi-independent Administrative Bodies

The central, regional and local authorities form the backbone of public administration in Germany. Nevertheless, there are several important administrative bodies, at each level of government, which may have a legal personality and fulfil major public tasks.

Corporation under Public Law (Körperschaft des öffentlichen Rechts)
The most important type of these semi-independent bodies is the corporation operating under public law. In German administrative law is traditionally defined as:

> a legal entity and an organizational combination of a number of natural or juridical persons (the members), which is entitled by law to form a will and act on its own irrespective of the change of its individual members.

The Federation, the *Länder* and the communes themselves are territorial corporations under public law (*öffentliche Gebietskörperschaften*). However, a very large number of other corporations exist under public law. Important examples are the chambers of the various professions, which exercise a sort of self-administration and self-regulation over their members. There are chambers for lawyers, doctors, pharmacists and craftsmen. Secondly, corporations can combine public and private personnel working within similar areas, like the chambers of commerce and industry, special corporations for regional planning purposes or for solving ecological or traffic problems connected with rivers, lakes or limited forest areas. Thirdly, the universities are corporations under public law in order to give them a sufficiently independent organizational basis within the constitutionally guaranteed freedom of science and research. Finally, the huge area of social insurance in Germany (old age, illness, social services, unemployment) is organized in corporations under public law with self-administration.

There is no coherent or unified system of laws which regulate these corporations. All of them are created either by law or in accordance with a legal provision, and many of them have their own legal personality. Several corporations without legal personality still have the power to pass binding Acts. The membership of these corporations can be compulsory or optional, and public and political control over their activities varies. Some of them may pass unilateral authoritative administrative acts, some not. All this would have to be analysed for a given entity by looking into the specific law applicable to that institution.

Establishment under Public Law (Anstalt des öffentlichen Rechts)
Whereas the basic idea of a corporation is the combination of various persons under an organizational structure of public law an establishment under public law (*Anstalt des öffentlichen Rechts*) is traditionally defined as an

> inventory of material or personal means, which in the hand of a body of a public administration is supposed to permanently serve a specific public interest.

Establishments of this type include the savings institutions of the local authorities and the providers of public utilities at the local level, which are often organized like private enterprises although they remain under public law (*Eigenbetriebe*). Most schools and many other cultural institutions (e.g. libraries, theatres and public broadcasting institutions) in Germany are establishments under public law, as well as a range of institutions in the field of scientific and technological research. The range of establishments under public law spans hospitals, prisons, abattoirs, water supply, sewage and waste disposal institutions to bodies with special functions in the administration of the economy or banking institutions of the Federation and the *Länder* (for example, *Kreditanstalt für Wiederaufbau*).

The creation of such an establishment requires either a law, or at least a legal basis, if it is to have its own legal personality. Whether endowed with a legal personality or not, the public body creating the establishment remains financially responsible for the activity of this institution. Consequently there is more or less strict control over the lawfulness and appropriateness of the activity of establishments. The methods of control and accountability vary considerably from one body to another.

Foundation under Public Law (Stiftung des öffentlichen Rechts)
The foundation is the third type of semi-independent institution under public law which does not have the same practical importance as the corporation or the establishment. Foundations under public law are normally created by a special law for the purpose of administering a particular property of cultural and/or historical importance, like for instance the *Stiftung Preußischer Kulturbesitz*, which contains a large number of artworks in the museums of Berlin.

Private Law Structures for the Organization of Public Administration

When exploring German public administration in the form of private institutions the complex legal position of these bodies means that definitional clarity if often hard to achieve. It might be more rewarding to describe, as a first step, some related phenomena in order to elucidate a more precise picture of what is meant by private law structures for the organization of public administration.

Delimitation to Nearby Legal Phenomena
First of all, it is necessary to distinguish between the incorporation of private persons into the fulfilment of administrative tasks under public law (*Beleihung*) and the use of private law structures for the execution of public administration. There are quite a few examples of these private organizations fulfilling public functions. The best known might be the Technical Automobile Inspection (TÜV), which has the form of a private association (*eingetragener Verein*) and is given the right to issue technical

control certificates, which is considered a formal act of public administration. Other examples for the incorporation of private persons into the fulfilment of administrative tasks are certain competencies of the captains of ships or aeroplanes. In the supervisory field, such as hunting, fishing, health control, etc., we find similar authoritative competencies of private persons. All this does not present constitutional problems because according to Art. 33 IV of the Basic Law authoritative competencies are only in general to be exerted by civil servants. Every incorporation of private persons into the fulfilment of public tasks needs a Statutory Act, be it a law itself, an Administrative Act or a contract prescribed in a law. Only clearly defined and limited competencies can be given to such an incorporated private person, the acts of which are considered as being administrative acts of the public body that has handed over the competence. Administrative courts are competent to control the acts of this type of public administration by private persons.

German texts on administrative law also distinguish between the simple use of private law for the activities of public administration on the one hand, and a private law structure for the organization of public administration on the other. So it is fairly common for a local municipality to use the organizational pattern of a civil law company without legal personality to run a theatre which acts on almost the same legal terms as a private individual. In this case the commune as a body of public administration has not changed its public nature, it has only decided to use the forms of private law for its activity because it is more suitable for the task. In doing this, however the public administration cannot escape the legal obligations that the Basic Law draws up for all public activity. So, of course, the citizens have equal right of access to the theatre although under private law in principle there is no such obligation.

'Government by contract' does not belong to the privately organized forms of public administration as very often the public administration will use the special knowledge and expertise of private institutions for public purposes, for instance in defence matters. However, in this type of co-operation we do not usually find a firmly established organizational basis nor an institutionalized influence of the public sector over private institutions. In that sense it is similar to the type of *ad hoc* arrangements that are found in Britain.

We might come closer to private law structures for the organization of public tasks if we look at publicly funded private non-profit organizations fulfilling tasks in the public interest. If the activity of the private non-profit organization remains outside the scope of direct administrative tasks and state organizations do not dominate these institutions by means of majority participation or contract, private law structures for the organization of public administration are not necessary. All that would be needed in such a case would be a parliamentary budget credit for the grant. However, quite important organizations in Germany fulfilling public tasks in the field of international relations like for instance the *Carl-Duisberg-Gesellschaft e.V.*, *Inter Nationes e.V.* or the *Geothe-Institute e.V.* have developed from mere private non-profit organizations to institutions that are closely linked to the Federal Republic of Germany.

Public enterprises are fairly similar to private law structures for the organization of public administration. In fact, it is almost impossible to define clearly the basic differences between various types of bodies in this area because neither the term enterprise nor the term public enterprise has firm boundaries. Sometimes we find structures of public law in this field of activity, sometimes those of private law. Frequently there are only historical reasons for one or the other type of organization. One common characteristic of these structures is the dominant influence of public administration which is exerted directly or indirectly by means of property rights, financial participation, statutes or other regulations.

Public Administration by Civil Law Bodies

Since public administration in Germany is in principle free to use any form of private institution to execute its functions we find a broad variety of juridical forms of privately organized public administration. Federation, *Länder*, communes and other independent bodies of public administration can, for instance, use the form of a stock company (*Aktiengesellschaft*), a limited company (*Gesellschaft mit beschränkter Haftung*), a registered association (*eingetragener Verein*), a foundation under private law (*Stiftung*) or even a partnership (*Offene Handelsgesellschaft*) or a limited partnership (*Kommanditgesellschaft*). Sometimes different forms of companies are bound together in a trust or a holding with the aim of avoiding tax disadvantages or to ensure appropriate public influence on the leading personnel of the private institution. One should note, however, that private statutory law is a competence of the Federal Parliament. *Länder* or communes cannot change the cogent rules of these statutes so they are only able to choose the private form that they find the most appropriate for the given task.

Organizations under the rule of private law have traditionally been used at all levels of public administration to fulfil a large range of public tasks. It is somewhat difficult to get a full picture of all the types of bodies and tasks at every government level, given the political independence of the 16 Federal *Länder* and the differences in administrative structure from one

Land to another. The Federation issues an annual report on its direct or
indirect participation (*Beteiligungsbericht*) showing which is the competent ministry, the type of activity of the institution, the other participants,
the financial importance of the participation, some basic figures of the
annual balances and the names of the leading and supervising personnel.
At the end of September 1995 the Federation recorded 405 such organizations. At the level of the *Länder* and the communes the number of organizations is thought to be much higher. It would be difficult to say that we
could find behind all these bodies privately organized public administration. Some are simply financial organizations in private business. There is,
however, a strong tendency, at least at the federal level, to get rid of mere
financial organizations because it is not considered to be a task of the state
to interfere in private business in this way. The Federation has thus considerably reduced the number of its organizations in the last few years, not
taking into account the huge action of privatizing the state industry of the
former GDR.

The tasks fulfilled by privately organized bodies of public administration on the national, regional and local level range from various activities
in the field of economics, social affairs as well as cultural institutions,
through institutions dealing with the aid to developing countries and
institutions for the promotion of research and development and urban
planning, to special private institutions which try to co-ordinate the
interests and activities of, for instance, communes, chambers of commerce, publicly organized broadcasting institutions or social insurance
organizations.

As to the legal classification of the activity of privately organized
institutions of public administration one can generally say that the choice
of a private law structure normally implies the application of private
law rules for the activity of the institution. Thus, the special rules on
unilateral administrative acts laid down in the Administrative Procedure
Law (*Verwaltungsverfahrensgesetz*) and the Administrative Courts Law
(*Verwaltungsgerichtsordnung*) are not applicable. Like other private
institutions these bodies would have to refer to civil contracts; and civil
courts are competent to decide in case of quarrel. There is, however, a
strong opinion in jurisprudence and literature that in choosing private law
forms of activity the administration cannot escape the obligation to
observe the basic rights of the individual that are stated in the German
constitution. One of the consequences of this is the widespread application
of the tender system for passing contracts in this area because otherwise
the fundamental right of the citizens and private enterprises to be treated
equal would be jeopardized.

Complete Privatization as an Alternative?

One of the fundamental issues at the borderline between private and public
law structures for public administration is the question: What makes a
specific task a public task? Where does the public sector begin and what
activities can be left to private business? I doubt that it is possible to give a
general answer to this question. Life is constantly changing and tasks that
in the past have been considered within the remit of public administration
could nowadays easily be carried out by completely private enterprises
because technical and economical circumstances have changed. Therefore
the choice of whether specific public interests can appropriately be
reached by market-oriented enterprises is largely political. Care has to
be taken, however not to create monopolies in privatizing public tasks; and
it must be ensured that the activity in the public interest will also be performed in difficult times when market conditions do not guarantee profits.
The difference in legal and constitutional infrastructure make correlations
between German quangos and their British counterparts difficult. It may
be that the traditional federal structure of Germany and the long-lasting
coexistence of private and public organizational structures of public
administration in Germany have led to a different debate. But before
drawing any conclusions it is worth embarking on a deeper analysis of the
reasons behind the use of private law structures for public administration
in Germany.

THE USE OF PRIVATE LAW STRUCTURES FOR
PUBLIC ADMINISTRATION IN GERMANY

This debate revolves around two key questions: (1) Is there a legal framework limiting the choice of organizational structure? (2) What political
arguments can be put forward in favour or against the choice of private law
structures for public administration?

Legal Framework and the Choice of Organizational Structure

As already mentioned, there is an old German tradition that in principle
the state and the other independent juridical persons executing public tasks
may use the whole spectrum of legal forms provided by the law, be it civil
or public law, to fulfil their functions. It is commonly felt that the authority
to decide upon the organizational structure, the personnel and the finance
implies a 'principle of organizational choice', which means that within the

limits of the law it is at the discretion of each body of public administration to choose forms of private or public law for organization as well as activity. If, however, the choice is made in favour of a private law institution, the public administration has to use, for its activities, the forms provided by civil law.

The federal constitution does not limit the choice provided that the organizational intrusion into the sector of private law does not interfere with specific aspects of the constitutional order. In the past there was a debate on the question whether the articles of the constitution about the basic rules for the civil service or the rules fixing the administrative competencies of the Federation and the *Länder* contain restrictions to the principle of organizational choice. Nowadays there seems to be a general opinion, however, that in using the term 'administration' (*Verwaltung*) the Basic Law does not rule on the applicability of civil or public law.

Therefore one has to take a close look at the sub-constitutional laws applicable to a given area of public administration to find out whether the nominally free choice between public and private law may be limited. The law concerning the saving banks of the local communes (*Sparkassen*), for instance, states that these institutions have to be established under public law with legal personality (*rechtsfähige Anstalt des öffentlichen Rechts*). But this does not hinder these institutions from behaving just like any private bank in relation to their customers. The communes are, however, financially responsible for their *Sparkasse*.

Some limits to the free choice of private law structures for the execution of public tasks are to be found in the rules governing the budget procedures on the federal and the *Länder* level including the communes. According to these rules the Federation and the *Länder* ought to form private enterprises, or take over responsibilities in private enterprises, only

- if an important public interest requires this,
- if the public purpose cannot be reached better and more efficient in other ways and
- if an appropriate influence of the juridical person under public law is given.

The laws of the *Länder* about the municipal administrative structure contain similar clauses. These clauses aim at avoiding a choice for public participation in private enterprises in cases where it might be detrimental to public finance. Even under these rules, however, a commune would still be free to decide in favour of the private structure if it is uncertain whether the civil or the public law structure would be more efficient. Since the commune and even the *Länder* are unable to change the legal rules applicable to different forms of commercial companies, because this is a matter of federal competence, the aforementioned clause about maintaining an appropriate public influence on the leading personnel might force the commune to choose the form of a limited liability company instead of a stock company since the law offers much wider possibilities there to intervene in the direction of the company.

Resuming the analysis about the legal framework influencing the choice of private law structures for public administration in Germany, one could say that especially at the level of the *Länder* and the communes there is a relatively wide legal range of possible decisions. In many cases it comes down to a political decision as to which administrative structure is chosen.

Arguments and Counter-arguments for Choosing Private Law Structures for the Fulfilment of Public Tasks

There is a strong opinion in Germany that the choice of a private law type of body offers a greater flexibility and thus possibilities for a more efficient organizational structure. One important reason for choosing private law structures is that there is much more flexibility in creating and dissolving an institution under private law than under public law. One of the reasons for this lies in the fact that the legal structures from which to choose are already pre-defined in private law. It is only necessary to draft an appropriate internal statute or a company contract and to have it registered in the register of companies or private institutions with legal personality. This does not take long and – most importantly – does not require changes of laws. The creation of public law institutions, on the other hand, is only rarely possible without amending a law or even passing a completely new law. Similar questions arise when a body created for a timed public task is to be dissolved after reaching its purpose.

The size of the advantage is, of course, bigger the shorter the planned timespan for the existence of the institution. On the other hand, the costs connected with the creation and dissolution of a private institution with legal personality, for example notarial charges, court and register fees, have to be taken into account.

Another important aspect to be considered is the status of the personnel. In choosing a private law type of institution the administration can avoid the application of the binding rules for the civil service and the application of the collective agreements for employees and workers in public institutions. Some argue that the application of the established rules lead to overstaffing, immobility and indolent personnel. The life-time career system of the civil service and the inflexible staff plans in public administration are said to hinder young dynamic forces and the pay system is criticised as not being sufficiently flexible or efficiency oriented.

These arguments are, however, by no means universally accepted. Some suspect that in certain cases the choice of a private law organization might also be influenced by the expectation of creating more profitable jobs for civil servants who have already fulfilled the same public task in a public law structure. Another counter-argument stresses the point that the private law rules about work contracts are by no means only advantageous in comparison to the rules governing the civil service. In Germany, as in other countries, the members of the civil service are recruited for a whole range of activities and can in principle be transferred to other posts even without their consent. In addition, large sections of the public sector workforce already work on the basis of private contracts which often contain special clauses offering a certain flexibility as to the pay and working conditions of leading staff.

There is also a body of opinion that believes that it is misleading to expect more efficiency from private law-type organizations because their staff may lack the necessary skills and expertise needed to co-operate successfully with the established parts of the public sector. Supporters of the idea of private organizational structures also stress the point that private law structures offer a greater flexibility as to the internal organiza-tion of the institution. They criticize the hierarchical internal structure and bureaucratic procedures frequently found in public law administration and suggest private institutions are more flexible and efficient forms of organi-zation. Indeed, the form of co-operation and staff motivation can be chosen, there is delegation of tasks to lower levels of the hierarchy, clearer decision-making processes, business type flow of information, etc. In the German discussion you would, however, also find the counter-argument, that public law structures are not closed to new modern and effective forms of management and organization.

Another interesting argument for the choice of private law forms of organization focuses on the need for flexible bodies for co-ordination and co-operation among various independent public entities with similar interests. This need is especially apparent at the level of local administra-tion. Public law does not provide forms for grouping common interests of local municipalities, for example in the political process of federal legisla-tion. So, similar to private lobby institutions or pressure groups, com-munes are working together in private law-type organizations to raise their voice in the process of legislation on the federal and *Länder* level. There are also privately organized research institutes working on specific subjects of common interest to local municipalities. Some *Länder* and even the Federation have a stake in some of these institutions because some aspects of this research are interesting to all levels of government, for example questions of housing or social problems.

An important point in the debate revolves around the flexibility of budgetary procedures. Public law types of administration are normally bound by the rules of public budget law with its annual procedure of fixing limited credits for a large number of specified tasks by parliament or the municipal council. The accounting system of private institutions, on the other hand, offers the possibility to use commercial forms of bookkeeping and accounting, of cost and performance accounting, of measuring the financial efficiency of the activity.

One has to admit that certain inflexibilities of the rules governing the budget of public institutions may be one of the reasons for inefficiencies in public administration. A frequently quoted example is the so-called December fever when budget surpluses are spent in a rush at the end of the financial year to avoid a cut in the following year. Another disadvantage stems from the fact that because the use of public funds is bound to budget approvals for a very wide range of defined allocations fixed for a whole year in advance, the priorities funds to be used efficiently cannot be set appropriately.

One argument is that private law structures are able to obtain private funds to finance or co-finance a public task. One has to be careful with this argument because sometimes private forms of pre-financing a public activity may only hide a growing financial burden for the public budgets of future years. It is interesting, given Britain's new Labour government's use of the Private Finance Initiative (PFI), that in Germany the permanent working group for budgetary matters of the finance ministries of the federation and the *Länder* have recently agreed a common initiative to help overcome the problems of private financing for public activities by agreeing on certain rules of transparency for all public budgets.

Often tax advantages play an important role in deciding on the structure of the organization. This may, however, cause problems as it cannot be accepted as an advantage for the state as a whole if, for instance, municipalities choose their organization structures for some of their activities mainly under the aspect of gaining tax advantages which the *Länder* and/or the Federation would have to pay through a reduction of their own tax revenue.

Sometimes the argument is used that special private law structures, e.g. the limited liability company, would offer better possibilities for limiting the liability of the state. This is doubtful because the choice of a private law structure in practice and even in law does not take away the financial responsibility from the public body behind this institution.

An important aspect in the discussion about the use of private law structures for public administration is certainly the question of how the individual rights of citizens are protected. The choice of private law forms of activity considerably reduces the procedural rights of the individual against misuse of public power. If the relationship between the administration and the citizen is governed by private law, the civil courts are competent to decide cases. The procedural rules applicable in these cases are in principle the same as for litigation between private persons and the special procedural rules for the administrative courts are not applicable. Civil courts in Germany do not have the competence for official fact-finding, an ascertainment of facts takes place only in as much as the contending parties disagree upon facts that are important for the decision, whereas administrative courts are obliged to ascertain the facts independently from what the litigant parties say. Thus, in civil lawsuits the individual in many cases bears the burden of proof where this would not be the case in the administrative procedure. In addition, the administration does not have as far-reaching obligations to hand over files or other documents to the court as in administrative court cases.

One of the most important aspects of the whole issue – and this is particularly relevant when compared with the contemporary British debate – is the question of whether sufficient democratic control can be maintained over the execution of public administration if a growing number of tasks are fulfilled by all kinds of bodies under private law. Transparency and publicity of administrative procedures are important practical aspects in effecting the basic constitutional principles of democracy and the rule of law. The more complex the structure of administration, the greater the danger of developments that try to avoid the light of democratic control, the greater the possibilities to hide activities. On the other side it might be advantageous to keep certain activities in the public interest away from the quarrels of party politics and leave it in principle to the judgement of experts in which way a certain public task should be fulfilled. Examples for this might be found in the field of culture, education and scientific research. There is nothing wrong with reducing democratic control in these cases as long as the development of such bodies does not go beyond the limits which democratically elected public bodies have set for them.

CONCLUSION

Looking at the discussion in Germany, we find ourselves returning to an old problem: how can public administration render the most effective service to the citizens and stay under sufficient democratic control at the same time?

In Germany there is no general programmatic attempt to change the structure of public administration into a growing number of privately organized independent sub-institutions or agencies. There is, however, a widespread feeling that the state and public administration should thoroughly examine the extent to which activities that are still considered public tasks could be handed back to private initiative and competition.

The choice of a private law structure for the fulfilment of public tasks does not in itself ensure the effectiveness of the execution of the task. It may even be connected with serious disadvantages. It is a never-ending responsibility of all those making decisions on the various levels of administration to thoroughly weigh all the arguments and counter-arguments for private or public law structures and to find on a case by case basis the organizational solution that is most suitable for the public task in question.

6 Quangocratization in the Netherlands

Frans L. Leeuw and Sandra van Theil

INTRODUCTION

In 1995 the Netherlands Court of Audit (NCA) published a survey of *all* Dutch quangos operating at the national level (Algemene Rekenkamer, 1995). The definition of a quango used in this study is, 'organizations, based on either public or private law, with public authority (i.e. have the right to make legally binding decisions that affect citizens and/or organizations) who are charged with a public task as their main task.' Quangos have no immediate hierarchical working relationship to a minister and are financed either from the State Budget or by levying. Using the NCA survey we will discuss some characteristics of Dutch quangos at the national level. Unfortunately, information on the numbers and activities of quangos at the local and regional levels has never been collected. Van Tilborg (in Coops, 1995) estimates that in approximately 48 per cent of municipalities privatization and quangocratization are often considered alternatives for the provision of goods and services, but actual figures are not mentioned.

The first section of this chapter will discuss the number of quangos at the national level and some of their characteristics. The chapter will then discuss the issue of accountability and end by summarizing the current quango debate in the Netherlands.

FACTS AND FIGURES

In 1993, 545 quangos existed in the Netherlands at the national level, of which over 40 per cent were established after 1980 (Algemene Rekenkamer, 1995). Figure 6.1 shows the increase in the number of quangos in the twentieth century.

Figure 6.1 shows that especially in the 1950s, 1970s and 1980s large numbers of quangos were established, though it is worth mentioning that quangos are sometimes established as clusters (i.e. the same task is performed by several organizations, for example in different regions). The survey contains 23 clusters, which account for 406 organizations, and

Figure 6.1 *The increase in the number of quangos at the national level in the Netherlands since 1910*

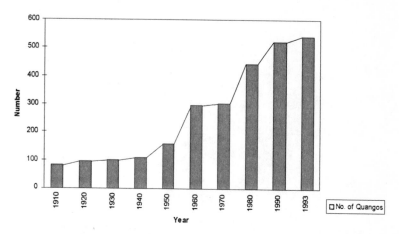

Source: Algemene Rekenkamer (1995).

139 'single' organizations. The spurts in the 1950s and 1970s are mainly caused by the establishment of such clusters of quangos (e.g. social security); the increase in the 1980s is mainly the result of an increase in the number of 'single' quangos.

As the survey of the Netherlands Court of Audit contains only quangos that existed in 1993, it is not possible to draw any conclusions on their lifespan. We have therefore made a comparison with an earlier study on the number of quangos from the Scientific Council for Government Policy (WRR, 1983). Although definitions in both studies are not entirely comparable, our study shows that only a very small number of quangos have been abolished (some 3 per cent) but mergers and reorganizations within the quango sector led to transformations in approximately 20–2 per cent of the cases. However, these organizations remain quangos. Apparently most quangos are here to stay.

Comparison with Bureaucracy

As one of the main claims underyling quangocratization is the decrease of the size of central government, it would be interesting to compare Figure 6.1 with data on the growth of bureaucracy in the Netherlands. Carasso, Koopmans, Raadschelders and Voermans (1994) have studied the number of bureaucratic units within ministries in the twentieth century,

Figure 6.2 *Bureaucracy and quangocracy in the Netherlands 1900–90*

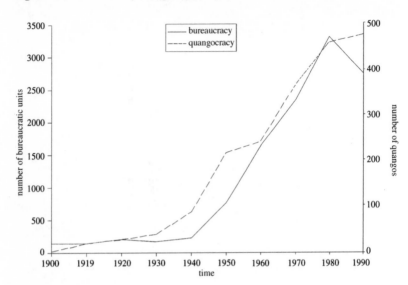

Sources: Carasso *et al.* (1994); *Algemene Rekenkamer* (1995).

using the State Directory which lists all bureaucratic units for each ministry. In Figure 6.2 we compare the increase in the number of bureaucratic units (bureaucracy) with that of the number of quangos (quangocracy). Both lines show remarkable similarities.

Figure 6.2 suggests that quangocratization has not led to a substantial decrease in the size of government bureaucracy, for it is not until the 1980s that the size of bureaucracy decreases. The figures for bureaucracy should, however, not be taken out of context, in this case the context of 'societal' growth. The effects of quangocratization on the size of bureaucracy could, for example, have been counteracted by economic and demographic changes that evoke bureaucratic growth (such as, unemployment evoking more benefits).

Types of Quangos

Quangos are characterized by a large diversity in legal basis, tasks and way of financing. Table 6.1 provides some random examples of quangos.

Legal Basis

The most common (almost 55 per cent) legal basis of quangos in the Netherlands in 1993 is public law. Within public and private law, different

Table 6.1: Examples of quangos in the Netherlands at national level in 1993

Quango	Task	Established in	Policy area
Bureaux for legal aid	Advice	1974	Justice
General pension fund for civil servants	Paying benefits	1922	Home Office
State examinations committees	Judging quality	1971	Education
The Netherlands Central Bank	Supervision	1814	Finances
Bureau for registration of architects	Registration	1988	Housing
Council for air traffic	Research	1993	Traffic
Chambers of Commerce	Coordination	1852	Economics
Chambers for Fishing	Licensing	1955	Agriculture
Social Economic Council	Make regulations	1950	Social affairs
Central organ for Health Service fees	Decision-making	1982	Welfare (health)
Service for broadcast contributions	Collecting fees	1941	Welfare (culture)

Source: Algemene Rekenkamer (1995).

legal forms are possible. For example, quangos based on private law are ususally charitable foundations. Since the 1980s the diversity of forms of quangos has increased markedly. Most quangos (90 per cent) have a legal origin of some sort (i.e. they are established by law or some other regulation). However, legislation underlying the establishment of a quango is not always complete; in approximately one third of the cases a goal for a quango is not formulated, only in half of the cases is a motive for the establishment mentioned, and in almost a third of the cases the financing of a quango has not been stipulated. If motives have been mentioned the two most important ones are:

(a) the belief (policy theory) that the efficiency of government will increase when tasks are carried out by quangos instead of central government; and
(b) the belief that due to quangocratization the distance between politics and people/society will be reduced.

Tasks

Quangos can be charged with different tasks, ranging from supervision, paying benefits to advice, research and quasi-judicature. Four main categories can be distinguished: financial transactions (such as paying benefits or issuing subsidies and grants); supervision (control, inspection, registration, quality assessment); regulations (self-regulation, issuing licences); and research, development and advice (RDA). The NCA study has listed 11 tasks, of which the most common are: quasi-judicature (21.7 per cent), judging quality (18.5 per cent), paying benefits (17.2 per cent) and supervision (13.2 per cent). Throughout the twentieth century, tasks such as supervision, paying benefits and judging quality have been the most common tasks. other tasks, such as making regulations, registration, quasi-judicature and advice have become popular only since the 1950s.

Budgets and Personnel

Quangos can be financed either through the State Budget or by levying fees. In the latter case fees can be set either by a minister or by the quango itself. The study of the Netherlands Court of Audit is based on analysis of State Budgets only. Only 60 per cent of all quangos are listed in the State Budget, which makes it difficult to draw conclusions with respect to the size of quangos' budgets.

Moreover, in most State Budgets no distinction is made between money spent *on* bureaucracy or quangos, nor on money spent *by* bureaucracy or quangos, let alone between money spent on quangos for personnel and on the execution of a policy programme by quangos. This lack of information can lead to false conclusions, such as most quangos have no expenses, revenues or personnel. Quangos whose personnel consists of civil servants seconded by central government departments are listed as having no personnel. This is the case for approximately 30 per cent of the (clusters of) quangos.

The Netherlands Court of Audit has formulated the following conclusions with regard to budget and size of quangos:

- in 1992 approximately 130,000 people were employed by quangos in the Netherlands;
- in 1992 almost DFL 38 billion (£12.6 billion) was spent on quangos by central government which amounts to 18 per cent of the total expenditures of the Dutch government in 1992;
- approximately DFL 160 billion (£53.3 billion) was spent by quangos in 1992 and approximately the same amount was received by quangos (revenues; 38 billion from state budget and 122 billion from fees and levying); and

- DFL 126 billion (£41.8 billion) was spent in 1992 on social security and health insurance by quangos (Algemene Rekenkamer, 1995: 15).

Policy Areas

Policy areas are operationalized as parent departments. There appear to be large differences between policy areas, not only in the number of quangos that existed in these areas in 1993 (Figure 6.3), but also in the rate of establishment of quangos over time.

The fields of social affairs, justice, agriculture, welfare, housing and planning, and education have the largest numbers of quangos, whereas defence and foreign affairs have only one quango each. Further analysis shows that in some fields growth displays a more stable pattern (such as infrastructure and agriculture) while in other areas quangos are established in spurts (such as housing and planning, and social affairs). In almost all fields an increase took place in the number of quangos in the 1980s. Leaving out foreign affairs and defence (only one quango each), there appear to be two kinds of pattern. On the one hand, there are policy areas

Figure 6.3 *Quangos in policy areas under parent department*

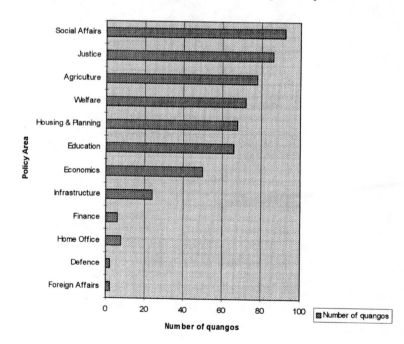

in which quangos are established to perform a specific task, examples are justice, housing and planning, and education. Quangos in these policy areas are typically established in spurts and preferably based on public law (with the exception of education). The major motive for the establishment of quangos in these policy areas is efficiency. On the other hand, there are policy areas in which quangos are charged with all kinds of tasks: agriculture, economics, social affairs, welfare and infrastructure. Most quangos in these areas are based on private law (except in the field of social affairs) and their establishment is based on motives such as: the need for independence and self-regulation; devolution and citizen involvement; or the continuation of a historically established tradition. In these policy areas quangos are established in small numbers at stable intervals (except social affairs). So far we have discussed several characteristics of quangos: numbers, size, tasks and organizational form. The next section of the chapter focuses on the accountability of quangos.

ACCOUNTABILITY OF QUANGOS

The assessment of information on the performance of quangos, i.e. the *accountability* of quangos, was the main topic of the NCA study. It is important to pay attention to this topic for three reasons. First, there is no *a priori* evidence that the goals of establishing quangos will be realized. Studies on intended and unintended consequences of policy-making show that goals sometimes run the risk of being so promising and challenging that politicians and bureaucrats, merely by stressing their importance in public, believe that they are already realized. Sieber (1981) gives examples and calls this overcommitment. To find out whether the assumptions behind the creation of quangos (efficiency, distance reduction) are true, auditing is necessary. Second, the creation of quangos may lead to unintended or undesired consequences that are actually counterproductive to the initial goals. Cream skimming is an example of such a consequence. And finally, a large amount of public funds is spent on and by quangos.

Accountability entails two dimensions: scrutiny and openness to the public (cf. Weir and Hall, 1994). Scrutiny is achieved if external control or evaluation is possible; that is, if quangos provide (written) information which can be checked by others (such as members of parliament, audit offices, Ombudsmen). Openness to the public is achieved if quangos' actions are transparent, for example if board meetings are held in public, and if citizens have opportunities to influence quangos' actions, for example,

through the use of a complaints procedure. Table 6.2 shows which requirements of accountability have been made for Dutch quangos.

As most (75 per cent) quangos are subject to the open government code
of practice, *scrutiny* is usually possible, for example, by the relevant
Ombudsman. However, 28 per cent of the quangos do not have to publish
an annual report, which we consider to be the minimal amount of accountability. In fact, in 18 per cent of the cases no requirements have been made
at all to ensure that quangos provide information on their performance,
while in 54 per cent of the quangos adequate and available information on
the performance is lacking (Algemene Rekenkamer, 1995).

As far as *openness* to the public is concerned, public meetings and complaint procedures are not required in most cases. In 1994 it was determined
that all quangos at national level are subjected to the General Civil Law (in
Dutch: *Algemene Wet Bestuursrecht*) which enables citizens to settle differences with (public) organizations. However, this does not imply that quangos do have a formal complaint procedure; according to Table 6.2 only
7 per cent of the quangos do. The data from a small survey by the National
Ombudsman (NO) in 1993 among Dutch quangos at national level con-
firms that there is little or no concern for the influence of consumers of
goods or services produced by quangos, in particular in the policy areas of
education, housing, traffic and agriculture (in both studies). The NO
survey covered 322 quangos and although over 75 per cent indicated that
they have to comply with general legal procedures in the event of complaints, a formal complaints procedure was present in only 35 per cent.[1]
The number of reported complaints is extremely low; 50 per cent of the
quangos in the NO survey reported that they had had only one complaint
in every 1,000 transactions (measured in the number of contacts with citizens), and approximately 20 per cent of the quangos reported one complaint in every 100 transactions. However, as most quangos have no formal
complaints procedure, they do not keep track of the number of complaints.

So far we have discussed the requirements of accountability. However,
requirements alone do not make a quango account for its performance
adequately. Table 6.3 lists a number of requirements and the number of

---

[1]The sample in the NO survey is not fully representative. Fifty-nine per cent of the
quangos in the study of Netherlands Court of Audit was questioned in the NO
survey, but quangos concerned more with accountability are overrepresented,
as indicated by the high number of organizations that publish annual reports
(84 per cent in this survey, 61 per cent in the study of the Netherlands Court of
Audit). Moreover, quangos from the policy areas of justice, home office and
finances were underrepresented.

Table 6.2:   Accountability of quangos at national level in the
Netherlands in 1993

Requirements	% Quangos (N = 545)
Publish annual report	72
Publish annual account	71.5
Publish evaluation report	13
Have board appointments-procedure	91.5
Hold public meetings	25
Subject to open government code of practice	75
Formulate complaints procedure	7

Source: Algemene Rekenkamer (1995).

Table 6.3:   Analysis of annual reports of quangos and
agencies at local and national level in the Netherlands

	% Organizations that report on	
	All (N = 84)	Quangos (N = 36)
Goals	78.5%	80.6%
Input indicators	87.3%	83.3%
Norms set for input	10.1%	5.6%
Output indicators	92.4%	97.2%
Norms set for output	17.7%	16.7%
Costs per good	31.6%	30.6%
Indication of productivity	25.3%	22.2%
Norms productivity	2.5%	0%
Effects of activities	49.4%	52.8%
Side-effects	12.7%	19.5%
Quality care	54.4%	41.2%
Quality indicators	15.2%	16.7%
Norms for quality	7.6%	8.3%
Budget	35.4%	38.9%

Note: Although 47 organizations participated in 1996 only
42 reports were evaluated.
Source: Arthur Andersen & Co (1995; 1996).

quangos that comply with these requirements. Strict requirements have not been imposed on all quangos but research would suggest that *if* rules are imposed most quangos will comply with them, although that in itself is no guarantee that the information on the performance is adequate; a quango that sends in a poorly prepared annual report does not provide us with more information than a quango that does not send in an annual report at all.

In 1995 and 1996 Arthur Andersen organized a contest among quangos and agencies at the national and local levels in the Netherlands on the best annual report. In 1995 37 organizations participated (20 quangos at national level) and in 1996 47 organizations (16 quangos at national level). Some random examples of organizations that participated are: Inland Revenue (winner in 1995), the student loan company (winner in 1996), public universities, food inspection service, service for broadcast contributions, land registry, police authorities, Arts Council. The annual reports were evaluated by the jury (i.e. points could be received if the items were present) on 139 items in six main categories:

1. Basic information (address, composition of board, structure of organization).
2. Goals (organizational goals, mission, vision, strategy, activities, future expectations).
3. Management (personnel, automation, maintenance, environmental care).
4. Performance (input, output, productivity, effects, quality of production).
5. Finances.
6. User-friendliness (layout).

Analysis of the data shows that the evaluations of most annual reports are not very positive. The best annual report was given 6.3 on a scale of 1 to 10 (with an average of 3.9 and a standard deviation of 1.2 on the same scale). Most organizations do well in the basic information, goals and management categories. Analysis of the data shows that most reports lack much information, especially with regard to performance indicators. Table 6.3 lists how many organizations reported on some main indicators of performance, as used in the evaluation. It shows that most organizations pay attention to goals, input and output indicators but in very few cases norms have been set for these indicators, nor has information been provided to compare production with former years. Effects of the activities are discussed in almost half of the annual reports, as is quality care.

The jury concluded that, although the reports in 1996 were on average evaluated slightly better than in 1995:

- the discussion of goals, mission, strategy, etc. could be greatly improved; these subjects are often vaguely formulated, only implicitly treated or scattered throughout the annual report;
- management topics are often mentioned but not discussed fully;
- most reports lack information on budgets; and
- although indicators are often formulated, insight into effectiveness and efficiency of organizations is hindered because of the lack of norm setting for indicators and comparisons of indicators over time (Arthur Andersen, 1995: 8–9; 1996: 8–10).

CONCLUSION

This chapter has demonstrated that the increase in the number of quangos, or quangocratization, has not led to a decrease in bureaucratization, nor to an increase in the use of performance indicators and performance assessment (cf. accountability). The results of NCA survey have triggered a previously absent interest in quangos. Government and Parliament want to increase the primacy of politics; more accountability, more uniformity in legal arrangements and more restrictions for the establishment of quangos. Some evaluations have already taken place, but a full legal framework has yet to be established.

REFERENCES

Algemene Rekenkamer (1995) *Verslag over 1994, deel III; 'Zelfstandige bestuursorganen en ministeriële verantwoordelijkheid'*. Tweede Kamer, vergaderjaar 1994–1995, 24130, no. 3 (Den Haag: sdu).

Arthur Anderson & Co. (1995) *Verslaggeving en prestatieverantwoording bij de overheid. Juryverslag F.G. Kordestrofee 1995* ('s-Gravenhage: Arthur Anderson & Co.).

——(1996) *Verslaggeving en prestatieverantwoording bij de overheid. Juryverslag F. G. Kordestrofee 1996* ('s-Gravenhage, Arthur Andersen & Co.).

Carasso, L.C., Koopmans, J.M.P., Raadschelders, J.C.N. and Voermans, I.F.J. (1994) *Organisatiedifferentiatie bij de rijksoverheid in historisch perspectief.* Bestuurswetenschappen, 6, 483–95.

Coops, R.H. (ed.) (1995) *Van overheid naar markt*. (Den Haag: Sdu).

Sieber, S. (1981) *Fatal Remedies* (New York: Plenum Press).

WRR (1983) Berge, J.B.J.M. ten, P. Haighton, P. den Hoed, H.F. Munneke en F.A.M. Stroink, *Organen en rechtspersonen rondom de centrale overheid.* Wetenschappelijke Raad voor het Regeringsbeleid ('s-Gravenhage: Staatsuitgeverij V35, delen 1–3).

Weir S. and Hall W. (1994) *EGO-trip: Extra-Governmental Organizations in the United Kingdom and their accountability. The Democratic Audit of the United Kingdom* (London: Charter 88 Trust).

7 Quangos in New Zealand
Enid Wistrich

Quangos in New Zealand developed and proliferated over a long period for much the same reasons as in other comparable countries: to carry out specific, often single, commercial or technical functions, to fund social and cultural activities without direct ministerial accountability, as well as to provide expert advice and research services, and to regulate private activities in the public interest. By the 1980s New Zealand had several 'non-core departments', including the Post Office and the Police (a national service), government trading corporations like the railways and broadcasting, statutory producer boards and mixed ownership industrial and commercial enterprises. There were also elected Hospital Boards, Maori Trust Boards (for tribal representation and development) and several hundred special-purpose authorities carrying out functions at local level, ranging from harbours and drainage to electricity power supply and pest destruction. The level of quasi-government organization was high and complex.

THE REFORM OF THE PUBLIC SECTOR

In 1984 a newly elected Labour government set out to restructure the state sector radically (Wistrich, 1992). The prime reason was to improve the growth and productivity of the economy and promote national wealth. The prescription for the public sector was greater efficiency and a more competitive environment. The first measures taken were to transform state organizations engaged in industry and commerce into profitable enterprises able to compete in market conditions. Then the public services were reformed in order to give greater value for money and improved systems of accountability and financial management. Government services were separated from the central departments and set up as operational units in the public sector, or contracted from the private sector. The reforms started with central government departments but very soon affected quangos. In the changes that followed some quangos were eliminated, some were joined to the local government service controlled by elected representatives, and some had their organizations and lines of accountability renewed and reorganized. In addition, a whole set of new quangos was established to meet defined purposes.

The picture appears complex but the key factor is a strong theoretical foundation and rationale for the reforms. In contrast to the 'incremental', casual growth and development of government and quangos up to this period founded on confidence in the state sector and the efficacy of government action, the reforms were 'rational', based on the neo-liberal preference for the market and competition, theories of public choice, transaction cost analysis and principal and agent theory derived from economists, theories of the business firm (Boston, 1991; Self, 1993). The New Zealand government had a blueprint, drawn up by the Treasury and published in the report *Government Management* (1987). It followed the ideas through which subsequent governments have continued to develop and refine. The principles that affect the reorganization of quangos are: first, the decoupling of policy determination from operations management in a system of 'purchasers' and 'suppliers'; second, a principal and agent relationship between ministers and departments, and departments and agencies, which report or are accountable to them; third, the avoidance in the agencies of the 'producer capture' and 'rent-seeking' of public choice theory.

Since 1987 central government has been reshaped to comprise 'core' departments which are responsible for policy determination, financing services, 'purchasing' services and monitoring service delivery. With three exceptions (the Departments of Welfare, Inland Revenue and Justice) service delivery is now the function of state owned enterprises, crown entities and private and voluntary sector organizations. Ministers are the purchasers of service output and departments or other agencies are responsible for supplying them according to the quantity, quality and price agreed in a contract of service. The chief executives of all government agencies are employers of their labour force and responsible for the work of their agencies.

THE ROLE OF QUANGOS

Quangos have been reorganized to fulfil several different kinds of function. One important group now run public utilities and commercial type enterprises, operating under the State Owned Enterprises Act (1986). In January 1996 there were 15 SOEs covering important functions: electricity production, television, radio, postal services and Crown forestry management. Others set up after 1986, such as Railways and Telecom, have since been privatized. The second largest group is a conglomerate one in terms of function but comes under the single legal category of 'crown entities' (formerly known as 'crown agencies') under the Public Finance Act (1989) and the Public Finance Amendment Act (1992). The 1989 Act defined them as:

> any entity over which the Crown is able to exercise control as a result of
> (a)   ownership of a majority of shares or
> (b)   power to appoint a majority of members of the governing body or
> (c)   significant financial interdependence

and excluded government departments, offices of Parliament and state-owned enterprises from this category.

Crown entities are usually established by statute and nearly all are controlled by boards of directors appointed by the Crown. They are responsible for their operational activities through chief executives hired by the boards. Their financial resources come from tax revenues as well as from private capital, fees and earnings in varying degrees.

In 1996 there were some 3,000 crown entities, but of these 2,690 were School Boards of Trustees. There were other multiple categories, for example 63 Crown Health Enterprises, 39 tertiary education institutions, 21 Business development boards and 9 Crown Research Institutes. But there were also 71 single crown entities with services ranging from regulatory (e.g. Accounting Standards Review Board, Takeovers Panel) to quasi-judicial (e.g. Police Complaints Authority, Race Relations Conciliator), to the arts (e.g. New Zealand Symphony Orchestra, NZ Film Commission), to social welfare (e.g. Housing Corporation of NZ) and to substantial enterprises (e.g. Auckland International Airport Ltd) (NZ Official Yearbook, 1996).

It is important to note the grouping of crown entities in clusters of organizations for specific service functions in accordance with the principles of government organization. For example, in the Health Services, the Department sets out policy, specifies outputs and provides finance. Regional Health Authorities purchase the services and the providers may be other crown entities, the Crown Health Enterprises, or Community Trusts owned by local communities. Other crown entities in this service area are the Public Health Commission which advises on public health services and purchases them, the Health Research Council, the Health and Disability Commissioner, the NZ Artificial Limb Board, the Blood Transfusion Trust and the Health Sponsorship Council. In another important functional area, transport, three different crown entities are responsible for safety, licensing and enforcing standards in, respectively, land, sea and air transport, a further one investigates accidents, another (Transit NZ) funds local authorities to build and maintain roads, and three more run the major airports. Education again illustrates the 'mixed' composition of government organization. First, the Education Department sets out policies and guidelines, and there is a separate department for inspection (The Education Review Office). Crown entities provide the Special Education Service and the Teacher Registration Board. But the same legal form is used by 39 entities providing tertiary education and 2,690 School Boards of Trustees elected by parents who now manage schools within their budget allocations.

If the definition of quangos is extended to include voluntary organizations largely dependent on public funds and government contracts for their funding, the number grows. A survey in 1991 of 65 member organizations of the New Zealand Federation of Voluntary Agencies found that two received all their funding from government and 11 received none, but the average received was about half their total income from government sources (Malcolm *et al.*, 1993). Voluntary organizations have many possible legal forms ranging from charitable trusts to 'incorporated' societies and companies (usually used for trading purposes). Their government funding may come from government departments, or from crown entities, in addition to contracts for service provision, from for example Regional Health Authorities.

Lastly, the quangos used for local authority work must be included. These are intended to be viable enterprises at arm's length from elected local councils. Local authorities have a statutory obligation to contract local authority trading enterprises (LATES) to construct roads and provide public transport. They may also use them to provide other trading services, e.g. refuse collection and sewerage.

The list is not exhaustive by any means. Advisory quangos abound, with greater or lesser degrees of importance. For example, under the NZ Nuclear Free Zone, Disarmament and Armaments Control Act (1987), a Public Advisory Committee on disarmament and arms control of eight meets three times a year. It is appointed and financed by the Foreign Affairs Department and is chaired by the Minister for Disarmament. In the area of Maori affairs, a successful initiative in Maori language teaching for young children (Te Kohanga Reo) is financed by government funds. Other quasi-public bodies exist which have been set up or empowered under various statutes but have not been drawn into the 'crown entities' category.

The overall picture has been described by the State Services Commission as 'the three-tier state sector'. It shows central departments confined to policy advice and some remaining 'core' services as its first tier, crown entities as its second, and private and community sector organizations as its third tier delivering services under contract to first and second tier agencies (SSC, 1996). This picture is rather too simplistic compared to the reality – where, for example, are local authorities or regulatory and advisory agencies? – but it shows the pattern which proponents of the new regime have designed and it offers a framework for management and accountability.

MANAGEMENT AND ACCOUNTABILITY IN THE NEW SYSTEM

Accountability in the New Zealand system is seen as a system of management which will relate service outputs, for which government units and agencies are responsible, to basic strategic aims set out by ministers. In 1993 a statement on 'Strategic Result Areas for the Public Sector 1994–7' outlined nine such areas. These are complemented by Key Results Areas for the departments setting out up to six (measurable) targets to be achieved in a two- or three-year period (SSC, 1996). Each departmental chief executive concludes a formal contract with the minister to cover these areas and is responsible for delivering them. Ministers thus become 'purchasers' of service for which departments are 'suppliers', and the service outputs are specified in the contract, including quality, quantity, price and timeliness. In its turn, each department makes purchase agreements with suppliers such as state-owned enterprises and crown entities, who again may purchase from other entities or private firms. Financial management systems introduced by the Public Finance Acts of 1989 and 1992 set out the reporting obligations and lines of responsibility and aim to establish management incentives for 'effective and efficient' use of resources (Pallot, 1991; Boston, 1993).

Within this system, state-owned enterprises have to agree their objectives and measures of performance with their Minister. They present an annual Statement of Corporate Intent which has been compared with 'much the same corporate data as is provided to investors in listed companies' (SSC, 1996), showing how they plan to achieve their objectives. Their performance is then monitored by the responsible department and by the Treasury. If there are socially desirable services which are not financially viable, they are discussed with the minister and departments and may be subsidized, with full transparency and public acknowledgement of the subsidy.

Crown entities follow a similar pattern, but there are variations because of the variety of types and tasks of the entities and the enabling legislation.

Under the Public Finance Amendment Act (1992), crown entities (including School Boards of Trustees) are required to include 'statements of service performance' in their annual financial reports. They have to set out their objectives and specify their outputs at the start of the year, and they must report on the outputs actually produced at the end of the year. A smaller list of crown entities, including some but not all of the first ones, are required to prepare 'statements of intent' which are sent to the responsible minister. These are comparable to the 'statements of corporate intent' prepared by state-owned enterprises, but are likely to include more non-commercial objectives. Crown research institutes fall within this category. Education and health agencies, and others set up under separate statutes, have their own specific accounting and financial management arrangements. The reports are all presented to the responsible minister and they and the annual reports are tabled in Parliament. A Crown Company Monitoring Advisory Unit set up in 1993 helps to monitor the reports, especially those of limited liability companies owned by the Crown.

Thus the reporting system, combined with new accounting practices, should deliver an overview of the managerial performance of the entities in relation to their objectives. There are, however, reservations about two aspects of the new systems. The first is whether the same reporting framework can be applied to the great variety of crown entities. School Boards of Trustees, for example, have very different activities and responsibilities to the Power Company Limited or the Civil Aviation Authority. (In practice, all School Boards' performances are now combined in one annual report.) Second, the arrangements for monitoring may become so complex and bureaucratic that compliance costs become burdensome and a disincentive to the private sector experts involved on the boards of entities (SSC, 1995). The State Services Commission is currently reviewing the accounting and reporting regimes of different groups of crown entities to ensure that they are appropriate to their activities. The Commission is also examining the methods of monitoring the 'ownership' interest of departments in the entities. An earlier effort to formulate 'ownership agreements' similar to the 'purchase agreements' for services is now being modified in order to reduce compliance costs (SSC, 1995).

POLITICAL ACCOUNTABILITY

The accountability of the entities to the public as citizens rests on the role of ministers and their responsibility to Parliament. Ministers are responsible for their departments' work in relation to the objectives agreed and outcomes achieved. But there is a different kind of responsibility held by other ministers as shareholding owners of entities supplying services and operations. For example, two ministers are each responsible for the Crown Research Institutes and the Crown Health Enterprises but two other ministers are responsible for the Departments of Science, Research and Technology and for Health. The same division of responsibility exists for state-owned enterprises. Crown Forestry Management and the Land Corporation have a Minister for State-Owned Enterprises, but other ministers are responsible for the overall functions, e.g. Forestry, Conservation, Environment. The new convention of responsibility is that functional area ministers are responsible for setting policy goals and monitoring performance but not for output and performance (Martin, 1993). The intention is to avoid producer 'capture' of policy advice (Self, 1993). This division of responsibility between policy and operations is one aspect of a long-running argument – the extent to which ministers can be held responsible for operational service. Whatever the formal position, the experience is that the public looks for a single figure to blame when things go wrong. For a minister to say that s/he has no access, as of right, to the operational unit responsible for the service (Martin, 1993) will be perceived as unhelpful, as well as possibly frustrating for the minister. We are back to the well-known distinction (or lack of it) between policy and administration or management, and how it affects political responsibility. This discussion also draws attention to arguments about the merits of the principal–agent model used in business applied to the public sector.

The select committees of Parliament have an important role to play in reviewing the reports of SOEs and crown entities. Those with commercial-type functions are regularly reviewed by the state enterprises select committee and their chief executives are called to attend and answer questions. Other crown entities may be called from time to time to appear before an appropriate committee. Certainly the reforms in accounting and financial management systems have required more detailed disclosure of both financial and non-financial information and related to them to outputs and objectives. This has contributed to the knowledge on which judgements can be based. However, parliamentarians need to be aware of and understand the information provided and devote the necessary time to the facts if they are to be used properly for evaluation purposes. Select committees have too few analysts or advisers to help them, but are assisted by the work of the Audit Office whose reports accompany the annual accounts submitted to Parliament (Pallot, 1993).

The workload of New Zealand's small Parliament of 97 members has thus been very considerable. Ministers often hold three or four portfolios each, while other MPs staff numerous select committees. This problem has been partly ameliorated since the 1996 election which increased the number of MPs by 20 per cent. It has been suggested that MPs need more support to carry out this aspect of their work (Laking, 1994). The burdens are heavier than they might be because functions in the public sector are very centralized. The 73 territorial local authorities with their elected councillors are allotted limited functions chiefly relating to roads, electricity and water supply, drainage and refuse collection. School Boards of elected trustees run the schools and are a good example of decentralized democratic management, but the arts, sport and leisure, road safety, business development and other functions are all currently under the remit of crown entities without any direct democratic input.

OTHER FORMS OF PUBLIC ACCOUNTABILITY

If political accountability is both limited and tenuous there are more direct ways in which citizens may become aware of the work of quangos and their rights in relation to them New Zealand's Official Information Act (1982) applies to all government agencies. Official information held by the agencies must be released unless there is a strong case for non-disclosure based on security needs, constitutional conventions or the need to ensure frank exchanges of opinion between ministers and officials or between officials. (Privacy of information is safeguarded under the Privacy Act 1993.) The openness of New Zealand government makes officials at all levels aware of the potential publicity their decisions may receive and strengthens public accountability. This access has been well used by interest groups and the press. For recourse in individual cases of malpractice, the Ombudsman Act (1975) is important. It applies to all state-owned enterprises and to some crown entities such as Crown Health Enterprises which are regarded as 'related organizations' of government departments.

CONCLUSIONS

New Zealand's highly systematic reorganization of the public sector structure and the systems of management makes it an interesting testing ground of the 'new' management. Quangos have their place within this system in the form of state-owned enterprises, crown entities and other statutory and government financed agencies delivering services or providing advice and regulation. The financial and management systems introduced have provided a sound basis for management accountability under a principal and agent model in a centralized system of government. Less attention has been given to political accountability, which rests on the long links to Ministers and Parliament, but the practice of open government ensures that information is available to all citizens.

REFERENCES

Boston, J. (1991) 'The Theoretical Underpinning of Public Sector Restructuring in New Zealand', in J. Boston *et al.* (eds), *Reshaping the State – New Zealand's Bureaucratic Revolution* (Auckland: Oxford University Press).
Boston, J. (1993) 'Financial Management Reform: Principles and Practice in New Zealand', *Public Policy & Administration*, 8: 1.
Laking, R. (1994) 'The New Zealand Management Reforms', *Australian Journal of Public Administration*, 53: 3.
Malcolm, M., Rivers, M. and Smyth, K. (1993) 'Emerging Trends for the Voluntary Sector', in G. Hawke and D. Robinson (eds), *Performance without Profit: the Voluntary Welfare Sector in New Zealand* (Wellington: Institute of Policy Studies).
Martin, J. (1994) 'The Role of the State in Administration', in A. Sharp (ed.), *Leap into the Dark – The Changing Role of the State in New Zealand since 1984* (Auckland: Auckland University Press).
New Zealand Official Yearbook (1996) (Wellington).
Pallot, J. (1991) 'Financial Management Reform' and 'Accounting, Auditing and Accountability', in J. Boston *et al.* (eds), *Reshaping the State – New Zealand's Bureaucratic Revolution* (Auckland: Oxford University Press).
Self, P. (1993) *Government and the Market? The Politics of Public Choice* (Basingstoke: Macmillan).
State Services Commission (1995) *Commissioner's Report for the Year Ended 30 June 1995* (Wellington).
State Services Commission (1996) *New Zealand's State Reform: a Decade of Change* (Wellington).
Treasury (1987) *Government Management: Brief to the Incoming Government,* (Wellington: Government Printer).
Wistrich, E. (1992) 'Restructuring Government New Zealand Style', in *Public Administration*, 70: 1.
Wistrich, E. (1992) 'Managing Sub-National Government in New Zealand', in *Public Money and Management* 12: 4.

8 Quangos in Denmark and Scandinavia: Trends, Problems and Perspectives
Carsten Greve

In Scandinavia, no acronym has been given to what British people refer to as quangos (Barker, 1982), PGOs (Hood and Schuppert, 1988) or EGOs (Weir and Hall, 1994). In Denmark and Scandinavia we usually talk about these organizations as 'semi-public organizations' or more generally about 'indirect public administration' (Modeen and Rosas, 1988). Many organizations in Denmark belong to an institutional *grey zone* between the public sector and the private sector (Marcusson and Peterson, 1990; Greve, 1995a).

Danish law does not define quangos. However, two laws are useful in relation to quangos: the Law on Public Administration and the Law on Access to Public Files. These laws define the structural boundaries of the state, but do not include organizations which are established under private law even though the tasks may be identical to the tasks performed by 'ordinary' public sector organizations. Quangos are then 'outside' the structural boundary of the state, performing tasks for public sector organizations. One possible way to define organizations in the 'grey zone' is to say that they are organizations which mix governance mechanisms such as authority, exchange and altruism (comparable to the three spheres of state, market and civil society) (see Bozeman, 1987). Briefly, organizations which may mix governance mechanisms are: special public agencies, state-owned enterprises, public foundations, self-governing institutions, voluntary organizations and associations ('non-profit') and private firms with long-term contracts with government ('for-profit'). Advisory bodies are *not* considered quangos in Denmark, but a part of the state itself. Many contract agencies could be considered as quangos. The aim of this chapter is to provide a brief overview of the quango state in Denmark and Scandinavia, outline its history, discuss the major trends and the problems associated with quangos in Denmark and Scandinavia. Where possible, links and correlations will be made between the British debate and the debate in Denmark.

OVERVIEW

Table 8.1 indicates the range of quangos that exist in Denmark. *Special public agencies* are a limited group of organizations, which are so special they seem to defy ordinary classification. The National Bank is the prime example, but this category would also include the Copenhagen Harbour and Post Denmark. Although the National Bank does not have the same formal independent status as the German Bundesbank it is still indepedent in action and politicians cannot interfere with its day-to-day decisions. Only a handful of special public agencies exist. Some, for example Post Denmark, are being considered for other organizational forms, hence they are likely to diminish in numbers. *State-owned enterprises* have recently been described by the Ministry of Finance (1996a: 69) as 'a Danish way of privatization'. It involves former public enterprises being made into private law companies owned by the state. *Public foundations* are also a varied species. Usually, a governing board is appointed and directs money to certain causes, for example in agriculture or the arts. Politicians cannot interfere with their decisions, but they can appoint new board members. *Self-governing institutions* describe a variety of organizations which are funded by the state,

Table 8.1: Quangos in Denmark

Type of quango	Examples	Current trend
Special public agencies	The National Bank Post Denmark	Diminishing in numbers
State-owned enterprises and other companies with public ownership or influence	TeleDenmark Copenhagen Airport	'Danish way of privatization'
Public foundations	State Foundation for Art	Independence preserved
Self-governing institutions	Kindergartens Folk High Schools	Independence preserved
Voluntary organizations	Danish Red Cross Danish Refugee Help	Creeping bureaucratization and rediscovered tool in social welfare provision
Private firms on long-term contract with the state	International Service Systems (cleaning) Falck (fire and ambulance service)	Increased use as a tool in welfare service provision

but which decide how to spend it independently. They include kindergartens, private schools and folk high schools (a special kind of Danish
school which pupils attend without sitting entrance exams). Christensen
(1988) counted 3,992 such organizations in the 1980s. *Voluntary organizations* can be any organization from sports organizations to the Danish Red
Cross or Danish Refugee Help. The trend concerning these organizations is
described below. *Private firms on long-term contracts with the state* represent a new trend with regard to social service provision. However, some
companies, like *Falck* described below, have been involved for several
decades in delivering public services, while being a private law company.

Summing up we can say that in Denmark – as in other countries – there
is no single type of quango but a range of bodies. The history of quangos
may point to the reason why, and it is to that question we now turn.

HISTORY

Quangos in Denmark and Scandinavia are not a new phenomenon. The
state and local government have long relied on quangos to perform certain
tasks. In the old days, colonies, e.g. the West Indies islands, were governed
by a quango. Voluntary organizations were used to deliver public service,
but their role was played down during the building of the modern welfare
state. In Denmark, ambulances and rescue services have been provided
mainly by a private company, *Falck*, since the beginning of the twentieth
century. Private schools and kindergartens exist side by side with public
institutions of the same kind. Denmark has a long tradition in combining
aspects of the public sector and the private sector.

A feature of the Danish case is the sloppiness with which co-operation
between the public sector and the private sector has taken place (from both
an administrative and political perspective). In Denmark, sweeping administrative reform has never been the order of the day. There is a lack of
interest in institutional reform (Knudsen, 1995). Consequently, an apathetic consensus has developed which has allowed problems to be solved
in an informal and flexible manner.

In other Scandinavian countries. the approach to institutional reform is
slightly different. Sweden has adopted a more coherent stance on the organization of its public administration, based on explicit administrative principles, although quangos have been developed more haphazardly (Tarchys,
1988). Norway seems more inclined to discuss and adopt general laws
for specific kinds of quangos such as public enterprises (NOU, 1991).
Finland tends to follow the German classification of independent public

law organizations, with four organizational types of indirect public administration: independent public agencies, public associations, state-owned companies and private subjects (Suksi, 1988: 510; Rosas, 1988: 92). Both Norway and Sweden have had research-based 'power commissions', whose official brief was to map the power structure, including the organizational features of the state.

Organizations that fit our current quango description have been around for some time. The administrative and political understanding has not been adequately equipped to deal with them. They have attracted little attention in Danish research on public administration with a few exceptions (Meyer, 1979: 107–15; Christensen, 1988). As a consequence there is no special legal categorization, and there are no coherent political guidelines as to how organizations should be drawn into policy-making, and which organizations the government can hive off. There is little estimation, evaluation and 'hard evidence' about the experiences with quangos and until recently, there has been little willingness to discuss these matters.

This situation is slowly changing. *Grey zone* problems are now being addressed in official government reports, for example on the state companies (Ministry of Finance, 1993; Werlauff, 1993). Contracting out has been the subject of a number of reviews (Ministry of Finance and Ministry for Home Affairs, 1995; Ministry of Finance, 1996: PLS Consult, 1997). The voluntary organizations' role in the Danish polity has recently being investigated by a committee established by the Ministry of Social Affairs (Betænkning [White Paper] No. 1332, 1997).

A recent conference, held jointly by a Select Committee in the Danish Parliament and a think-tank on the Public Sector's Condition and Future in April 1996 on *The Grey Zone*, widened the discussion in Denmark to a larger audience among politicians, civil servants and grey zone organizations themselves as well as the press. Further discussions were generated by the think-tank, and in its final report, the chairman expressed amazement at the critical and constructive public debate that had taken place (Beck Jørgensen *et al.*, 1996).

A major research programme on 'Democracy and Institutional Change' began in 1996 in Denmark, and one project within the programme deals with 'autonomization of public agencies and quangos'. Research in voluntary organizations is taking place in various universities and research centres throughout Scandinavia (Selle, 1996). The place of new organizational forms in changed governance structures attracts researchers' attention. Privatization, corporatization and contracting out are slowly beginning to be explored.

TRENDS

Four main trends can be identified in the Danish case.

Establishing State-owned Companies and Contract Agencies

The first trend is quite dramatic. In the early 1980s the privatization issue was never put firmly on the Danish policy agenda (Andersen, Greve and Torfing, 1996). However, since 1990 the government has established many state companies under private law. In 1996, 47 state-owned companies existed in Denmark, and they employed 27,000 people (Ministry of Finance, 1997) out of a total of roughly 150,000 in the state sector and 800,000 in the whole public sector. Norway also has long experience with state-owned companies (Grøndahl and Grønlie, 1995). Post Denmark (equivalent to the Royal Mail) with 25,000 employees, is organized as an 'autonomous public enterprise' (hence its inclusion above as 'a special public agency'). Statistics have not existed in this area before. However, the Danish Statistical Office has recently published the first statistics on the subject of public enterprises with the explicit aim of shedding light on 'the part of the Danish economy which is owned or directly controlled by the government or local government'. It shows that half of public investment is made in public enterprises. Public enterprises are defined widely and cover the unmapped (until now) area of enterprises in local government. Two hundred public company reports are used to compute the data material (Danish Statistical Office, 1997).

The explicit assumption of the reform on state-owned enterprises is a clear politics – administration split. The Ministry of Finance speaks about 'encapsulated politics' placing the whole reform firmly in the New Public Management frame of thinking. Trying to keep politics away from the companies raises grave concerns for democratic accountability (Greve, 1997).

Contract agencies can be considered a stepping-stone towards becoming a quango for some public agencies. Many of these organizations are governed by a 'market logic' as well as the traditional 'logic of politics' (see Bozeman, 1987, for a discussion of the theory of types of governance logic). A brief elaboration of their status and role is demanded. Contract agencies have taken off since 1991, with 20 agencies being established (Ministry of Finance, 1996). They cover educational institutions, research institutions and national museums, such as the State Museum for Art. An administrative reform in the 1960s divided ministries ideally into policy making departments and 'directorates' (agencies). Therefore, agencies as such were not a big idea in Denmark, nor in the rest of Scandinavia. The concept for a written contract was new though, and it was inspired by the Next Steps development in Britain. The 1960s reform was not implemented fully in all government departments, leaving the field open to a new wave of contract agencies. There have been trends and counter-trends with regard to centralization and hiving off (Beck Jørgensen and Hansen, 1995). Experience so far Shows that contract governance can be a useful tool in the public sector, provided that it is used with care (Thaarup, 1996). Research-based evaluation with contractual government is scarce.

Contract agencies are still part of the state and the minister remains responsible, as with the same Next Steps in Britain (Pliatzsky, 1992). Therefore, contract agencies are sometimes not included in 'quango counts'. I do discuss them now, because they seem to be part of the Ministry of Finance's current reform strategy for the public sector where 'autonomization' is a key word. The Minister of Finance (1996) has heralded the contract concept as the way forward for governing the public sector. In a recent report on governance forms in the Danish civil service, the Ministry of Finance made comparisons with the contract idea in Sweden, New Zealand and Australia (Ministry of Finance, 1996a). Throughout the public sector, 'contract mania' appears to have broken out with central government departments and local governments experimenting with a variety of contractual forms of governance.

Contracting Out (Involving Private Firms to Gain Access to Public Markets)

The second trend concerns contracting out. While the idea did not generate much action in the 1980s, proposals and policies for contracting out have dominated Danish public debate in recent years. Building on the ideas put forward by Savas (1987) and popularized by Osborne and Gaebler (1992), the split between an organizer and a provider has come into focus. A prag-matic stance is being embraced by key actors such as politicians and companies. In early 1996, however, the Social Democratic Prime Minister Mr Nyrup Rasmussen made it clear that social service contracting out was not on the agenda. Contracting out remains a hotly contested issue for the governing Social Democratic Party. Some local governments are experi-menting still. Two strikes connected to contracting out have seriously limited the scope for future attempts in this area of restructuring the public sector. Although guidelines have been laid down by a Council for Contracting Out, core government activities specified (Ministry of Finance,

1996c: 26–7) and think-tanks have endorsed the possibilities (Ugebrevet Mandag Morgen, 1995), the results remain poor.

Private sector companies see contracting out as one way to make inroads into the Danish public sector. New markets are being developed, for example concerning development of devices for helping handicapped people. Subsidiary companies are being created by established firms to gain access to the public market, notably in welfare services.

Joint-Venture Co-operations and 'System Export'

The third trend is that joint-venture companies are being set up at a rapid pace. The Ministry of Industry (1994, 1995) has actively been encouraging public–private partnership. In 1996, public–private co-operation was listed as one of five key policy areas for the current and future industrial policy in Denmark (Ministry of Business and industry, 1996a). A law passed in 1992 permits local governments to participate in commercial activities in company form. In 1995, 240 companies were used for this purpose, concentrating on energy, gas, traffic and solid waste disposal (Ministry for Business and Industry, 1996b). In Sweden, 1636 companies with local government participation existed at the local and regional level in 1992–3 (Johansson *et al.*, 1994). The competition law is fashioned so that public and private companies can compete on level ground. The Association of Local Governments, a powerful body in Danish politics, has issued guidance and support to 'systems export'. Reviews are showing many local governments are engaged in this kind of activity (Association of Local Governments, 1995).

Voluntary Organizations Being Used to Provide Public Service

The fourth trend is that voluntary organizations are becoming more professional and are copying the bureaucratic way government departments are organized. This trend has been going on for some time, but is especially pertinent where the receipt of large chunks of public money is involved. For example, many sports organizations, which used to be grassroots in character, are now led by experts and professionals (Klausen, 1989). Unlike their American non-profit counterparts, Scandinavian third sector organizations have a tradition for internal democratic decision-making and relying on voluntary workers (Christensen and Molin, 1995; Klausen and Selle, 1995). Almost 300 voluntary organizations were located recently, many of them performing social policy tasks for the government and local governments (Anker, 1905). Voluntary organizations are increasingly used as a tool for alternative models of social welfare provisions throughout Scandinavia (Betænkning 1332, 1997; Henriksen, 1996; Selle, 1996). If they are to compete with private firms for contracts, problems may arise for the organizations' integrity.

To take stock of the current situation: There are a number of trends which are causing the 'grey zone' to expand. New organizations are moving into the grey zone. However, some organizations are just passing through on their way to full privatization. A recent example is the public enterprise *Postal Giro*, which, after being transformed into a state-owned company, merged with one of the big commercial banks. Few quangos have been 'hived back' into the public sector. One state-owned company, *TV-2 reklame* which sells advertising slots on TV, was recently absorbed by the TV station *TV-2*, which is another quango! The question is whether the grey zone is being developed in a qualitative manner as well. What kind of problems does the grey zone in Denmark raise? It is to this question I now turn.

PROBLEMS

A number of problems can be raised with regard to quangos, for example, pay, excessive profits, economic efficiency and patronage by political parties. Here I shall concentrate on governance and democratic accountability.

Problems of Governance

Politicians' Inclinations to 'Dump' Problems in the Grey Zone
Many unpopular decisions can be covered up when organizations in the grey zone are established. Closing hospitals is never popular. A recent quango set up as a company and owned by the state and the local governments in Copenhagen advocated that one central hospital should be closed down – a decision that would have been met with fierce popular opposition if it had been taken in a democratic assembly. Companies are also in charge of building bridges between the islands of Sealand and Funen, and Denmark and Sweden, as well as planning a whole new part of the capital which should make Copenhagen and southern Sweden into a vibrant enterprising zone.

Avoidance of responsibility is another well-known problem. Agency executives and politicians can shift the blame if things go wrong. Recently this happened when the Danish State Factory for Army Clothing was shut down, following conversion to a private law company in 1992, after more than 200 years in operation Politicians blamed the board and the chief executive for not running the company efficiently. The CEO accused the politicians of a woolly brief in the first place, and for not accepting the consequences of competition.

Number and Range of Tasks Performed by Quangos
As yet, no clear discussion has taken place on what kinds of tasks should be entrusted to quangos. The contracting-out question has not really moved beyond issues such as cleaning and elderly care. The purchaser–provider model allows for many tasks previously considered public in nature to be produced by an external private firm. Yet, practical problems arise when specific tasks are contracted out, and the Ministry of Finance (1996c: 28–30) recently acknowledged that there are no easy answers as to which 'grey zone' tasks can be delegated to private firms.

Differentiating between user-directed services and common-weal services has been suggested (Anthonsen and Beck Jørgensen, 1992). Instead of the public sector, the term 'the common sector' has been proposed, indicating a widened responsibility for public tasks (Dalsgaard and Jorgensen, 1994). We might fear a new 'public capitalism' (Beck Jørgensen, 1995) where each individual organization is pursuing its own goal.

Creation of Winners and Losers
In the grey zone, there are clearly going to be organizations that benefit from the new state of affairs, not least grey zone organizations that aim to move into new markets. In the Danish discussion there is a tendency to describe the whole exercise as a 'positive-sum' game, that is, everyone involved benefits. One test for the grey zone is whether the public is prepared to accept that state companies go into receivership, and private sector firms move into another business area. The closing down of the Danish State Factory for Army Clothing left both MPs as well as private stakeholders in a fury. According to a newspaper report, the head of a private firm was heard to say: 'We never imagined dealing with the state meant losing money.'

Unions' attitudes to working in the grey zone are different. Some unions went along with state companies being established, but were disappointed when they found out privatization was coming (e.g. *GiroBank*). Other unions have mobilized against privatization. The railways union lobbies for keeping the Danish State Railways within the public sector, arguing that a co-ordinated transport policy is needed.

Loss of Expertise in the Public Sector

One further problem is the loss of expertise to organizations in the grey zone. Danish ministries have information asymmetries which means the expertise about the service in question lies with the provider (private firm) and not the purchaser (central department). This has important consequences for the construction of contracts, targets and performance indicators as the purchaser relies on the information offered by the provider and it is in the provider's interests to underestimate, in order to secure easy targets, and overestimate the costs. The solution to this problem would be for the purchaser to set up shadow teams to provide an independent channel of advice and information as to what were or were not stringent targets, but the establishment of such a team would probably exceed the efficiency savings of contracting out the service in the first place.

The result of this may be a kind of a 'contracting state' (Harden, 1992), reflected in the now well-known 'hollowing out of the state' discussion (Milward and Provan, 1993). The real fear, seen from an administrative and democratic point of view, is a kind of 'headless chicken' state, in which public governance becomes difficult, if not outright impossible (Hood, 1996).

Problems of Democratic Accountability

'Normal' democratic control procedures are being undermined. The limited use of the Law on Public Administration and the Law on Access to Public Files has already been mentioned. The Ombudsman and some of the National Audit Office powers cannot be applied to all quangos in Denmark. In some state companies, a part of the shares have been sold and listed on the Stock Exchange. The National Audit Office does not gain direct access to these companies.

Ministers and Parliament are being decoupled from the actual service delivery. Although they have general oversight, they lose day-to-day contact. Members of Parliament can ask questions in Parliament, yet they could risk being turned down if the question concerns state companies, for example. Politics has escaped the 'fence' of Parliament to be exploded into a variety of organisations (Pedersen *et al.*, 1994). Is a new kind of 'democratic control/accountability' regime being established? New players, or old players assigned to new roles, are now engaged in democratic control.

Parliament has strengthened its function in an ambitious plan, set forward by the newly elected chairman of Parliament. The state's donation to political parties was raised fourfold. The impact on the political process by the boost in parliamentary research staff will be interesting to monitor. Regulatory bodies, say, the Competition Council or new independent watchdogs, like the National Telecom Agency in Denmark, are also part of the new democratic control regime. The National Audit Office has stepped up its role with scrutinizing the behaviour of organizational innovation and grey zone organizations. The National Audit Office has called for common guidelines for establishing state-owned companies (1995), and has criticized the events leading up to the first closure of a newly established state-owned company (1996).

In general, government departments are being equipped to be much more active in shaping their own strategy, and to cooperate with organizations outside of the public sector. In a seemingly pragmatic effort, the Ministry of Finance (1995) published a 'toolkit for welfare' with various management tools. The impact on public agencies as well as quangos has yet to be established.

Citizen and user participation in quangos such as the special public agencies and the state-owned enterprises has been poor. However, in other quangos such as the voluntary social organizations, user participation is considered vital. There seems to be a lack of institutional integration between various forms of democratic representation, such as experiments with user participation in primary schools (Sørensen, 1995).

The prospect for developing democratic accountability forms will remain gloomy if the government's current enthusiasm for New Public Management continues. Little effort has been made to think in terms of control by process. In the state-owned companies, the new boards and managing directors seem less inclined to pay special attention to democratic control. When chairmen of boards are private sector 'heavyweights', as is sometimes the case, they do not like the idea of being 'pushed around' by politicians or bureaucrats. So far, outright conflict between ministers and chairmen of boards has not occurred. But the commercial mission of, for example, the ferry company *Scandlines* (a state-owned company) seems to run counter to some politicians' idea of how a state-owned company should be run.

How interested are politicians or government departments in developing new ideas about democratic control? Here, one must look at the chief aims of establishing quangos. The Ministry of Finance, for example, seems more interested in keeping public expenditure under control and they see state-owned companies as one such means, because they can control the companies' expenditure much more closely as a private company than a public enterprise (Greve, 1995b). Grey zone organizations themselves might be hesitant to be 'dragged into' taking responsibility for public

104 — Carsten Greve

policy-making. Voluntary organizations seem especially wary of 'tenders in brown envelopes' in fierce competition with private companies.

PERSPECTIVES: A WAY FORWARD?

Public–private co-operation can be a good thing for society at large. The grey zone can be made colourful (Greve, 1996): first, we need to distinguish more between different kinds of quangos; second, we need to find a way to make quangos a legitimate part of governing in a democratic society. However, it does require certain elements, currently absent from the debate. Politicians need to send clear signals as to their intention in establishing quangos. Core public tasks need to be pointed out. A clear legal framework is needed, maybe not as one all-encompassing law, but adopting clear principles may lead in the right direction. Mistrust between public and private leaders must be addressed, and proper learning processes established.

There is now a promising mood for discussing problems with quangos in Denmark. The government stresses the need for public–private co-operation, and the Ministry of Industry seems to be taking a lead in this respect (Ministry of Industry, 1994, 1995, 1996). The argument is that the public sector should be developed and not hived off in parts or made into a 'minimal' state. Politicians of all parties are being open-minded and experiments are taking place with new governance tools at both national and local levels. The press coverage on the grey zone is extensive compared to a few years ago. Researchers are contributing ideas. It is all more important because organization in the grey zone are eager for stable signals. To be sure, both the economic aspects of whether there are efficiency gains or not, and the legalities of how to combine grey zone organization and equality before the law must be dealt with. But in the end, participants in the discussion must come to grips with the political issue: What kind of a public sector do we want as citizens or voters? Also administrative questions must be put forward: What are the governance problems with many organizations in the grey zone? As well as the crucial democratic concerns: Can accountability to Parliament and the people be maintained?

REFERENCES

Andersen, Kim Viborg, Greve, Carsten and Torfing, Jacob (1996) 'Reorganizing the Danish Welfare State 1982–1993. A Decade of Conservative Rule', *Scandinavian Studies* (USA) Vol. 68, No. 2 (Spring), pp. 161–87.

Anker, Jørgen (1995) *De frivillige social organisationer* [The Voluntary Social Organizations] (Copenhagen: SFI) (report no. 12).

Association of Local Governments (1995) *Kommunal Systemeksport 1995 – analyse af omfang og indhold* [Local Government 'System Export'] (Copenhagen: KL).

Barker, Anthony (ed.) (1982) *Quangos in Britain* (Oxford: Oxford University Press).

Beck Jørgensen, Torben (1995): 'The New Public Capitalism – A Comment on Recent Reform Proposals', in H. Hill and H. Klages (eds) *Quality, Innovation and Measurement in the Public Sector* (Frankfurt: Peter Lang).

Beck Jørgensen, Torben and Hansen, Claus Arne (1995) 'Agencification and Deagencification in Danish Central Government', *International Review of Administrative Sciences*, Vol. 61, No. 4, pp. 549–63.

Beck Jørgensen, Torben *et al.* (1996) *Den offentlige sektor. Fra nutidens vilkår til fremtidens muligheder* [The Public Sector. From the Conditions of Today to the Possibilities of the Future]. (Copenhagen: Project on Public Sector – Condition and Future).

Betænkning no. 1332 [White Paper 1332] (1997) *Frivilligt socialt arbejde i fremtidens velfærdssamfund* [Voluntary Social Work in the Welfare Society of the Future] (Copenhagen: Ministry for Social Affairs).

Bozeman, Barry (1987) *All Organisations Are Public. Bridging Public and Private Organisational Theories* (San Francisco: Jossey-Bass Publishers).

Christensen, Jan (1988) 'Denmark', in Tore Modeen and Allan Rosas (eds) *Indirect Public Administration in Fourteen Countries* (Aabo: Aabo University Press), pp. 65–82.

Christensen, Søren and Molin, Jan (eds) (1995) *I den gode sags tjeneste. Frivillige organisationer i Danmark* [Serving a Good Cause. Voluntary Organisations in Denmark] (Copenhagen: Copenhagen Business School Publishing).

Dalsgaard, Lene and Henning Jørgensen (1994): *Det offentlige. Sektorens og de ansattes værdier of værdighed* [The Public Sector and the Values and Dignity of the Employees] (Copenhagen: Danish Lawyers and Economists' Association).

Danish Statistical Office (1997) *Statistik for offentligt ejede virksomheder 1991–1995* [Statistics for Public-owned companies 1991, 1995], News from the Danish Statistical Office, No. 11, 16 January.

Greve, Carsten (1995a) *Den grå zone* [The Grey Zone] (Copenhagen: Project on Public Sector – Condition and Future).

Greve, Carsten (1995b) 'Statslige aktieselskaber og Finansministeriets rolle' [State-owned Enterprises and the Role of the Ministry of Finance], *Administrativ Debat*, No. 4, pp. 13–15.

Greve, Carsten (1996) *Gør den grå zone farverig* [Make the Grey Zone Colourful] (Copenhagen: Project on Public Sector – Condition and Future).

Greve, Carsten (1997a) 'Summary of the Conference on the Grey Zone' (in Danish), in Parliament: *Parliamentary Report No. 6 from the Select Committee on Democracy and Power in Denmark* (Copenhagen), 19 March.

Greve, Carsten (1997b) *Styring og demokratisk kontrol af statslige aktieselskaber* [Governance and Democratic Control of State-owned Enterprises], PhD thesis. (Copenhagen: Lawyers and Economists Publishers).

Grøndahl, Øyvind and Grønlie, Tore (eds) (1995) *Fristillingens grenser* [The Limits of Autonomization] (Oslo: Fakbokforlaget).

Harden, Ian (1992) *The Contracting State* (Milton Keynes: Open University Press).

Henriksen, Lars Skov (1996) *Lokal frivillig organisering i nye omgivelser* [Local Voluntary Organizing in New Environments] (Aalborg: Aluff Publishing).

Hogwood, Brian (1995) 'The Growth of Quangos. Evidence and Explanations', *Parliamentary Affairs*, Vol. 48, No. 2, pp. 207–25.

Hood, Christopher (1996): 'Beyond "Progressivism": a New Global Paradigm in Public Management?' *International Journal of Public Administration*, Vol. 19, No. 2, pp. 151–77.

Hood, Christopher and Gunnar Folke Schuppert (eds) (1988) *Delivering Public Service in Western Europe. Sharing Western European Experiences of Para-Governmental organisations* (London: Sage).

Johansson, Anders *et al.* (1992) *Nye driftsformer i kommuner og landsting* [New Enterprise Forms in Local and Regional Governmente] (Stockholm: Trygghetsfonden).

Klausen, Kurt Klaudi (1989) 'Den tredje sektor: Frivillige organisationer mellem stat og marked' [The Third Sector: Voluntary Organisations Between State and Market], in Hviid Nielsen, Torben og Kurt Klaudi Klausen (eds.) *Stat og marked* [State and Market] (Copenhagen: Lawyers and Economists' Publishers), pp. 227–82.

Klausen, Kurt Klaudi and Selle, Per (eds) (1995) *Frivillig organisering i Norden* [Voluntary Organising in the Nordic Countries] (Copenhagen: Lawyers and Economists' Publishers).

Knudsen, Tim (1995) *Dansk statsbygning* [Danish State Building] (Copenhagen: Lawyers and Economists' Association Publishers).

Marcusson, Lena and Petterson, Oluf (1990) 'Orienteringspunkter i den grå zonen' [Points of Orientation in the Grey Zone] *Nordisk Administrativt Tidsskrift*, Vol. 71, No. 3.

Meyer, Poul (1979) *Offentlig forvaltning 3. udg.* [Public Administration 3rd edn] (Copenhagen: C.E.G. Gads forlag).

Milward, H. Brinton and Provan, Keith G. (1993) 'The Hollow State. Private Provision of Public Services', in Ingram, Helen and Rathgreb Smtih, Steven (eds) *Public Policy for Democracy* (Washington, D.C: Brookings Institute).

Minister of Finance (1996) 'The Future Governance of the Public Sector', in *The Fri Aktuelt*, 14 May.

Ministry of Finance (1993) *Erfaringer med statslige aktieselskaber* [Experiences with State-owned Companies] (Copenhagen).

Ministry of Finance (1995) *Værktøj til velfærd. Effektive institutioner* [Tools for Welfare. Efficient Institutions] (Copenhagen).

Ministry of Finance (1996a) *Budgetredegørelse. Tillæg: Styringsformer i den offentlige sektor* [Budget Report. Addition: Governance Forms in the Public Sector] (Copenhagen).

Ministry of Finance (1996b) *Intern kontrol og resultatopfølgning* [Internal Control and Performance Follow-up] (Copenhagen).

Ministry of Finance (1996c) *Udbud og udlicitering* [Tender and contracting out] (Copenhagen).

Ministry of Finance (1997) 'Orientering til finansudvalget om statens aktiebesiddelser and the special public enterprise Post Denmark' [Orientation to the Select Committee on public funds re: shareholdings of the state, and the special public enterprise Post Denmark] Ministry of Finance, 23 June.

Ministry of Finance and Ministry for Home Affairs (1995) *Erfaringer med udbud og udlicitering* [Experiences with tender and contracting out] (Copenhagen).

Ministry of Business and Industry (1994) *Offentligt-privat samspil* [Public–Private Cooperation] (Copenhagen).

Ministry of Business and Industry (1995) *Offentlig–privat – lige konkurrence* (Public–Private – Fair Competition) (Copenhagen).

Ministry of Business and Industry (1996a) *Erhvervsredegørelse, 1996* [Danish Industrial Policy, 1996] (Copenhagen).

Ministry of Business and Industry (1996b) *Redegørelse til Folketingets Erhvervsudvalg om kommuner og amtskommuners deltagelse i erhvervsdrivende selskaber m.v.* [Report to Parliament's Select Committee on local governments, participation in commercial companies] (Copenhagen).

Modeen, Tore and Rosas, Allan (eds) (1988) *Indirect Public Administration in Fourteen Countries.* (Aabo: Aabo Academy Press).

National Audit Office (1995) *Beretning om omdannelse af 8 statsstyrelser til aktieselskaber 1989–1994* [Report on the transformation of 8 public institutions into state companies] (Copenhagen).

National Audit Office (1996) *Beretning om Statens Konfektion i fri konkurrence* [Report on the Danish Factory for Army Clothing in Market Competition].

NOU (1991) *Lov om statsforetak* [Law on Public Enterprises] (Oslo: Statens Forvaltningstjeneste).

Olsen, Ole Jess (1993) *Regulering af offentlige forsyningsvirksomheder i Danmark* [Regulation of Public Utilities in Denmark] (Copenhagen: Lawyers and Economist's Publishers).

Osborne, David and Ted Gaebler (1993) [1992] *Reinventing Government. How the Entrepreneurial Spirit Is Transforming the Pubic Sector* (New York: Plume).

Pedersen, Ove Kaj m.fl. (1994) *Demokratiets lette tilstand* [The Light State of Democracy] (Copenhagen: Spektrum).

Pliatzky, Leo (1992) 'Quangos and Agencies', *Public Administration* Vol. 70, Winter, pp. 555–63.

PLS Consult (1997) *Erfaringer med udlicitering i kommuner og amter* [Experience with contracting out in local and regional government] (Copenhagen: Schultz).

Rosas, Allan (1988) 'Finland', in Modeen, Tore and Rosas, Allan (eds) *Indirect Public Administration in Fourteen Countries* (Aabo: Aabo Academy Press), pp. 86–104.

Savas, E.S. (1987) *Privatization: The Key to Better Government* (New Jersey: Chatham House).

Selle, Per (1996) *Frivillige organisasjoner i nye omgvender* [Voluntary Organisations in New Environments] (Bergen: Alma Alter).

Suksi, Marku (1988) 'Om den meddelbara offentlige forvaltningens struktur i Finland' [Indirect Public Administration in Finland], *Nordisk Administrativt Tidsskrift*, Vol. 69, No. 4, pp. 510–29.

Sørensen, Eva (1995) Democracy and Regulation in Institutions of Public Governance. Unpublished PhD thesis. Institute of Political Science, University of Copenhagen.

Tarschys, Daniel (1988) 'PGOs in Sweden', in Hood, Christopher and Schuppert, Gunnar (eds) *Delivering Public Services in Western Europe* (London: Sage), pp. 63–74.

Thaarup, Bent (1996) *Kontraktstyring* [Contract Governance] (Copenhagen: Project on Public Sector – Condition and Future).

Ugebrevet Mandag Morgen/Strategisk Forum (1995) *Velfærdsalliancen* [Welfare Alliance] (Copenhagen).

Weir, Stuart and Wendy Hall (eds) (1994) *EGO Trip. Extra-governmental organisations in the United Kingdom and their accountability* (University of Essex: Democratic Audit/Scarman Trust).

Werlauff, Erik (1993) *Statsselskaber* [State Companies] (Copenhagen: Ministry of Industry).

Part III

The Insider's View

9 The Housing Corporation: Multiple Lines of Accountability

Anthony Mayer*

Many arguments about the lack of accountability of non-departmental public bodies – or quangos as I shall call them–are ill informed. A number are coda for the transfer of power from central government to the organization of whom the advocate is a member. This chapter addresses the illusion that quangos lack accountability. It then considers the role of quangos and the case for and against the transfer of power from them. In conclusion it makes suggestions as to improvements to the accountability regime in which quangos currently operate.

INTRODUCTION

The Housing Corporation is a quango set up by statute proposed by the Secretary of State for the Environment, Transport and the Regions and approved by the House of Commons. It was established in 1965 by the then Labour government. Since then its powers have been amended and extended through successive legislation and most recently through the Housing Act 1996.

Its core tasks are two-fold: to pay grants to registered social landlords (RSLs) to build homes at sub-market rents, and to regulate these landlords. In addition, it has a role, defined in the Housing Act 1996, to facilitate the proper performance of registered social landlords. The Corporation has an independent board of a maximum of 15 members, appointed by the Secretary of State according to the requirements of the Code of Public Appointments. The board has special responsibilities to direct the affairs of the Corporation and to advise the Secretary of State on matters relating to social housing policy. Crucially, it hires (and can fire) the Chief Executive. The Chief Executive is a member of the board and also the

---

*The views expressed here are the author's, and should not be taken to reflect the views of The Housing Corporation.

Corporation's Accounting Officer. I have been in post since April 1991, having got the post through open competition.

DEFINITIONS OF ACCOUNTABILITY

Accountability – or lack of it – is a slippery concept. It means different things to different people. Depending on their perspective, people will emphasize different aspects of it. Put baldly, accountability is a relationship between two bodies, one of whom has the availability of sanctions against the other. It is axiomatic that any and all quangos should be called to account for their actions and should operate in a way that takes account of the legitimate interests of its many and varied stakeholders, which in our case include government, Parliament, tenants, local authorities, private lenders and RSLs.

EXTERNAL ACCOUNTABILITIES

The Corporation has formal accountabilities to the following bodies.

The Department of the Environment, Transport and the Regions

The Housing Corporation has no independent right of existence. If the Secretary of State for the Environment Transport and the Regions decided we should cease to exist, then subject to the approval of the House of Commons statute could so secure.

We operate under a Management Statement and a Financial Memorandum agreed with the Department of the Environment, Transport and the Regions (DETR). These are published documents to set out what we can and cannot do, our degrees of freedom and our stewardship reporting requirements. Every year ministers give us output and value-for-money targets for our funding of new social housing, which we are required to meet. Our annual report is laid before Parliament, and we are also required to produce annual stewardship reports for each area of work, in addition to formal in year reporting arrangements.

Every five years ministers commission a wide-ranging review of our work, known as the Finance, Management and Policy Review (FMPR). This makes recommendations on our operating practices, which we are required to implement. The FMPR is preceded by a Prior Options Study (POS) under which, like all quangos, we are required to justify our existence. The report on the last review was published at the end of 1996. It reflected the conclusions of the POS that the Corporation was the most appropriate vehicle to regulate and fund registered social landlords. A further mechanism for securing the accountability of the Corporation to government is through the requirements of government accounting rules and other government-wide codes of practice. These codes include, not only our Code of Best Practice for Board members, but also a Code of Practice on Access to Housing Corporation Information, our staff rules and procedures for handling complaints.

The focus for the ongoing working relationship between the Corporation and the DETR is the sponsoring directorate, headed by a Grade 3 civil servant. If a problem arises, it is almost invariably that post-holder who is the first port of call. In terms of exercising the external accountability function, this is the key relationship. Most of the time, it is conducted in co-operative and cordial terms. But in the final analysis, we exist to do jobs for government; if we fail to do so, or if there is a risk of our failing, then an element of censure on a direction from DETR is inevitable. This is perfectly proper given the relationship.

The National Audit Office and the Public Accounts Committee

The National Audit Office is empowered to review any or all of our activities or decisions as part of its annual programme of inspection work and in the discharge of its responsibilities to undertake value-for-money studies. They have unrestricted access to all our working papers. Their reports go to the Public Accounts Committee who are entitled to summon and cross-examine me and the DETRs Accounting Officer, censure our performance and publish recommendations for remedial action. In 1993 the NAO published *The Housing Corporation: Financial Management of Housing Associations* which led to a hearing in 1994 before the Public Accounts Committee. Enquiries by the PAC can and do make a difference to the ways in which we operate. For example, following the 1994 hearing we made a number of improvements to strengthen and improve our financial regulation of RSLs.

The existence of even the possibility of a PAC hearing exerts a strong discipline. Preparations for a hearing can take up most of the time of the senior executives involved for up to a month. By definition, in a hearing which lasts for no more than a few hours, issues tend to be covered quickly and those of most immediate public or political interest given greater prominence. But the Committee have a right to recall witnesses;

the hearings can be televised and there is a report after the hearing. Quango Accounting Officers take the PAC process lightly at their peril.

Select Committee for the Environment

The Select Committee for the Environment is entitled to review any of our activities and our performance in carrying out these activities. It is entitled to summon us to give written and oral evidence and to publish reports on this evidence and that of others. In 1993 we were called to assist in the Committee's major review of the work of the Corporation and in 1995 we assisted the Environment Select Committee's review of Housing Need.

On both occasions the Committee were assisted by an expert assessor whose role was to help them focus on the key issues. From my admittedly limited, if first-hand experience, each committee member appeared well briefed and able to ask relevant and probing questions. No one member dominated proceedings and there was no evidence of party political infighting.

Members of Parliament

In a typical year I sign around 100 letters to Members of Parliament about constituency cases. Unless they wish otherwise all MPs' correspondence is replied to by myself or my chairman. We have, to my knowledge, never refused a request for information on account of collection and collation costs. If an MP remains concerned about a case, it is standard practice to ensure further contact to try to resolve matters. In all but a handful of cases there is a satisfactory and amicable resolution. If an MP remains dissatisfied then he or she retains the right of recourse to the minister, the Ombudsman or the courts.

The Courts

All our funding and regulatory decisions are subject to judicial review. Section 6 of the Housing Act 1996 has made it explicit that a body aggrieved at our failure either to register them as a social landlord, or to de-register them, may appeal to the High Court. The more active involvement of the courts in securing fairly reached and reasonable administrative decisions by public bodies has been one of the major constitutional developments over the last 20 years. The Housing Corporation has not yet been the subject of a judicial review, but as with PAC hearings, the existence of the possibility of a judicial review exerts its own strong discipline.

New policies must be subject to proper consultation. Decisions must be reasonable and taken properly within the Corporations internal procedures.

The Parliamentary Commissioner for Administration

Individual members of the public can complain to the Parliamentary Commissioner for Administration (the Ombudsman) through his/her MP. Complaints can either relate to failures in our administrative machinery or to refusals to disclose information. The Ombudsman has free access to all relevant working papers, publishes his findings, and in respect of proven maladministration, can request us to make remedies. The relationship between the PCA and the Housing Corporation is case-specific. It is not close; there has only been one case in my tenure.

External Auditors

Our external Auditors are appointed by the Secretary of State and report to him annually on the propriety, effectiveness and efficiency of our activities and structures. Their annual management letter is considered by our board, and the expectation is that any and all recommendations are implemented.

Internal Accountabilities

So much for external accountabilities. The Corporation's board is the fulcrum of a range of internal accountabilities. Board members are appointed by the Secretary of State and are all independent. Independence is secured in two ways. First, the appointments process has entailed the preparation by DETR officials of a shortlist of candidates with the required skills and expertise across the social housing spectrum. The minister chooses from this shortlist. There are no 'fast-track ministerial nominees' and no 'political' appointments. The appointments process has been further opened up in the last year to conform to the government code of practice on appointments: all board appointments are now advertised. Second, under the Management Agreement with the Department, the board are given a specific remit to 'provide independent strategic advice to the Minister on social housing issues'. The board run a government agency not a government department. While throughout the year they provide the minister with advice and comments on social housing matters, it is implicit that, ultimately, it is the minister who decides, the board which implements. 'Informal pressure' by ministers is not on the agenda.

In addition to advising the Secretary of State on strategic policy issues and directing the Corporation's activities, the board provides an essential check on the activities of the executive. The board's Registration and Supervision Committee takes all decisions relating to the registration and deregistration of social landlords and oversees all cases where a registered social landlord is being supervised. The board's Finance and Audit Committee is responsible for the approval of the Corporation's operating budget and for the annual programme of the Internal Auditor.

An essential adjunct to accountability is openness. Unless the Corporation's actions are known by its stakeholders, and its decision-making is transparent, it cannot properly be called to account. The Corporation seeks to maintain open and constructive relationships at both regional and national levels. Each board member has a responsibility to maintain close contact with one region and chairs formal consultation meetings with the main regional social housing players. In addition they arrange smaller or less formal opportunities to listen to views at the regional level on policy and practice. Such arrangements enable board members to take part in a two-way process. There is a similar set of meet-ings with representative and professional organizations at national level and a formalized consultation process on all new policy initiatives.

'Regionalism' will have major implications for the quango-state in the coming years. Our arrangements for securing regional liaison are, so far, informal and set to be 'fit for purpose'. The advent of Regional Development Agencies, although not it seems to be directly involved in housing, will require us to reassess our stance. There is a dilemma here. On the one hand formalizing our regional focus would further promote 'bottom-up' investment strategies which reflect regional housing needs. It would also, by widening the involvement of institutions and people at the regional level, extend and improve our accountabilities. On the other hand, if regional bodies with housing investment allocation responsibilities were set up, there would necessarily be tensions with local authorities (who set their own housing strategies which we help implement) and with the minister (who sets overall national housing strategies). These tensions would need resolving and the benefits of regional bodies involved in hous-ing would clearly need to outweigh the costs. In the meanwhile, once Regional Development Agencies are set up we will need to work closely with them to ensure that our patterns of investment reflect and enhance agreed regional economic and regeneration strategies.

Finally, on the issue of openness, we recognize that in respect of each and every funding and regulatory decision, a party affected by it has a right to an explanation and a justification. More generally, each year there are publications to account for performance in all our functions and to give policies and targets for the following year. Other booklets provide information about the operation of the Corporation.

As well as demonstrating our own accountabilities, we also need to ensure that those we regulate and fund also maintain high standards of accountability. The Corporation's regulatory regime sets performance standards against which registered social landlords are reviewed each year. The standards cover all areas of activity including accountability and consultation. Accountability covers the way organizations conduct their affairs as well as dissemination of information. Consultation requirements are more closely defined and require that tenants and leaseholders (service recipients) should have the opportunity to exercise genuine influence over the service they receive.

TRANSFER OF OUR POWERS?

There are commentators who argue that the range of accountabilities set out above notwithstanding, anything short of full democratic accountability is unacceptable: our funding responsibilities should be transferred to (democratically elected) local authorities or to the regional offices of the (democratically elected) government.

There are no persuasive points of principle to make against this argument. We exist to do jobs for the Secretary of State. The reason for our continuing to fund registered social landlords is pragmatic: the Secretary of State has yet to be convinced that anyone can do the job better. We have so far spent £20 billion of the taxpayers' money on new social housing and have helped to promote a further £10 billion private finance. Year after year we spend 99.9 per cent of the funds allocated to us and we meet, and invariably exceed, the government's lettings and value-for-money targets.

There are others who argue that to minimize any potential conflict of interest, our regulatory and funding responsibilities should be split. There is an argument of principle here. How can I properly be accountable to the Secretary of Sate and to Parliament for the £20 billion of taxpayer funds invested in registered social landlords unless I can ensure that their stewardship lies in safe hands? There is also argument of practice: our funding and regulatory roles reinforce each other. We can turn off the funding tap if the performance of a registered social landlord is unacceptable. And our regulatory roles enable us to ensure that registered social landlords who receive public funding are suitable recipients of it.

If, despite all of these considerations, a Secretary of State were to be convinced that our power should be transferred to others, then so be it. We exist, survive and prosper in a climate of all too real accountability!

IMPROVEMENTS TO THE ACCOUNTABILITY REGIME

Finally, what, if any, improvements might be made to the accountability regime in which we exist?

First, more could be done to make our accountability to Parliament more transparent and structured. There is no doubting, as shown above, the wide range of mechanisms which are in place to ensure that we are accountable to government and Parliament. For the most part these largely remain invisible to many who have an interest in our work. In addition, the inquiries by the National Audit Office for the Public Accounts Committee and the reports by the Select Committee of the Environment focus on specific issues and not the full range of our activities. We do lay annual reports before Parliament which review the whole spectrum of our work. These could helpfully be the subject of annual hearings by the Select Committee for the Environment. To make the annual review process effective there would need to be a premium on publicity and dissemination of the hearings. The Committee itself would also need more resources and research staff to maximize the effectiveness and focus of the review process.

Second, the Ombudsman could be given more sanctions. If maladministration is found, then under the present arrangements an apology follows, together with a review of processes to ensure the error is not repeated. But this is all rather low-key, especially if the error was one-off, historical and unable to be remedied. What about a fine or compensation arrangements or formal powers to ensure that weak procedures are strengthened?

Third, there is scope for more formal contact between quangos. Other than annual meeting of accounting officers sponsored by the DETR, there are currently no formal or even informal relations between the Housing Corporation and other government agencies. The principles and practices of our range of accountabilities have been developed largely in isolation of other bodies in similar or even identical bodies. There must be ample scope for the sharing of experience with a learning and/or advisory process depending on whether we are behind or ahead of the game.

Finally, the quango debate could be better informed. The more there is authoritative, empirical research on the accountabilities and achievements and methods of working of quangos, the better would be the understanding of their role and contribution to the workings of government. There are a number of areas of research to consider. For example, there may be lessons to learn from looking across the experiences of different quangos to get a better understanding of what makes for good relationships with sponsoring departments; of the nature of the role of boards and of the impact they have. There is also useful investigation that could be carried out about the relationships and methods of working at regional and local level between different spending bodies.

10 Of Ministers, Mandarins and Managers

Brian Landers

INTRODUCTION

On Sunday, 15 October 1995, I joined other members of the Prisons Board and marched, uninvited, into the Home Secretary's office to express our dismay at his intention to sack the Director General of the Prison Service, Derek Lewis. Michael Howard listened to the unanimous opposition of career civil servants, prison governors, private sector managers and distinguished non-executive directors and then carried on exactly as before. The reality of the Prison Service's 'independent' agency status was never clearer, not quasi-autonomous non-governmental but pseudo-autonomous governmental: psago not quango.

On joining the Prison Service I received a leaflet headed 'Home Office Organizational Structure'. It showed the various Home Office divisions reporting through Grade 3s and Grade 2s up to the Grade 1 Permanent Secretary. To one side, and not linked in any way to the rest of the organogram, was a box labelled 'Executive agencies of the Home Office. Independent bodies reporting directly to the Home Secretary'. HM Prison Service was in that box. The implication to me was that the agency was independent from the Home Office bureaucracy but not from ministers. This was not the view of many managers in the Service, who naively wanted to be independent from both, nor of the Home Office mandarins who wanted the agency to be independent of neither. Ministers appeared to be unsure what they wanted. The failure to agree on the meaning of the one word 'independent' bedevilled the agency from its inception.

The theory of agencies is that the most effective way for ministers to have their policies implemented is to entrust them to independent professionally managed agencies focusing solely on service delivery. The agencies would be set challenging, precisely defined performance targets. Achieving the targets was in itself supposed to demonstrate the virtues of independence. The Prison Service achieved all its targets, far surpassing historical performance in key areas such as reduced escapes, yet Lewis was fired and the agency effectively reintegrated into the Whitehall machine.

The question is why, when equally sensitive agencies, such as the Scottish Prison Service and the Defence Research Agency (later DERA), successfully transformed themselves did we seem to fail so spectacularly. Lewis, in his book, *Hidden Agendas*, appears to place the whole blame on one man: Michael Howard. The truth is far more complicated. There were other key personalities, not least Lewis himself, and members of the Home Office mandarinate. More fundamentally there were institutional pressures that meant that from the start the agency's carefully crafted Framework Document was a sham.

These pressures involved the interplay of ministers and civil servants, of policy and operations, of public sector 'ethics' and private sector 'best practice'. Examining the Prison Service case is of more than historical interest because these competing pressures above all reflect differing theories of accountability. Who is responsible to whom for what? It is no coincidence that the one potential pressure that played no effective part in the workings of the Prison Service, despite repeated assertions to the contrary, was Parliament.

To analyse these pressures I intend to consider separately the objectives of the three key players – Ministers, mandarins and managers – and then focus on the issue of accountability and the role of Parliament. I also want to digress into a discussion of 'policy' because it is the secrecy of policy advice which I believe is the most severe constraint on public accountability.

MINISTERS

For most politicians (with Michael Howard being very much the exception) the salience of penal policy is rarely high. Prison operations are however different. The treatment of Myra Hindley or Private Clegg is considered a legitimate subject for political involvement. Prison escapes and riots are held to be events requiring ministerial accountability. This is not the case in other countries, nor is it the case in similar circumstances in this country. There was no clamour for the Defence Secretary's head following the fatal military blunders in the Falklands Campaign. Nor has a Home Secretary been at risk following serious police failures, such as the Yorkshire Ripper.

Ministers can react to the political salience of prison operations in one of two ways: delegate or control. Kenneth Clarke favoured the former, thus the agency's creation; Howard the latter. Clarke was limited by the perceived legitimacy of political responsibility for operations. For that reason he could not create real operational independence, such as that enjoyed by the police (the model favoured by Lewis). Howard, on the other hand, wanted direct control but would not accept responsibility from which there were no avenues of escape (my proposal that a minister should act as a Greenbury-style non-executive chairman of the Prisons Board was met with horror).

The Prison Service agency was created not in response to any theory of accountability but because it fitted the current political dogma and because the then Home Secretary was emotionally inclined to delegate. When he was replaced with someone nearer to being a control-freak any political pressure to make it succeed vanished (with the exception of occasional rumblings from the Deputy Prime Minister). When Anne Widdecombe was appointed Prisons Minister it seemed that the agency concept might be reinvigorated, but she lacked political clout. I remember her grilling us on one occasion about our deteriorating performance after Derek Lewis was fired (as shown by our failure to achieve our Key Performance Indicators, supposedly the benchmark of agency success). She had just got Lewis's successor to admit that he had stopped bothering about the KPIs (without telling ministers) when she was cut short by Michael Howard himself, who airily dismissed the relevance of KPIs at all.

There were, on the other hand, concerted pressures to make it fail, primarily from within the mandarinate.

MANDARINS

The Home Office has largely escaped the management fads that have peri-odically washed over Whitehall. It saw no reason to change the way it operated. In *Hidden Agendas* (1997, p. 34), Lewis describes a meeting of senior Home Office officials, at which I was present, in which there was some opposition to the lack of 'intellectual foundations' for the Home Secretary's policies. As usual Lewis is too discrete. What was actually said, at its most extreme, is that the Home Office's problem was that minister's policy proposals did not reflect proper Home Office policy and the new Permanent Secretary ought to concentrate on educating ministers rather than trying to change the Office.

The Home Office had a stunning self-confidence which extended to the way it had run the Prison Service. As a newcomer it was obvious to me that there were appalling problems. Some common practices were simply unacceptable: slopping out, conditions for remand prisoners, imprison-ment of the mentally ill, juveniles in adult prisons, 24-hour lock-ups, widespread intimidation. Simple international benchmarking showed security standards to be deplorable. Financial controls, as I once told horror-struck colleagues preparing for a Public Accounts Committee hearing, were 'shambolic'.

This was not the view of the Home Office establishment. I made myself very unpopular by suggesting that the Whitemoor escape might have had something to do with the quality of management we had exercised over the prison. There always had been high-profile escapes, I was told, and there always would be: rather like saying that planes have always crashed so why try to prevent pilot error.

Although many senior civil servants opposed agency status (indeed some members of the Prisons Board professed this quite openly) loyalty to ministers transcends all else. Once the decision to create an agency had been made, all but a few put their best efforts into making it appear to succeed. Their first task was to design an agency which, in reality, changed as little as possible.

It is important to realize that in numerical terms the Prison Service is not a minor adjunct to the core Home Office; it very largely is the Home Office. Of the 53,000 Home Office staff 40,000 work in the Prison Service (with another 5,000 in the Immigration Service; which managed to resist agency status). These numbers underestimate the importance of the service because many support staff in areas such as personnel and accounts would transfer out in the usual agency model. In order to maintain job opportunities for the career civil servants at the top of the Home Office it was essential to ensure they retained their dominant position in the new agency.

This was quite contrary to the approach of the Scottish Prison Service which expressly separated itself from the Scottish Office requiring its senior managers to choose between careers in one or the other. It was also contrary to the expectations of many prison governors who had expected agency status to open up career opportunities for themselves. (Although Derek Lewis was often referred to as the first outsider to head the Service in fact his successor was the first insider in the role, all previous Director Generals having been mandarins passing through or retiring into the Service.)

To keep the bulk of the Agency's top management in civil service hands required a rationale. Professional, operationally focused management was supposed to be an Agency's supreme virtue. Whitehall's most sacred word was summoned: 'Policy'.

POLICY

'Policy' is the holy grail of senior civil servants. 'Policy' is the core of their mystique, the magic process which they uniquely understand and

which takes priority over all else. If the mandarins were to retain control
of the agency, it could only be because they alone could 'do' policy.
It therefore followed that policy responsibility had to remain with the
Agency. Under the Framework Document the Director General became
'the Home Secretary's principal policy adviser on matters relating to the
Prison Service'. I believe this policy responsibility was unique among
agencies. It was crucial to the blurring of accountability which surrounded
the Agency, often in unexpected ways. For example, the Prisons
Ombudsman was blocked from investigating complaints about individual
prisoners' categorization (which determined what sort of prison they were
sent to) because this was a 'policy' matter on which the Agency 'advised'
the Home Secretary and policy advice was beyond the Ombudsman's
remit.

Giving senior management 'policy' responsibility meant that the whole
organization was inevitably focused on the demands of Westminster rather
than on internal operations. Why, I once asked, were all the area managers'
offices in London? Suppose there were a riot or escape on their patch? But
that, I was told, is precisely when they had to be in London: how else
could they brief ministers?

It is worth examining what Whitehall means by policy and why it
so jealously protects it from public scrutiny. What it does not mean is what
those outside Whitehall mean. It does not mean, for example, economic
policy or criminal justice policy. The history of Britain in the twentieth
century has, after all, demonstrated fairly conclusively that policy in the
normal sense of the word is something that Whitehall has been particularly
bad at.

Policy in normal conversation has to have a content. You can have a
foreign policy or an economic policy, but to just say you have policy is
meaningless. But the policy senior civil servants are fixated with has no
content. Policy in Whitehall-speak is a process not an output. And the
process is Westminster politics. Senior civil servants are Westminster
groupies. Their satisfaction comes not from developing policy in the normal sense but from serving ministers, being in the know, in short just from
being there.

What civil servants crave when they talk of policy is the buzz of travel-
ling in ministerial cars and the mystique of the red boxes, the adrenalin
spurts caused by impossible deadlines and constant press scrutiny, the
manufactured excitement of parliamentary debate and the shadow boxing
of parliamentary questions. The machinery of politics itself is narcotic to
which the mandarins are addicted. Policy, in the normal English sense, does
not come from civil servants. All the brainpower, research and accumulated

wisdom of the Home Office policy-makers did not actually generate any major policy initiatives in my time there, despite record levels of crime and glaring inefficiencies right across the criminal justice system.

There is a view, captured in a memorable phrase of Harold Laski's, that 'policy is secreted in the interstices of administration'. On a small scale this is undoubtedly true. A prison governor makes a decision in a particular circumstance and suddenly you have a precedent that others follow. In my experience policy on a grand scale does not arise in this way. It comes from a few determined individuals who stand apart from the civil service mainstream. Many of the major prison policy changes came from Derek Lewis. Two fundamental policies, mandatory drug testing and differential regimes, had been around as ideas before Lewis arrived. What changed is that he brought to an organization that had been content merely to administer his vision of a prison service striving constantly to improve. It was that vision of change that led to the impetus for policy change. The initiatives that did not originate with Lewis came from the Home Secretary himself.

Lewis has described the development of policy on home leave (Lewis, 1997: 115–17). This started with a desultory internal review but escalated as a result of media comment on some blatant abuses of the system. There then followed more than a year of skirmishes between Lewis and the Prisons Board on the one hand, and Howard and his political advisers on the other. Unusually it was the intervention of the Prisons Minister, Michael Forsyth, that eventually led to the impasse being resolved. Typically neither external pressure groups (including MPs) nor the core Home Office played any significant role.

I am not suggesting that this pattern of policy development was typical because I am not sure that any pattern is typical. What surprised me is that, rather than there being a well-established policy formulation process, practice seemed to be determined overwhelmingly by the personal characteristics of the minister. Michael Howard had a very definite personal agenda, an adversarial style and clear intellectual superiority to most of his advisers. As a consequence policy input from elsewhere was minimal and when proffered, for example by Derek Lewis, was rarely welcomed. Many of Howard's predecessors and Cabinet colleagues clearly made less of an impact both on policy and on policy processes.

The fact that it was policy in the Whitehall sense rather than the English sense that was passed to the Agency became plain when serious policy was suddenly required. By the autumn of 1995 the Conservative Party was losing the initiative on law and order, being outflanked by a Labour Party 'tough on crime, tough on the causes of crime'. On 12 October, Michael Howard announced to the Party conference a radical change in sentencing policy. Mandatory sentences would stop thousands of hardened criminals being let off by out-of-touch judges and ensure that they remained behind bars where they would pose no threat to the public. Of all those most directly affected by these proposals only one part of Whitehall was not consulted. The Party conference speech was a bombshell to us. The biggest prison building programme in modern history was proposed, costed, planned and decided upon without any consultation with the Agency.

At that time, just days before Lewis was fired, our relations with the Home Office in general, and with the Home Secretary and Permanent Secretary in particular, had almost completely broken down. The proposals had been put together by a team from which the Prison Service had been deliberately excluded. This was despite the Framework Document and despite the Woolf Report's insistence that the Prison Service 'accept a more central role ... in sentencing policy'. Even the costings, which were critically important, were put together by Home Office officials with no input from my own Finance Directorate. This case also demonstrated why, in my view, the mandarinate is so anxious to avoid policy advice being subject to scrutiny: its quality, its reflection on ministers and its honesty.

Immediately after the Party conference we received a memorandum from a senior Home Office civil servant explaining what had been going on out of our sight. Attached to it was a mass of correspondence between the Home Office and Treasury outlining the basis for the various cost assumptions that had been made. Two things interested me. One was the frank admission that the figures were not particularly robust and in one case were simply wrong. (Typically, the mistake had been picked up by Michael Howard himself after being passed by heaven knows how many officials.) The other was the admission that the Home Secretary in his speech had departed from the line agreed with Treasury and with civil servants and that nobody yet knew precisely what he meant. For example, all the costings had been done on the basis that the new minimum sentence regime applied to 'domestic' burglaries, but the Home Secretary had dropped that reference. If the change was intentional the financial impact would be considerable.

Had these documents been open to public inspection the embarrassment to civil servants and ministers would have been enormous. It has been argued therefore that to disclose this sort of advice would inhibit policy formulation and the free flow of ideas. In my view what would happen is that if ministers and advisers knew the advice would be freely available, much more effort would be devoted to the quality of that advice, surely to everyone's benefit.

The issue is, however, about honesty as much as quality. The mandatory sentencing debate proceeded on two levels with the same people arguing in opposite directions. In public the benefit of mandatory sentencing was that more criminals would be locked up. However, in private we were searching desperately for arguments that would convince the Treasury that the prison budget would not have to go up because the effect on the prison population would be marginal, that is we would not be locking up more criminals. Had the precise planning assumptions been made public a proper debate could have taken place which would have brought to light the irreconcilable differences between low cost and high impact and forced a choice to be made.

MANAGERS

If most ministers and mandarins were lukewarm to the concept of agency many, although certainly not all, managers inside the service were enthusiastic. Often the enthusiasm was naive in the extreme. Some seemed to believe that Agency status would mean no ministerial involvement in anything. Just as the 'refusniks' amongst the mandarins believed that without them the prison service would collapse, some prison governors believed that without ministerial and civil service interference the service would become a beacon of liberal practice unconstrained by the need to make financial choices or respond to public concerns of any kind.

Much of the enthusiasm was founded in the conviction that traditional civil service values inhibited efficiency. A particular concern was with civil service personnel rules. I remember one colleague complaining that agency status was supposed to have freed him from the precepts of the Civil Service Commissioners, the 'guardians of mediocrity' as he called them. Certainly the civil service definition of 'Open and fair competition' for posts bore no relation to what I understood by the term in the private sector.

For example when an employee of a private prison (with extensive public prison experience) applied for a senior job in the Agency we were told by the Home Office not to interview him as the job advert had not said it was open to the private sector (we could, however, have interviewed someone from the Scottish service). To interview the applicant would have been 'unfair' to anyone else in the private sector who might have wanted to apply but had not realized they could do so. On another occasion I gave an

outstanding manager extra responsibilities and was then told I had effectively changed his job so I would have to advertise it and make him apply
for his own job: not the conventional approach to staff motivation.

Demarcation disputes were a particular issue. There are around a dozen
trade unions in the agency, each jealously protecting their turf (exactly
how many depends on how you define 'union'). The governor of one
prison appointed a civil servant to a job traditionally held by a member of
the PGA (the Prison Governors Association); he was ordered by our own
headquarters to reverse the appointment. I tried to promote a governor into
a civil service job but this was vetoed by the Home Office. I was told the
appointment 'would not be acceptable to the First Division Association'
(one of the civil service unions).

In the absence of consistent ministerial pressure to force through change
mandarin inertia easily overpowered managerial impatience. I characterized what the Home Office called 'Toto', the Top of the Office, as perma-
frost management – a frozen layer that stifled all hope of growth below.
The most trivial signal of Agency autonomy was relentlessly extinguished.
Even the word agency was effectively banned. When I noticed soon after
I joined that the Whitley Council which brought together prison service
management and the POA, our largest union, was still called the Prison
Department Whitley I assumed it was an oversight and suggested it be
relabelled, after all the Prison Department no longer existed. I was told
this would not be possible, the POA would never agree. This, I later
discovered, was simply not true, it was the civil servants who successfully
blocked the renaming. Three years later it is still the Prison Department
Whitley (perhaps I should be surprised that HMPS is no longer deemed to
stand for His Majesty's Prison Service).

PARLIAMENT

Such bureaucratic manoeuvring would be of little consequence were the
context not so important. The business of the Prison Service is the liberty
of individuals. It matters when human beings are kept in degrading conditions because money Parliament has allocated to the Prison Service is
wasted. It matters when inmates are kept in prison longer than the Courts
intended because sentence calculations are done on bits of paper in
cramped offices. It matters when criminals re-offend because their offend-
ing behaviour was not efficiently addressed in prison. It matters when
penal policy is developed with no regard for the evidence as to its likely
effect.

All these things should matter to us all, but above all they should matter to those we elect to represent us. To make an effective contribution, however, MPs require information. They have two avenues to that information which are not open to the general public: Parliamentary Questions and scrutiny by Parliamentary Committee. Both are almost totally ineffective.

PQs were the bane of our life, even the totally potty had to be answered. Religious peers consumed hundreds of hours of very senior time with questions on the accuracy of our computer records on Buddhist inmates or our policy on Scientology. On one occasion I received a panic-stricken message from the Home Office. Glenda Jackson MP had asked a Parliamentary Question which they could not answer. She wanted us to 'list the number of traffic violations involving Departmental vehicles, the nature of the violations and the total amount of fines arising from those violations in each year since 1986'. Why she wanted to know it was not ours to ask. If she wanted ten years' history on such trivia we had better find a way of producing it. Unfortunately we could not. The idea of each prison keeping records of any traffic violations for ten years was just too absurd to contemplate, although marginally less absurd than the belief that we might have some procedure to magically summon up such data from a central database just in case an MP wanted it. We politely responded that to produce such information would involve disproportionate cost.

Many questions were far more sensible but they were received with the same disdain. The key consideration when answering PQs was to avoid anything that might embarrass ministers. This is absolutely ingrained in civil servants. In my experience nobody ever proposed an untrue answer but it was not at all unusual deliberately to hide information which the MP had clearly been seeking if it might prove embarrassing. If the question was not specific enough, then we would respond in harmless generalities; if it was too specific, we would answer only the precise point raised, ignoring any side-issues.

Parliamentary Committees should have been able to overcome these issues. I twice witnessed Westminsters most feared Committee, the Public Accounts Committee, in action. What was notable in both cases is that they missed the most fundamental issues due to an evident lack of effective briefing, the rather mixed quality of the Committee membership and their own procedures. In the first case Derek Lewis was questioned on the contract for The Wolds, Britain's first private prison. Commercially such contracts are very dangerous because the winner is effectively granted a monopoly – put crudely, whenever we wanted to change anything they had us over a barrel. The Wolds was built as a remand-only prison and, after the contract was agreed, the requirement was changed. We then had to negotiate revisions from a position of total weakness. The PAC simply missed the issue.

The second time I appeared as a witness. The Agency had 'overspent'. This was a technical offence that meant not that we had wasted taxpayers' money but that we had paid a few invoices just before the year end rather than just after. There were, however, very serious and long-standing financial control problems in the Agency which someone had clearly briefed one of the Labour MPs about. In particular the MP, Alan Williams, had been given a memorandum I wrote to ministers warning them of the problems to which they had not responded. Williams, however, ran out of time because, instead of letting members pursue their questions to their logical conclusion, each member has a strictly limited allocation. As Williams appeared not to have shared his briefing with anyone else, nobody followed up his points. Even worse, the Committee degenerated into gesture politics of a particularly unedifying sort with at least one MP who quite plainly did not understand the basic accounting issues being debated.

Like PQs the PAC took up an enormous amount of time. A full-time defence team worked for weeks preparing briefings for us. The Permanent Secretary cleared his diary and waded through enormous quantities of paper. I received special one-to-one training at the Civil Service College from a former Permanent Secretary. We rehearsed with a host of Home Office and Treasury advisers. And at the end of the day we were adjudged to have 'won' because the real issues remained uncovered and our minister had not been embarrassed (although I received some unflattering headlines).

CONCLUSION

I can only make judgements about the wider issues of quasi-government and public accountability on the basis of my personal experience of the Prison Service. Although not a typical agency the pressures under which it works are seen, in less exaggerated forms, elsewhere.

It seems to me that the split between operations and policy is fundamentally important not only to optimize operational efficiency but to maximize public accountability. The Home Secretary alone must be responsible for policy and for that to be effective the definition of policy must be unambiguous. The Prison Service alone must be responsible for operations and for that to be effective there must be a clear public process for holding the service accountable. The arguments about the dividing line between policy and operations could be easily resolved by defining policy as anything embodied in legislation, Prison Rules or the annual vote. Everything else is policy implementation, that is operations.

Policy would, by definition, be public and subject to public scrutiny. Covert ministerial interference in the Service would become impossible. The Home Secretary, supported by Home Office civil servants, would be subject to advice and lobbying from anyone interested, including the Prison Service. The Prison Service would however be no more the ministers 'principal' adviser on penal policy than the police would be on criminal policy. The service's policy advice hopefully would be more informed and should certainly be published. This would not only improve democratic accountability but also tend to improve the quality of policy advice which, in my experience, too often lacks rigour especially in quantitative analysis and informed international benchmarking.

I would chop the Prison Service itself into manageable pieces, giving each independence within a statutory framework and subject to a post-Nolan Board of independent directors. They should provide custodial services to the courts on a formal contractual 'purchaser–provider' basis and ideally should be directly accountable to an elected authority (either Parliament or regional assemblies). That accountability would not be through Ministers but through an independent Parliamentary inspectorate combining the roles of the Chief Inspector of Prisons, the Prisons Ombudsman and the service's existing Standards Audit.

It is only by making the penal policy process truly transparent and ensuring that prison operations are subject to rigorous independent inspection that we can effectively protect the rights and liberties of both victims and offenders.

11 Local Government and the Unelected State

Andrew Purssell[*]

The conventional view about local government and the transfer of many of its powers and responsibilities to unelected bodies is well summed up in the Association of Metropolitan Authorities' 1994 discussion document 'Changing the Face of QUANGOs':

> Democratic government in Britain today is threatened by the growth of a 'new magistracy' of appointees who sit on public bodies, spend taxpayers' money and take decisions (often in private) which should properly be the preserve of elected politicians from local government. Elected councillors have been removed from other bodies on which they used to sit as of right. QUANGOs now account for approximately £49.7 billion of public expenditure (about 20% of the total) – more than is allocated to local government in England and Wales in revenue Support Grant.
>
> (Association of Metropolitan Authorities, 1994: 1)

The document goes on to acknowledge that appointed bodies, like the poor, have always been with us, but that recent years (for which, the clear implication of the document being, one can read the last 20 years) have seen a qualitative change:

> Whereas in the past many appointed bodies had a purely advisory or limited decision-making role, and often included elected politicians in their membership (including councillors at the local level), today a new species of public agency has come into being, holding executive powers and discharging functions previously under the control of democratically elected politicians. (ibid.)

From this one would get the impression that the future of democracy itself, to say nothing of the health of local government, was at a moment of unique danger. The document correctly points out that recent years had

---

*The views expressed here are the author's, and should not be taken to reflect the policy of the London Borough of Barnet.

seen grant maintained schools, training and enterprise councils, housing action trusts and urban development corporations take functions from local authorities, each with boards of appointees taking on decision-making powers once held by councillors elected by local people. In other areas, councillors had been removed from positions of influence over local decision-making, as in the case of district health authorities, or had their influence diminished, as on the new police authorities. What all these developments had in common, of course, was that they had all happened since 1979.

It is true that the mid-1990s saw a crescendo of concern about certain trends in the way this country is governed. This was not new. There has been concern about whether the institutions of the British state are up to governing a rapidly changing modern democracy in which many once universally accepted views of the world are increasingly challenged over the last 50 years or more. On the Left this has been manifested in the attempt to graft tripartism and welfare institutions onto the constitution and various (substantially unsuccessful) tries at modernization, such as the Department of Economic Affairs, the abortive Crossman reform of the House of Lords and the 1970s devolution proposals. The ambiguity of the British Right – torn between defence of tradition and promotion of economic efficiency – is reflected in its views about the constitution. For some our institutions are incapable of being improved upon; for others they (or at least some of them) can simply get in the way of bettering the fortunes of UK plc. There was little disagreement within the Conservative Party in 1979, however, that the country was becoming ungovernable and that the institutions of the state were, for one reason or another, part of the problem.

Constitutional reform – as generations of Liberal Party activists will ruefully confirm – was, however, for years one of those issues that rarely caused mass concern among the electorate. When Charter 88 was established, the then leader of the Labour Party dismissed it and what it said as being of exclusive interest to the middle class. However, a succession of events, starting, perhaps, with the abolition of the Greater London Council, through the fiasco of the Community Charge (when all the checks and balances that are supposedly built into the constitution failed to work) to the succession of scandals within central government and the unelected bodies to which it had increasingly looked to deliver public services which were ably exploited by opposition parties in the run-up to the 1997 general election did bring the way government and the state work to the fore and possibly contributed to the extraordinary scale of the rejection of the Conservative government.

It is important to consider this longer perspective when looking at the question of local government and the growth in unelected bodies providing public services locally. For far from this being an issue that arose in the last 20 years, what we have now is the culmination of a process that started some 40 years ago; the 'new magistracy' of Professor John Stewart's luminous phrase is not so new. If there are problems of democratic deficit and fragmentation at local level the reasons for this process need to be analysed and confronted. If they are not, any changes may simply go the same way as all the other attempts at reordering local governance (and there are surely fewer areas of public policy that have been more pored over for so little lasting effect than local government).

The fundamental problem is that there is not, and has never been, any vision about what local government is – or should be – *for*. It has been established, remodelled and abolished to meet social, administrative or political demands of the moment. As Keith-Lucas and Richards put it:

> At no stage of English history has any government held a consistent and logical policy on the range and limits of municipal services. Local government was not evolved to provide a coordinated system of administration for a logically defined range of services; it emerged, piecemeal, in answer to a succession of separate needs and demands. (1978: 35)

That this is so can be seen by tracing the history of local government and the services it has at one time or another provided. From the beginnings of local government in its modern form, it was the priorities of the centre that dictated form and function. The Municipal Corporations Act of 1834 was a product of the same utilitarian reforming impulse that brought about the New Poor Law and the public health measures inspired by Sir Edward Chadwick. Nineteenth-century radicalism also helped bring about the creation of county councils (despite Lord Salisbury's suspicion). In view of the present controversy, it is ironic that modern local government replaced a wide range of elected and nominated bodies. Outside London, county administration was in the hands of the old magistracy at quarter sessions. In London, as Jerry White has pointed out, a range of organizations provided public services before the London County Council and the metropolitan boroughs were created.

The form and functions of the new authorities reflected the increasing belief among those (especially radicals and socialists) pressing for social reform that local authorities would be the best means of delivering it. In 1888 the Executive of the Fabian Society identified the opportunities the local government reorganization of the time provided for promoting socialism. Annie Besant announced that the new county councils 'created

the machinery without which Socialism was impractical: units of government which could easily be turned into units of ownership' (MacKenzie
and MacKenzie, 1979: 108).

The highwater mark of local government responsibilities came in the
1920s. Many local authorities provided gas, electricity and water to their
areas; over half the country's hospitals were run by local government and,
following the Local Government Act 1929 which abolished the Boards of
Guardians that administered the Poor Law and transferred their functions
to the county councils and county boroughs, had some responsibility for
administering local welfare. In Winifred Holtby's novel *South Riding*
(1936) county councillors are shown receiving a report from the County
Medical Officer with regard to infectious diseases, visiting a county council mental hospital and deciding on the relief to be given to the poor. It was
hardly an exaggeration to say that 'apparently academic and impersonal
resolutions passed in a county council were daily revolutionising the lives
of those men and women whom they affected' (Holtby, 1936: xi). But by
the time *South Riding* was published, the high tide of municipal power was
starting to turn. Outdoor relief of the able-bodied poor was transferred to
the Unemployment Assistance Board in 1934. The first steps towards
nationalization of electricity had been taken in 1927 with the creation of
the Central Electricity Board.

However, by far the greatest impetus to the transfer of functions away
from local government to unelected bodies was given by the Attlee
government elected in 1945. Instead of the piecemeal approach to social
change which arguably lent itself to implementation through local authorities, the new government wanted to see nationalized services provided
uniformly across the country in a way that was arguably impossible across
local council boundaries, with clear control from the centre (the poor performance of some local authorities', particularly in responding to wartime
emergencies, was probably also a contributing factor). The National
Health Act 1946 removed municipal hospitals, maternity homes, sanatoria
and mental hospitals from local government control and vested them in
nominated regional hospital boards. The National Assistance Act 1948
centralized local authorities' remaining social security functions. Region-
ally appointed boards replaced local authorities in the provision of gas and
electricity. As Keith-Lucas and Richards suggest, local governance itself
was nationalized in the new towns as the New Towns Act 1946 provided
for the appointment of new town corporations (another precedent that
would be built upon 35 years later).

Thinking about the provision of public services developed roughly along
the lines set by the Attlee government for the next 20 years. The view that

Britain's relatively poor economic performance was due to the failure to apply the most modern techniques of management became common; there was also the view that only organizations of a certain size would be able to use these methods to their greatest effect. Again, this encouraged centralization – the Water Act 1973 saw the transfer of water supply and sewerage functions to regional water authorities and the National Health Reorganization Act 1973 saw the loss of local government's residual personal health responsibilities.

Seen in this light, the actions of the Conservative government elected in 1979 are striking more for their continuity with what went before, than as a break with previously accepted practice. The difference was in the ideologies that motivated the steps taken (but even here there were continuities – some have pointed to the real break coming in 1976 under the previous government). First, the new government was determined to reduce public expenditure, a substantial proportion of which was ascribable to local government services and activities. This led to changes to the local government finance system and imposition of controls to ensure (or at least try to ensure) that authorities trod the line. Second, ministers had a view of public sector management influenced by the 'public choice' school – that elected politicians and bureaucrats would seek to increase their budgets and importance and that interest groups would demand 'rents' from elected politicians at the expense of the wider public good. Some writers in the public choice tradition had suggested greater use of single-purpose organizations. This type of thinking found practical realization in the transfer of functions away from local authorities, or the removal of local government influence from bodies such as local health authorities.

The catalogue of powers and responsibilities removed from local authorities to unelected bodies is well known; in the education field, councils lost higher and further education responsibilities and saw the introduction of legislation allowing individual schools to 'opt out' of local education authority control; primary responsibility for providing social housing was switched to housing associations, and local authority tenants were given freedom to choose their landlord. In a striking extension of the new town concept, local land use planning and development functions were transferred to appointed bodies in certain urban areas. Ministers knew what they wanted done, knew how they wanted it done (in ways as close to the market as possible) and did not trust local authorities often dominated by their political opponents to fall in line. When the prospect of conferring community care responsibilities on local authorities arose, it was done in the most grudging way possible, and with many strings attached. In 1991, amidst the collapse of the community charge, serious consideration was given within Whitehall to nationalizing all local spending, leaving local authorities as effectively administrative agents for central government (Butler, Adonis and Travers, 1994: 300). It is unsurprising that by 1994 unelected bodies accounted for approximately 20 per cent of public expenditure – more than was allocated to local authorities via revenue support grant.

What has been the effect of these changes? First, large areas of public service provision which have major impacts on the places people live have been removed from direct public influence. Ministers have argued that initiatives such as grant maintained schools actually enhance local accountability, but this is difficult to sustain in view of the requirements in the legislation establishing them about the way in which they should operate and the fact that they have to look to another unelected body – the Funding Agency for Schools, based in York, for funding. Secondly, the local public sector has been fragmented – there is now a bewildering range of organizations providing local services, a situation exacerbated by the fact that some of those services are now provided by private sector (or, as in the case of Training and Enterprise Councils, quasi-private sector) organizations, which can make co-ordination difficult and does nothing to promote public understanding about what is available from where (which was hard enough when all that required explanation was that council housing was a district council function while social workers were employed by county councils). Finally, one form of accountability for decisions – however tenuous the link between councillors and their electors may sometimes have been – was removed or weakened and nothing effective was put in its place. Granted, unelected state bodies were notionally covered by ministerial accountability to Parliament, but in practice this has not proved particularly effective, not least as it allows for shuffling of responsibility by changing the boundaries between what is 'policy' (and thus something for which ministers could properly be expected to take responsibility) and what are 'operational issues' (for which the management of the body concerned should take responsibility).

Just how significant an impact this can have on real people was seen in London's Docklands in the 1980s, where the local authorities' planning powers were vested in a ministerially appointed development corporation which pursued development of the area in a particularly single-minded way, paying little heed to the welfare of those living in the area (particularly in the early years of its work). As David Widgery, a local general practitioner, pointed out with regard to the Canary Wharf development:

A development corporation without direct accountability to the public or responsibility beyond selling off land to the highest bidder ends up

hoist by its own petard, accepting offers with absolutely no civic, archi-
tectural, or community merit and putting a brave face on it. It then finds
itself obliged to produce a roadlink which is immensely destructive to
an established community.

(Widgery, 1991: 224)

Worse, the effects of the LDDC's work have distorted the London economy
(the Corporation of the City of London responded to the growth in office
development to its east by encouraging more office development in *its*
area) and will have a baleful effect on public transport for decades as the
Jubilee Line extension project swallows up resources that could be used
more productively elsewhere. Widgery writes movingly of the powerless-
ness of those living in the shadow of the development of Docklands as
they were moved out of their homes to make way for the road to Canary
Wharf or had to live with the dust and noise of construction.

Docklands is an extreme case. Another example is provision of health-
care, where there has been a trend towards closure of local hospitals and
centralization of health provision. There is very little a community affected
by this can do; worse, there is no forum within which health authorities
can even enter into debate about possible benefits of centralization. Valued
local facilities are lost, causing some real hardship, and to add insult to
injury the reasons for it happening are never properly explained.

From local government's perspective, the removal of functions and
influence were bad enough. However, these changes were generally
accompanied by what at times seemed to be sustained denigration of local
government's record in delivering the services that were taken away from
it. No one who has worked in or with local councils will be under any
illusion that some of them have been, and are, dreadful service providers;
corrupt, inefficient, wasteful and dominated by their workforce. However,
some at least of the criticism is unfair. Many of local government's really
bad ideas (including the oft-cited estates of tower blocks) have their ori-
gins in central government initiatives or encouragement, and there is little
evidence that the unelected bodies that took over from them have
performed any more efficiently than the councils from which they took
over. In any event, the result was that the one body locally that is widely
recognized as having a degree of legitimacy in directing local affairs
because of it electoral mandate found not only that its ability to carry out
this role was reduced because of a loss of functions, but also that its very
legitimacy was put in question. This was particularly important in a situation where local authorities' capacity to do certain things for their areas
was confined to seeking to influence other organizations. Some unelected

organizations did not want to be influenced, and the climate of opinion about local government (especially in Whitehall and among 'opinion formers') that these trends encouraged did not help.

What can be done to remedy these problems? Some of the more obviously objectionable features of the system of unelected governance can be addressed through application of the programme of reforms suggested by the first report of the Nolan Committee to the process of appointment, openness (including publication of annual reports and audited accounts), codes of conduct, training and provision for 'whistleblowing' to unelected bodies and the more detailed proposals of the committee's recommendations on local spending bodies. Some of these have already been taken up. The Labour Party has made vague references to tackling quangos, and the new government has made an encouraging start by providing for oversight of unelected bodies by elected authorities in its proposals for devolution in Scotland and Wales and for a Greater London Authority. There is little sign, however, of this government having any less enthusiasm for the quango than its predecessor; indeed it is proposing to establish very powerful regional development agencies in England which will (initially at least) be run by ministerial appointees and be accountable to locally elected representatives only in Greater London. Nor does there seem to be any impetus to turn back the clock and return functions to local authorities. The fundamental issues about the role and relevance of local authorities remain.

The record outlined above brings into question what local government is *for*. If the trend has been for central governments to denude councils of power, why is this, does it matter, and if it does, what should be done about it? Over the period described earlier, British society has become more differentiated and less deferential. In general, people are better educated and more assertive. The emphasis on people as consumers has given rise to a greater consciousness of quality and demands for services that are tailored far more to individuals' circumstances. There is a growth in knowledge of, and interest in, the environment (especially when something happens locally that affects – or may affect – it). At the same time, what happens locally is more and more shaped by a multiplicity of economic and social forces operating on a regional, national or international scale. There is a need for a local institution which provides a space within which competing interests and perspectives can be debated so that a framework for the future shape of the area can be devised that is at once coherent, but also sensitive to the differences within society, and which can then do something effective about implementing that framework.

Peter Ambrose argues that democratic participation in the processes that shape the environment is important because their effects are not distributionally or environmentally neutral. Local environments are interactive systems – changes to one aspect will have major impacts on others, and while Ambrose is primarily talking about the built environment, this applies to other things as well – closure of a local hospital, or alterations to the admissions policy of a local school, for example. The one local organization with the visibility and perceived legitimacy to shape these processes are local authorities – it is to them that people affected by these changes that people look (as has been seen in the local authority in which this writer works, where a decision to close local hospital accident and emergency facilities have become a major issue between the parties in the Council – even though this is not a service over which the Council has any control). If such means do not exist, and the environment is shaped in ways that ignore or override the interests and concerns of local people, those feeling ignored or marginalized will find other ways of expressing themselves. Is it totally accidental that it was in Docklands that the British National Party elected a councillor at a by-election in 1993?

Should this role be taken on by local authorities? It seems to me that there is no other realistic candidate, given councils' democratic legitimacy and visibility and their (albeit constrained) powers to realize plans, to regulate and enforce. Taking it on will mean local government looking at ways in which it can reach out to involve people and interests not reached via traditional elective politics (the political parties have a responsibility here as well – bandying rhetoric about living in a post-political age and how apathetic people are about politics can be a self-fulfilling prophecy, and it is encouraging to see the parties talking about innovations like primary elections for candidates for Mayor of London). It will mean empowering those who may otherwise find their voices drowned out by the more powerful or articulate. It will mean being rather less self-absorbed than we in local government so often are.

The solution is not simply to turn the clock back. There is a good case for returning some functions vested in appointed bodies to local authorities (there are already moves towards changing the relationship between local education authorities and grant maintained schools, the constitution of the new police authorities could be reviewed), allowing greater local authority influence by extending local authority representation on the governing bodies of sixth form colleges and colleges of further education and the Environment Agency and considering a local government role in new areas, such as health care commissioning. Some unelected bodies, such as urban development corporations and housing action trusts could be left to wither on the vine. However, major reforms would take some time, even if ministers were sympathetic. Local government has come perilously close to abolition over the last 15 years, and it has to clearly re-establish its relevance *now*. It has to ask itself why governments have wanted to transfer functions elsewhere, whether the unelected bodies might not have had some advantages over traditional local authority structures and how it can act now to ensure the needs of local people can be met. Many authorities are taking practical steps to ensure this despite the fragmentation of the local state, compiling directories of local service providers, setting up committees to monitor local service provision, working with unelected bodies by helping them communicate with and consult local communities or joining with them to lobby the centre for more resources. This could be extended by imposing a statutory duty on all organizations providing local services to work together, perhaps to cooperate with local authorities in preparing community plans setting out a strategic framework within which all would work, and to make clear what they have done towards attainment of these objectives in annual reports.

In the longer term, local government needs to make the case for providing the forum within which local priorities will be set. As argued above, this will require an active engagement with all those it serves, especially the least confident and articulate, who are often those from which we have most to learn. Local government also has to prove that it can be an efficient and effective deliverer of services (in some places it undoubtedly has a lot to live down). There are those who argue that councils should get out of the business of actually *doing* things themselves because this would remove the temptation to become dominated by producers and overlook the needs of local people. This seems to me to be an argument for impotence – what relevance or credibility would something that would effectively be an elected think tank have? The services the local council provides are, after all, one of the reasons for it having such visibility and importance to people in their everyday lives. It is local government's failure (or alleged failure) to deliver on this that has been one factor behind its loss of influence (the editorial of the 1997 'Labour Party Conference Special' edition of *New Statesman and Society* urges the prime minister to devise a 'strategy and clear view of local government' before proceeding any further with devolution and points out that a recent Audit Commission report 'made plain' that 'local authorities are even making a mess of running services such as public libraries' even if not 'all the problems are of their own making'). If it is conceded that local authorities cannot effectively provide services, what chance is there of persuading anyone, let alone central government, that the time has come for local government to be given the assured place in the constitution that it lacks?

And in the end that is what is required if this debate is not to be repeated every time a government of whatever party gives thought to whether – for whatever reason is currently important – a function currently with local government would be better placed elsewhere. Without a written constitution entrenching the position of local government in a way analagous to the Council of Europe Charter of Local Self-Government (which sets out certain 'rights' for local authorities, and which the Labour government has now signed), this could take the shape of a parliamentary select committee dealing with relationships between central and local government, which would have the responsibility to report on any proposal affecting local authoirities' functions, powers or financing. As in Ireland, local authorities could be given the right to nominate members to a reformed House of Lords. These issues may not be beyond the horizon of political debate; the same *New Statesman and Society* editorial referred to earlier urged the prime minister to take a strategic approach to the future of local government:

> These are not easy problems to solve, but they will not be solved by ad hoc political opportunism: a parliament here; a mayor here, a 'regional chamber' there. Two things are urgently needed: a worked-through strategic outline of what the government thinks its constitutional programme is intended to lead towards … and some clarity on whether Blair intends to scrape away further at the powers and financial responsibility bestowed upon local government or to commence with a will on the long, patient process of rebuilding the bottom tier of the British political system.
>
> ('The Other Side of Devolution', *New Statesman and Society*,
> 26 September 1997: 5)

The government may have changed, but the underlying realities have not. There are signs that the present government is not wholly unconvinced of public choice school arguments (According to Andy McSmith, the outline of what eventually became *The Blair Revolution* by Peter Mandelson and Roger Liddle promised to give examples of 'hard decisions Labour dodged' in the past 'because it was in hock to producer interests' (see McSmith, 1996: 288). It has public policy pledges that it shows every intention of using any means necessary to attain.

There is a formidable agenda for local government to address, one it clearly overlooks at its peril. Happily, the signs are that its *is* being addressed, often with considerable imagination and originality. The collection of essays edited by King and Stoker (1996) shows that fundamental questions about what local government should be about that go beyond the sterile debates about local democracy are being asked. New ideas – such as those about associative democracy and community – need to be assessed critically (there is much to be said for and against both of these concepts) and practical proposals for change built on such insights should be developed.

As Winifred Holtby pointed out in the introduction to her novel, local government can be the front line thrown up by society in the war against ignorance, illness and social exclusion; the battle is not faultlessly conducted, nor are the motives of those who take part in it all righteous or disinterested. But it is one eminently worth fighting.

REFERENCES

Ambrose, P. (1994) *Urban Process and Power* (London).
Association of Metropolitan Authorities (1994) *Changing the Face of QUANGOs.*
Butler, D., Adonis, A. and Travers, A. (1994) *Failure in British Government* (Oxford).
Holtby, W. (1988) *South Riding* (London).
Keith-Lucas, B. and Richards, P. (1978) *A History of Local Government in the Twentieth Century* (London).
King, D. and Stoker, G. (eds) (1996) *Rethinking Local Government* (Basingstoke: Macmillan).
MacKenzie, N. and MacKenzie, J. (1977) *The First Fabians* (London).
McSmith, A. (1996) *Faces of Labour* (London).
The New Statesman (1997) 'The Other Side of Devolution' 26 September.
White, J. (1993) *Fear of Voting: Local Democracy and Its Enemies 1894–1994* (Oxford).
Widgery, D. (1991) *Some Lives!* (London).

12 Quango Watch – a Local Authority Perspective

Andrew Peet

In July 1996 my fellow councillor, June Evans and I, were asked by the leader of Tameside Metropolitan Borough Council to form a working group under the aegis of the policy and resources committee to look at the subject of quangos. Clearly, within the Council there was a great deal of concern about these mysterious bodies which, it was perceived, wielded great power and spent vast amounts of money. An atmosphere of suspicion bordering on paranoia existed. *Something* should be done. But what?

First it was necessary to decide what a quango is. My initial thought was to survey a number of groups to see what perception these groups had of quangos. Accordingly I chose a group that should have had some idea: members of the local District Labour Party, many of whom were councillors; Labour Party members through a ward meeting; and as a control, constituents with no party affiliation or position within the local authority structure. The questions I asked were these:

- What does the acronym quango stand for?
- Who can be a member of a quango?
- How are members appointed?
- Are members of quangos paid?
- What connection is there between quangos and the Council?
- What connection is there between quangos and central government?
- Who funds quangos?
- Where does this money come from?
- Is there a quango regulator?
- Does the existence of quangos affect your life in any way?
- Would you like to know more about what they do?

The results were interesting, to say the least. The District Labour Party delegates were very reluctant to return their answers. Did this mean that they were reluctant to reveal ignorance of the subject? Those that did displayed extreme suspicion about the whole issue, but a general feeling that these bodies were the mouthpieces of a Conservative administration prevailed. The returns from the general public displayed an overall lack of knowledge, but an underlying suspicion that one might have expected. The respondents from the ward members displayed a wide range knowledge from the informed to uninformed.

Next, I tried to answer my own question 'What is a quango?' Accordingly I reported to the Policy and Resources Committee in the following vein:

> Having been given the brief of 'Quango Watch', my colleague and I set to work. We were determined that this should be a member-led initiative and not an officer-driven one. At first, Quango Watch seemed to have an obvious area of concern, but following an extensive literature review, external discussion and attendance at the 'DEMOS' conference it became apparent that there was considerable complexity. The latter conference reinforced our belief that there was considerable uneasiness about the very name.

As we saw it, there were three main areas to consider: Who?, What? and How? These were the areas that we put to our parent committee:

WHO SHOULD WE BE WATCHING? IN OTHER WORDS, WHAT IS A QUANGO?

Many organizations and bodies now feel that they do not fit into a category that has become synonymous with patronage and lack of control. John Plummer, speaking at the DEMOS conference, suggested that witnesses to Nolan were keen: first, not to be seen as quangos; and second, to distance themselves from each other. One organization after another sought to remove themselves from the title 'quango'. This disassociation from the term quango highlights the complexity of the issue. Few groups claim to be quangos and therefore the definitions that are referred to below are illustrative of how various bodies prefer to be seen.

1. The original 'Quasi-Autonomous Non-Governmental Organizations' is a contradiction in itself as, if it is only *partly* autonomous, then the remainder of its control and funding must come from without itself. It is clear that this control and funding comes from central government, thus highlighting the problems of the 'Non-Governmental' title.
2. Nolan I and II use the terminology of Executive Non-Departmental Public Bodies (and NHS bodies) being public bodies with executive powers whose boards are appointed by ministers (9000 board members, spending £40 billion a year) and Local Public Spending Bodies defined as '"not for profit" bodies which are rarely elected and not appointed by Ministers. These provide public services, often delivered at local

level and are largely or wholly public funded' (4500 bodies; 70,000 voluntary board members; spending £15 billion of public funds p.a.).

3. Other local authorities define a number of bodies, typically four, for example:
    (a) a body created to provide a public service, e.g. English Tourist Board;
    (b) an organization delivering services previously provided by the borough council, e.g. the sixth form college;
    (c) an organization delivering public-funded services previously considered to be public, e.g. united utilities.
    (d) A regulatory body for any of the above e.g. OFWAT.
4. The common dictionary definition of a quango is: 'An organization or agency that is funded by the government but acts independently of it.'
5. Our own definition would be: 'Any organization previously under the control of the local authority (or whose nature would have placed it so), which is no longer accountable to any locally elected body but still with access to public funding.' In other words, non-elected spenders of tax pounds.

WHAT EXACTLY ARE WE WATCHING?

Lord Nolan's brief can be summarized into two essential areas: appointments and propriety. We made clear reference to both these strands. Lord Nolan stated: 'There is much public concern about appointments to quango boards and a widespread belief that these are not always on merit. The government has committed itself publicly to making all appointments on merit.' The transcripts of the oral evidence given to the Nolan Committee might not be Booker prize material but it often contains the most illuminating conversations and debates. Take, for example, the following extract of a conversation between Professor Anthony King (Nolan Committee) and Stanley Kalms (Chairman of the Dixons Group):

Professor Anthony King: Since you talked about quangos, can we talk about quangos? Which one are you on at the moment?

Stanley Kalms: I am on two. I am Chairman of the Kings National Health Trust, which is a large hospital in Camberwell, and I am on the Funding Agency for Schools and chair their finance committee.

King: Now can we take just as an example the Funding Agency for Schools? How were you recruited for that job?

Kalms: I have a long history of involvement in education – that is perhaps one of my major outside interests. I heard that the Funding Agency was being formed, I indicated to people who walked the corridors that it was an area that I ought to be involved in. As such I was asked to come along and be interviewed.

King: You say you indicated to people who walked the corridors. Who were they?

Kalms: In this case I happened to mention it to a minister at an earlier stage and I happened to mention it to the Chairman-elect and said to him, 'I think this is an area where I can make a contribution because I have a knowledge and an interest in the subject.'

King: So in this case you were not head-hunted – you hunted your own?

Kalms: I hunted myself, yes.

King: Yes.

Kalms: But at a fairly senior level. I doubt if it would have been effective if I had just dropped a word somewhere else.

(Second Report of the Committee on Standards on Public Life, May 1996, Cm 3270, vol. 1, p. 389, paras 1823–6)

We both felt that while this may well be common practice in senior management appointments (as suggested by Stanley Kalms in his introductory speech to Nolan), these are methods quite alien to the general public or to local government. I am not waging any sort of campaign against the Chairman of Dixon's; he simply provided an apposite example from the mass of evidence in the Nolan transcripts.

Propriety should encompass the areas of behaviour, honesty and policy.

We felt that these were crucial areas to address and that it would be difficult to improve on Nolan's outline, but we drew the committee's attention to the fact that not only had vast amounts of public funding been removed from local authority control, but that vital policy decisions affecting the lives of everyone in the borough had been taken from those who the people have chosen to make such policies and whom the people hold accountable. No quango board is subject to surcharge for poor decisions, or presents itself to the electorate for reappointment.

HOW ARE WE WATCHING?

Cllr June Evans made an excellent report on questions relating to the 'How?' – highlighting the fact that we would prefer to approach quangos in a spirit of co-operation and the difficulties of eliciting information from bodies who may be less than open and the political implications.

One of the initial steps we took was the creation of a quango register to catalogue all such organizations relevant to our area. An officer prepared a list that was discussed to decide on the format that it should take. We saw two examples, one from Bury and another from Kirklees. It is interesting that in Kirklees they have chosen to combine what Tameside is doing through its Service, Delivery and Assurance Committee in examining their own organization with the scrutiny of outside bodies. Through contacts made at the DEMOS conference we have also been able to see the direction being taken by a number of other local authorities: Lewisham and Basildon, for example.

We then sought from the Committee an approval of our definition of 'Who?'. We also confirmed that the 'What?' would include looking at appointments, propriety and policy-making, all of which will clearly mark our boundaries; and the continued support of the 'How'.

We then had a working definition of what we considered to be a quango, perhaps not what others might have chosen, but fitting our brief. From this evaluation of direction there had also come a clear understanding of the importance of the key issues of transparency and accountability. Moreover, it was clear that this should not be a one-way street: as a Council we too must abide by the standards that we chose to apply to others. The setting up of the Service, Delivery and Assurance Committee with its brief to be an continuous internal audit of all the Council's business is evidence of that – providing, that is, that there is a certain degree of political freedom. Ideally, there should be complete political freedom, ensuring that ideological agendas do not bias the work of such a group. At least this was a start along the road that will no doubt be strongly influenced by the Nolan Committee's work as time goes on.

In other authorities, the work of quango groups is not only linked to, but is part of a Quality Assurance Committee. Our examination of this methodology seemed to indicate that in making this link so close, the issue of quangos as we understood them appeared to have been subsumed by the introspective aspect of such a Committee. External considerations seemed to be mainly along the lines of examining areas of public/private partnerships, which although part of the whole quango scene, was moving the goal posts still further, although I am not entirely sure in which direction.

COUNCILS AND QUANGOS: TOWARDS A NEW RELATIONSHIP

The problem for local authorities in relation to quangos is that they feel they draw their authority and their mandate from the people, which is tested by periodic elections. Their actions, decisions, remuneration and even private lives are subject to public scrutiny as laid down by Act of Parliament, and by the local press. If they are dishonest, or even mistaken, they can be held to account. Ultimately, councillors can be personally surcharged.

Not so with quangos. Public perception of these bodies is that they are shadowy creatures run by we know not who, in a manner of their own choosing. Unless a criminal act is proven in the courts, they are untouchable, relying on the 'golden handshake' method of rooting out those who, for whatever reason, they feel should be dispensed with. They are not to be trusted, yet huge sums of public money are in their control. It was in this atmosphere of mistrust that Quango Watch was established.

However, it is all too easy to condemn the quangocracy as a Conservative plot to undermine local authorities. This view ignores the fact that the original flurry of quango creations took place under a Labour government and that at the beginning of the Thatcher era, the Iron Lady herself pledged herself to dismember them. That she did away with some but created many more speaks volumes for the usefulness that central government finds in the system. Perhaps my original thoughts on the dichotomous nature of the beasts had some validity after all. 'Quasi' suggests a shadowy, unnamed, but fairly clear hand in the creation, appointments to and overall guidance of these most useful arms of government. At the time of writing, it is early days in the evolution of a new Parliament, but there is currently little sign that quangos will be anything else but useful to the new administration.

There is an increasing awareness within local government that we work with and alongside the quango; they may after all be useful. The present impossible position regarding the state (or lack) of repair of council housing stock is an appropriate and current example of the new ways of thinking which are sweeping through the whole administration. Without engaging in the political debate surrounding this most emotive issue, let me illustrate one mode of thinking. We have a very large housing stock with a potential repair bill running into multi-million pounds. We have several million pounds of capital receipts, but not enough to effect all repairs even if the government were to release the capital all at once, which seems unlikely. As a local authority we are constrained by long-standing regulations against the raising of monies for this purpose. A private company with similar assets would be welcomed by any bank. Why not then set up a company (or quango!) based on a public/private partnership to administer this housing? The subsequent release of funds would be more than enough to complete all repairs and leave a fund available for school building and road repairs, which are also in a lamentable state.

These are not the wild ideas of a right-wing group as can be seen by Margaret Beckett's insistence that local authorities 'look closely at alternative ways of funding their housing stocks...'. The world has changed since the days of Wilson and Callaghan, and new solutions must be found for what appears to be an old problem but is in fact a brand new one. It has to be admitted that die-hard left-wingers perceive most pronouncements from the Blair administration as the rantings of a right-wing group!

Thus, local as well as central government can see virtue in quangos and it becomes even harder to understand the universal paranoia surrounding them. But let us return to the Nolan themes: accountability and transparency. If we knew who were on these quangos, how the appointments were made, what exactly they did and could hold their funding up to scrutiny, then there would be far less suspicion about them. There would still remain the issue of democratic accountability, but I feel that most would be appeased by these measures. The issue is increasingly less one of whether or not their should be quangos and more one of whether they can be made accountable.

One of the issues that does remain is concern over political control. Is there anything wrong with the concept that cannot be addressed by replacing board members who hold opposing political views with new members of the governments shade of opinion, or do we need new methods of ensuring political balance or neutrality? Some evidence from the Nolan Committee highlights the problem of political balance (para. 1829):

Professor Anthony King: When the Funding Agency for Schools was set up last year you may well remember that John Patten, who was then the Secretary of State, was accused of packing the agency with Conservative supporters. Did you at that time think there was any evidence to support that view?

Stanley Kalms: Well, I think that in an agency such as the Funding Agency you clearly have to agree with the philosophy of grant maintained schools, otherwise this is not the place to be. If you don't agree with it you should be off the committee and attacking it. So clearly those who are on that particular quango are supporters of the system. It doesn't necessarily imply that they are Conservatives but it does imply that they are supporters of grant maintained. I suspect that they are not all Tories.

There is no doubt that this represents a method of ensuring a committee that will reach a speedy consensus on how to spend its £2 billion annual budget, but I suspect that for many this will reinforce the views already held about the dangers inherent in the quango system. Labour itself will be coming under similar attack but it will be reacting, it is hoped, in a post-Nolan world where these issues have been held up to the light of scrutiny.

CONCLUSION

In considering reforms of quangos our own authority is engaged in an exercise to examine our own practices. Do we provide the services that the public expect of us? Are there better ways of providing that service? Do our committee systems show efficiency and fairness of decision? Are certain committees necessary at all? Most importantly we intend to set up a Nolan Standards Bench, a body of independent composition that will be responsible for the scrutiny of the whole Council, particularly those areas that are already engaged in investigation of methodology, such as the Audit Department. The irony is that thinking about service delivery raises the question of whether is some areas quangos may be a better option than local authority delivery. However, our conclusion is that this can only be done if quangos reach similar standards of accountability. Perhaps, then, one of the answers lies in the ironical suggestion that what is needed is the setting up of another quango, 'OFQUAN' or an acronym to that effect, to regulate the system. That should allay the fears that have built up during the lifetime of these most durable of government bodies.

13 A National Health Service in Quangoland

Peter Baldwin

The provision of health services in Britain has never been undertaken directly by the state. As an historical perspective will demonstrate, the relationship between government and the provision of health care has always been hands-off. Nevertheless, during the 1980s there was a tendency for the provision of services to be fragmented, and this raises questions concerning the nature of accountability and whether health needs are being adequately met.

As a way of setting the twentieth-century scene it is necessary to take a brief look at events in the preceding centuries. The historical perspective demonstrates how the state has always relied on a range of voluntary and local-level bodies for the provision of health services. While the Army and Navy relied on Commissioners for the sick and wounded to administer their hospitals throughout the eighteenth century, civilians had to rely on charitable foundations or, from 1782, on the work of Boards of Guardians for the Poor. Under the Poor Law Amendment Act 1836, the poor could look to a nation-wide system of Boards of Guardians. These Boards were elected locally but supervised by a central government body comprising three salaried members and a secretary, who was none other than Edwin Chadwick. The role of those Boards was the more necessary because, following the Napoleonic Wars, the downturn in the economic cycle left the population in the countryside, apart from the squirearchy, with scant means and services. Simultaneously the population of the cities and towns was growing apace, heavily concentrated in rudimentary housing, on low wages and with minimal services. In these conditions cholera and other infectious illnesses, such as tuberculosis, became rife; and social class was no protection. The Crimean War produced similar conditions and results for the Armed Forces, but within the direct and undeniable responsibility of ministers.

There were two main results. One was a long process, which ran on far into the twentieth century, of definition and concentration of public health functions into the hands of locally elected authorities now conceived as multifunctional, with powers to raise revenue from rates on property and to borrow on the security of those rates. Public health functions came to include notification of infectious diseases and generally the prevention of infection from disease, unsound or adulterated food or the condition of dairies, cowsheds or milkshops; investment in and operation of systems of clean water supply and their protection against pollution; of public baths and washhouses; and of sewerage, drainage and sanitary conveniences; collection of refuse and disposal of waste matter of all kinds; abatement of nuisances; control of vermin; regulation of offensive trades, and of factories and workshops generally; housing of the 'working classes'; recreation grounds; lighting; ventilation; regulation of the construction of buildings; and establishment of hospitals.

Local authorities acquiring these functions appointed, under statute, qualified medical practitioners as salaried Medical Officers of Health to supervise their execution. The scene was thus well set for local epidemiological research into infection, if not into other causes of ill-health, and for prophylactic if not remedial action (Riden, 1987). The other legacy was the creation of the nursing profession in consequence of the masterful leadership of Florence Nightingale, with its systematic concern with hygiene and its own necessary and distinctive contribution to therapy and personal care. A further important development at this time was the transfer of the duty of care of mentally ill and mentally handicapped people from justices of the peace to local authorities. This duty was often discharged by local authorities who co-operated to maintain very large, long-stay hospitals.

Despite such improved organization conscription for the First World War produced disconcerting evidence of the connection between poverty and ill-health. This was accentuated by the economic depression in the early 1930s. Moreover, the Second World War increased social and political pressure for welfare reform and in 1942 the Beveridge Report was produced. This widely supported report proposed fundamental reform of social security and health services and subsequently provided the basis for most of the social legislation of the 1945 Labour government. This social revolution included provision for the National Health Service. However, because of the urgent requirements of post-war reconstruction and straitened national finances, more than a decade was to pass before its institution could be supported by substantial new investment from public funds.

The National Health Service Act 1946, did not entirely restructure the provision of health care; rather, the new arrangements were imposed on existing institutions. Before the NHS primary medical and dental care was provided by general practitioners operating in private, fee-earning partnerships, or alone, and in premises of their own. The same doctors often provided the medical staff of self-financing cottage hospitals; and these hospitals often had strong traditions of voluntary service. Secondary and tertiary care was provided by specialist consultants, and junior doctors under their supervision, operating in or from larger hospitals and sanatoria which were provided sometimes by charitable foundations (frequently appealing for funds) and sometimes by local authorities. Remuneration of these consultants was usually by fees, sometimes charitably waived; sometimes by salary, especially in teaching hospitals which acquired the means to pay from the school's income from tuition fees, endowments and grants.

The concept visualized for the National Health Service was equal access for all to an equal national standard of medical and dental care delivered free of charge at the point of need. In the preparation of the legislation two issues were subject to fierce debate. One was directed towards the question of whether doctors and dentists should become salaried. The second was concerned with who should be their paymaster. Broadly, the representations on behalf of general practitioners were resistant to the concept of salary as distinct from fees for service; and the representations on behalf of consultants and junior doctors serving in the larger hospitals were not unfavourable to remuneration by salary provided that it would be paid by central government and not by local authorities. Out of this debate emerged the form of legislation which has provided for the pay of doctors. General practice was to be financed from central government funds under contracts between the practitioners and territorial authorities. Hospital services were to be funded, including salaried staff, from central government funds channelled again through territorial authorities which only in very recent times have become the same as those responsible for funding general practice.

Even the initial establishment of the health service raised important questions of accountability and democracy. The NHS created a large-scale bureaucracy whose authority derived through the national ballot box. In effect it was the Secretary of State who was accountable for the running of the health service. The only democratic control was, in effect, indirect through the minister. Democratic control through local authorities was completely excluded from the original, and subsequent, structure of the NHS. With the exclusion of elected local authorities from responsibility for any element of the National Health Service the Secretary of State stands as the sole link between that service and elected authority.

The problem that derives from this arrangement, and it is a constant theme in relation to ministerial responsibility, is that the Secretary of State is answerable in principle to Parliament for everything done, or omitted to be done, in the exercise of the functions imposed by statute on the organs of the National Health Service. In practice, however, ministers in

Parliament have increasingly relied on a view that anything done or omitted to be done which can be regarded as within delegated managerial responsibility of an authority subordinate to them is to be treated in Parliament as a matter of that subordinate authority's responsibility. Hence, while they are constitutionally accountable, they have often pushed responsibility downward, in effect turning health authorities into quangos. This delegation of authority raises the question of how and to whom these authorities are responsible and answerable. There are no alternative constitutional prescriptions for these chains of accountability. One of the consequences is the increasing tendency of the public to contemplate litigation on matters of medical or dental treatment.

From time to time the possibility of more democratic control of the National Health Service has been considered at the behest of central government, for example by the Guillebaud Committee in 1953–6 (Cmnd 9663, 1956), in the Porritt Report of 1964 (Medical Services Review Committee, 1964), by Redcliffe-Maud through the Royal Commission on Local Government in 1966–9 (Cmnd 4040, 1969), and in a Green Paper entitled 'National Health Service: The Administrative Structure of the Medical and Related Services in England and Wales' published in 1968. When Richard Crossman was Secretary of State for Health the practice of appointing some serving local councillors to National Health Service Authorities began, but was discontinued when it was found that the perspective of responsibility for wards was unhelpful for the wider purposes of deploying the resources of a National Health Service Authority to the best effect, in terms of equal access to an equal standard of service.

The capacity of local authorities to carry real responsibility for any very large extra service was reduced when the second Thatcher administration introduced the poll tax. The impact of the new tax was to increase disproportionately the share of local expenditure met ultimately by the Exchequer, and thus to intensify the involvement of central government in the exercise of judgement on local deployment of resources within whatever service.

An unrelated development has brought local authorities back into association with the National Health Service. This was the decision of the third Thatcher administration, on the advice of Sir Roy Griffiths, to transfer funds from the Department of Social Security to local authorities. This change extended their involvement in the provision of social services which they had acquired following the Seebohm Report (Seebohm, 1968). The consequence of the Griffiths' policy was a requirement for local authorities and health authorities to co-ordinate the use of their budgets when the needs of individuals crossed functional boundaries, e.g. social services and health services. For example, general medical and dental practitioners and community nurses are variously financed, but often deal with the same individual. Therefore it is important to meet individual needs despite functional differentiation in service delivery. It is an interesting question where responsibility and answerability lie in ministerial, council chamber and official circles for success or failure in delivery of service in these circumstances. There may be no clear answer to this question so long as separate budgetary systems are involved in providing service for individuals. We owe much to human care and co-operation among staff in local government and the National Health Service at levels below those who are legitimately responsible and answerable for the system.

This is an arrangement within the National Health Service's statutory structure which, on the face of it, emphasizes the direct responsibility and answerability both of its appointed authorities who commission and finance services to be provided by its Trusts and of the members of those Trusts. This arrangement comprises the community health councils to which the local population can complain about the form or behaviour of any element of their hospital or hospital-based services. But, apart from the involvement of the Secretary of State in appointments to all these bodies, formal disagreement between a Community Health Council and the National Health Service Authority is to be referred to and be decided by the Secretary of State. In that sense ultimate responsibility still rests with the Secretary of State.

This statutory system of horizontal answerability of territorial authorities to other quangos, such as the Community Health Councils, was not the only point of territorial communication between Health Authorities and the public. There was also the required practice of the Regional and District Health Authorities to open a public gallery to their meetings, excluding only items of business, such as disciplinary procedures, which had to be debated in private. The public gallery was discontinued when the creation of the 'internal market' in the National Health Service in the 1990s introduced considerations of commercial confidentiality into the processes of territorial planning and decision-making.

Following the Griffiths Report the government decided to divide the organization of the Department of Health between its core of policy advisers, including the Permanent Secretary and the Chief Medical Officer, and the National Health Service Executive. As a result the general managers of all the National Health Service authorities were brought into a *de facto* system of answerability to the chief executive of the National Health Service Executive. Such a system was the express intention of Sir Roy Griffiths' plan for creating a chain of general management through the service, on the commercial pattern familiar to him, alongside the service's statutory system of territorial authorities. As a consequence, the chief executive of the National Health Service Executive was seen as responsible and answerable on managerial matters, as distinct from policy matters, such as NHS pay. However, the existence of practical links between the chief executive and the general managers of the National Health Service authorities calls into question any argument that the Secretary of State is entitled to regard the members of those authorities as ultimately responsible and publicly answerable. The executive staff of the authorities and Trusts receive a regular flow of instruction directly from the National Health Service Executive for which the Secretary of State is incontestably responsible and answerable in Parliament, since it is part of his or her Department of State. The changing structure has not, therefore, formally changed the lines of accountability; they continue to lead directly to the Secretary of State.

Traditionally, and in keeping with the constitution, the Permanent Secretary of the Department of Health was accustomed to share with the Secretary of State responsibility for the execution of policy throughout the National Health Service, and in other functions related to health, while the Secretary of State uniquely carried responsibility for the policy itself. The only other administrative civil servant in the Department with the same range of responsibility as the Permanent Secretary was the Department's Accountant General, among whose functions was the conduct of audit anywhere where the Department's voted funds were spent, including the National Health Service. That the Permanent Secretary and the Accountant General should have this range of responsibility in common should be no surprise since to put into execution either decisions taken on policy grounds excluding finance or decisions taken on financial grounds excluding policy would be equally unwise. The arrangement followed the classic form of accountability to Parliament under which Department's Permanent Secretaries are appointed also as their Accounting Officers – a role which, as I can vouch from experience, need not be inordinately difficult provided that the Principal Finance Officer (by whatever title, including Accountant General) performs to the highest standard.

Again, from experience, it is apparent that in the past the distinction between financial and political responsibility was maintained when the Chairman of a National Health Service Authority was called upon to answer in terms of financial accountability before any political authority. Chairmen were placed in this position during the 1970s and early 1980s when the government required that the making of executive decisions on behalf of individual National Health Service Authorities should be done on the basis of a consensus between the Authority's chief administrative, medical, nursing, financial and works service's officers. With the introduction of general managers in the mid-1980s the need for consensus was removed and lines of accountability diverged. Chairmen were then engaged in answerability to the Ministers who appointed them (and who would determine succession) while General Managers were separately engaged in a chain of mandatory instruction from the National Health Service Executive. Only an ill-defined distinction between policy and execution stood between the two chains of answerability.

The Chairmen's threads in the fabric of responsibility acquired some definition from a regime operated by Sir Norman Fowler as Secretary of State. He held meetings, of what he called his NHS Cabinet, with the 14 chairmen of Regional Health Authorities in England to explain, and sometimes to consult upon, his policies. These meetings were attended by his ministerial colleagues and senior official advisers. The chairmen co-ordinated their contributions, including their criticisms, by choosing every two years one of their number as chairman of chairmen. They also provided standing secretarial support and conducted their own consultations before the Secretary of State's meetings. From my own experience as chairman of chairmen I would suggest this process provided the opportunity to infuse policy with issues of with practicability and equity (which, of course, is a principle of the NHS).

This was not a closed circle of communication. To obtain the views of hospital and hospital-based services, including those for the mentally ill or mentally handicapped, regional chairmen ensured there were regular consultative, and sometimes directional, meetings with the chairmen of the district health authorities. There was also, once or twice a year, consultation with the chairmen of the corresponding community health councils. The recent absorption of the regional dimension of National Health Service organization more closely into the Departments machinery has spread the fabric of direct answerability between the territorial authorities and the department both more widely and more thinly. At the same time the authorities' public galleries have been closed. It is natural, then, that the traffic of answerability should travel more than ever by the routes of the National Health Service Executive and the authorities' general managers, while audit in the national interest is conducted by the National Audit Commission rather than by departmental auditors. Thus, responsibility has shifted within the NHS quangocracy but not towards greater public accountability.

The issues that arises from these changes is how, in the context of the breaking up of service delivery, do we retain accountability? Who is accountable and is it possible to ensure that the NHS, rather than becoming a set of self-governing administrative units, is an instrument for policy? A major danger is that wider issues of health, such as poverty, bad diet, smoking and alcohol, etc., will be lost as NHS Trusts are concerned solely with delivering their services and not wider elements of health policy. The search for greater efficiency impairs the ability of the government machine to identify and formulate questions requiring decisions on policy when these questions are broader than a single body. The reforms and quangoization of the NHS has created a fundamental problem of coordination.

The problems of co-ordination are highlighted by the case of BSE. For several years the Ministry of Agriculture, Fisheries and Food was carrying responsibility for the meat trade from the farmers' fields to the fast-food chain and the retail counter. It exercised that responsibility by making enforceable, but not regularly enforced, regulations. Then came the need for the Secretary of State for Health to inform Parliament and the public of the possibility that the disease in cattle is transferable in lethal form to human beings. In the international furore that followed the announcement, huge unforeseen costs to the British economy were incurred. Yet the policies for controlling the spread of the disease among cattle and for preventing its spread to human beings should have been united throughout in a single structure of enforced measures backed by continuing agreement between the Secretaries of State and by the collective responsibility of the Cabinet. However, the fragmentation of health policy-making prevented such a structure existing.

A contributory cause of the lack of co-ordination – perhaps the most serious one – has been a change in the role of the Cabinet Office. It has shifted from being a policy co-ordinating body to a policy executing body. For example, it is responsible for the Citizen's Charter. But its original and unique function is precisely to arrange in good time, and on the appropriate scale of collective authority, for those elements of the machinery of government, to come together to consider matters which cross departmental boundaries. It has to be in question how far it is still the internally acknowledged duty of the Cabinet Office to organize this service in the process of British government.

The problem of co-ordination at national level has been exacerbated by the fragmentation of services at local level. With the advent of the National Health Service local authorities lost the function of establishing hospitals. The Health and Safety Commission and Executive took over several other public health functions. The office of Medical Officer of Health in local authorities was discontinued. With it went the opportunity of that office for local research into the epidemiology of infection. On the face of it there was all the more reason to look then to National Health Service authorities to pursue local epidemiological research as the foundation for decisions on the deployment of their resources; and in particular to their capital resources for anticipating future needs as well as for making good clinical deficiencies in existing provision. There have been good epidemiological analyses from this source. However, the first Major administration preferred to take back distribution of capital resources into the Department's regional structure. The second Major administration went further and incorporated the regional authorities into that structure. It remains to be seen how far local epidemiology and other local insights will prove to be the touchstone for distribution of public funds and involvement of private capital.

This problem of fragmentation essentially derived from an earlier period. The third Thatcher administration decided that the purchasing of services should be separated from the function of supplying health care. In addition, services would be delivered by Trusts which would compete with each other on commercial principles for the commissioning authorities' custom or, in other word, for their funds. Whatever else may be said about this process there is no logical reason whatever for supposing that the results of commercial competition will match even approximately the pattern of service which would be suggested for the near or further future by rigorous epidemiological study of local need. It may be good for the bottom line of this year's and next year's accounts for the Barset District General Hospital Trust to decide, on grounds of cost to itself and to its potential funding authority or authorities, not to provide for a particular form of treatment; but it will not be good for the patients in the locality who find that they need precisely that treatment, especially if Trusts elsewhere are also reluctant to provide it. By definition, indeed, the concept of competition involves selection of activity which must risk leaving need unmet; and in so far as competition is advocated on grounds of promoting efficiency, this is at the price of risking a wasteful use of capital.

The focus of Trusts on the market and costs means that wider epidemiological issues are often ignored. However, a wider, more long-term view of health care provisions demonstrates that concentration on more general health issues will actually save resources. Through local epidemiological research and greater preventive measures the demands on the health service will be reduced. By using this approach Chadwick reduced the annual cost of Poor Law Relief in the value of the currency at the time from £27 million in 1831 to £5 million in 1851, despite the provisions of the Public

Health Act 1848, and the costs of dealing with cholera outbreaks. Such interdisciplinary thinking and informed action should happen now.

The problem for government is that there are a whole set of health needs that are as yet unmet, and demographic trends, changing epidemiological patterns and new technology will determine whether the scale of unmet need in this nation and/or the world will grow during the twenty-first century. Moreover governments increasingly believe that they have met the limits of public expenditure and so are concerned with curtailing the costs of health care. With this prospect of uncertainty at best and intensified need at worst there is a premium on encouraging voluntary effort as the only means of supplementing the contributions of government and the market and of reaching need beyond the capacity of either.

Because of the failures of government, processes of reform and the market, there is a reliance on quangos and voluntary effort within and beyond quangos. Government has shifted from voluntary service, to local authority provision, to national control to quasi-markets and diverse service delivery. However, the greater diversity of service delivery raises two crucial questions: How are services to be co-ordinated to ensure that nonstandard health issues are met and resources used efficiently? What are the chains of accountability that exist both upwards to ministers and downwards to users? The NHS has always provided services through diverse institutions, but the introduction of markets has led to greater problems of cooperation because different elements of the health service are now competitors. It also presents market accountability as an alternative to ministerial accountability, but it is not clear that the market can always see or meet the health needs, or democratic needs, of the citizen.

14 The Accountability of Training and Enterprise Councils
Alistair Graham

INTRODUCTION

Training and Enterprise Councils have been in live operation since April 1990 and in their seven years of existence they have established their credibility as strategic players at local level in the areas of economic development, regeneration and developing a skilled workforce. An essential part of establishing that credibility has been the importance of addressing the issue of how TECs can satisfy their contractual commitment to the government of the day, and at the same time to be genuinely accountable to the local communities they serve.

The creation of TECs in 1989 represented a significant devolution of power to local level and is one of the few examples of a government of any political persuasion devolving responsibility for the delivery of part of its economic objectives to such a level. This devolution arose because the attempt by central government to deliver a world-class workforce by the Manpower Services Commission and then the Training Agency was not seen to be successful as measured by organizations such as the National Institute for Social and Economic Research. Detailed studies carried out by the Institute throughout the 1980s on the level of skills and productivity of the British workforce compared to Britain's main economic competitors showed serious deficiencies in both skills and productivity levels. What was remarkable about the decision to create TECs was that it placed senior private sector leaders in the front-line of creating thriving local economies sustained by skilled workforces. This means the issue of TEC accountability has to be seen in the context of the boldness of the experiment the previous government initiated in decentralizing part of its economic machine.

WHAT ARE TECs?

There are 80 TECs in England and Wales. In Scotland there are 22 Local Enterprise Companies (LECs) which are similar organizations, but which

162

also have a wider responsibility for physical as well as human resource development. TECs in England and Wales work within an annual education and funding contract between each TEC and the Secretaries of State for Employment, the Environment and Trade and Industry. This is a legal contract, incorporating five documents and is over 400 pages in length. The reason why the Secretary of State for the Environment is a signatory is because a number of the government programmes which are run by TECs are included in the Single Regeneration Budget (SRB). This was an attempt by the Conservative administration to bring a wide range of government programmes together to achieve a more coherent approach to local economic development and regeneration issues. The Department of Trade and Industry has an interest through business support services contracted with TECs, but delivered by Business Links. In Scotland, Local Enterprise Companies (LECs) receive their funds, and are supervised, through an intermediary body called Scottish Enterprise, which in return is responsible to the Secretary of State for Scotland.

TECs (and LECs in Scotland) are independent private companies limited by guarantee/shares and therefore subject to company law. They spend primarily public funds including money from the EU, either from the European Social Fund or European Regional Development Funds. TECs in their operating agreement are defined as 'independent companies which have been set up as Training and Enterprise Councils for the purpose of providing training, supporting enterprise and undertaking other activities'. The agreement provides for a three-year corporate plan and a one-year business plan to be produced by each TEC in accordance with guidance provided by the Secretary of State for Employment.

The previous government's strategic guidance to TECs for producing their corporate plan for the period 1997–2000 included a foreword by the Prime Minister and was signed by the six Cabinet ministers covering Education and Employment, Trade and Industry, Environment, the Home Office and Transport. The introduction spells out the role government sees for TECs.

> Continuing to help British business to win in world markets is a priority for Government. Competitiveness is the key – competitiveness of the economy as a whole, and of each individual and each business. This document confirms the important role we expect TECs to contribute to play in driving forward competitiveness at local level.
>
> In the five years since the completion of the network, TECs have made much progress. You have increased the breadth and quality, and reduced the cost, of the services you provide. You have built strong

partnerships with a wide range of organisations, including those involved with you in establishing the Business Link network. You are involved in a host of projects and activities designed to strengthen your local economies.

Your strength is that you are *strategic bodies led by business*. You bring a business perspective to local issues and encourage partners to take a broad view of the needs of the area. It is crucial that TECs continue to work in partnership with local authorities, Chambers, Careers Services, Employment Service, education and training providers and others in the local area to develop and achieve your shared objectives.

While the primary focus of TECs is on meeting local needs, that can only be done effectively if local action is set within the regional and national context. TECs will need to continue to build effective partnerships with organisations at regional level, including Government Offices. Government Offices promote a coherent approach to competitiveness, sustainable development and regeneration in both urban and rural areas. They co-ordinate the preparation of regional competitiveness frameworks that set out an agreed plan of action to improve prosperity. TECs are key partners in this activity and through your own corporate plans can make a bridge between local action and the wider needs of reach region.

As Government's key private sector partner at local level, we will seek to give you as much flexibility as we can to address the three key priorities we have set you:

- to create and maintain *dynamic local economies* with strategic partners, in particular with local authorities;
- to support *competitive business*, through effective investment in innovation and the development and management of people, and increased use of business support services through the network of Business Links; and
- to build a *world class workforce* and create a learning society with the skills essential to successful businesses and individuals.

TECs were given a broad endorsement by the incoming Labour government. David Blunkett wrote to TEC chairs in a letter dated 29 May 1997 outlining the new government's approach:

As you know, the new Government aims to build a better educated, as well as more competitive, Britain. A Britain in which everyone is equipped to find and keep a decent job. I want to work in genuine partnership with you and the other partners involved in education, training and employment to bring about substantial improvements in standards, achievements and equality of opportunity for all.

I recognise the value TECs can bring to local partnerships and I am impressed by the significant voluntary, unpaid contribution being made by TEC Directors. We have an ambitious agenda to fulfil – and I'm not going to pretend that it will be easy – but with your help we can bring about substantial improvement.

TECs will continue to have a broad remit, working closely with this and other Departments. Your work with other partners in the wider economic development of your local areas and the Regions will also be crucial. Your work will be a key part of the local delivery of the New Deal for the unemployed, for our programme of lifelong learning, and our agenda of employability.

It is vital that we draw on the expertise of TECs – your close understanding of business, the labour market and the training sector – to best effect in helping each individual, business and community succeed in an increasingly competitive global economy.

In the coming weeks I will be making announcements to bring about positive change. We will be producing a White Paper on Education and will make announcements about Employment and the New Deal. We are also likely to publish a further White Paper later in the year, setting out a more comprehensive view of lifelong learning.

I want to underline the importance I attach to the contribution of TECs. There are many examples of innovative and effective practice. I would particularly point to your success in driving forward Modern Apprenticeships and Investors in People; in leading in the development of the Business Link network and in making Training for Work more effective. I do, however, see scope for TECs to improve their performance so all perform to the level of the best. Areas where I see scope for improvement include the effectiveness of local partnerships and the way in which you account to your local communities. Working with the TEC National Council and yourselves, I wish to ensure the spread of best practice to every TEC. I have asked the TEC National Council to bring forward proposals as soon as possible about how we might progress to achieve this.

The letter flagged up two key issues; ensuring consistency of performance across all TECs, and accountability to local communities through good quality partnerships.

It is the key role of thinking globally and acting locally which makes the issue of local accountability of TECs so vital. Given their limited resources (on average a TEC has an annual budget of £20 million and falling year by year), it is not possible to make an impact locally with such limited funds unless each is working in close harmony with a wide range of local institutions, such as local authorities, chambers of commerce, further education colleges and the local business community. In such a partnership, TEC plans should flow from a shared analysis of the position of the local economy and an agreed approach to defining and meeting local needs.

TECs can be summarized as follows: non-profit-making private companies; holding a 'licence' to operate locally from government; contracted on an annual basis to provide a range of services including management and labour market information, for a number of government departments including Education and Employment, Trade and Industry and Environment; governed by a board of 15 or 16 unpaid directors, two-thirds of whom must hold the office of chairman or chief executive of a company or be a senior operational manager, at a local level of a company. The chair of the board is nominated by the board. A significant proportion of funding is performance-related and they have freedom to spend surpluses on local projects in line with agreed Corporate and Business Plans and to attract/ earn additional funds from public and private sectors. Most TECs act as strategic facilitators seeking to develop successful partnerships rather than engaging in direct delivery and are subject to extensive audit checks.

TECs, therefore, have to be accountable both to government, from which they derive their existence and funds, and to the local community which has a major stake in the success of their activities. Critics see them as just another example of unaccountable quangos which cannot, by their very nature, be part of the local community. It has to be accepted that for the purposes of the current national debate, they have to be seen as 'quangos' as they primarily spend public funds and are perceived as such even if they have some characteristics unlike other quangos such as having company law status.

An example of this approach is the 'Accountability Index' produced by Chris Sheldon and John Stewart for the Association of London Authorities. This scores each type of London-appointed quango against the key accountability characteristics of local authorities, namely: whether they are directly elected; whether they come within the remit of one of the public sector Ombudsmen; whether there is extensive statutorily defined public access to policy and decision-making meetings; whether there is extensive statutorily defined public access to information; whether members of the body are liable for surcharge; whether members of the body have a statutory requirement to declare any interests which may conflict with their duties; whether these are monitoring officers charged with a statutory duty to ensure probity and financial regularity. On such an index, TECs come out badly because the members of their boards are not directly elected and they do not operate within a statutory framework. However, that sort of accountability index does not get to the heart of accountability relevant to bodies such as TECs. No bodies dominated by private sector people are going to subject themselves to direct elections.

In a chapter in the Hansard series in Politics and Government, *The Quango Debate*, edited by F.F. Ridley and David Wilson, I stated: 'TECs are accountable and this accountability should be extended. There is a widespread recognition in TECs that there is a democratic deficit to be addressed.' Since writing that in 1995, TECs have responded to the following codes, frameworks and reports which strongly influenced their approach to accountability.

- Report of committee on the financial aspects of Corporate Governance (known as Cadbury Report).
- Greenbury Report on executive pay.
- TEC National Council – a framework for the local accountability of Training and Enterprise Councils in England and Wales.
- Second report of the Nolan Committee on Standards in Public Life: 'Local Public Spending Bodies'.

Another dimension to the continuing debate about local accountability is the proposed creation of Regional Development Agencies in 1999, which it is intended will be private sector-led bodies working closely with Regional Chambers comprised primarily of elected local authority representatives and which, in due course, may become elected regional assemblies. Many of the responses to the government's consultative document have suggested that the funding for TECs should flow through Regional Development Agencies together with the funding of other local/regional bodies in the same way as LEC funding flows through Scottish Enterprise.

The debate about the function and operation of RDAs has some way to go and it is too early to say that the creation of RDAs will radically change the framework in which TECs operate.

TRADITIONAL FORMS OF ACCOUNTABILITY

There are a variety of forms of accountability through both Parliament and the provisions of the Companies Act. The arrangements for TECs to be accountable to Parliament via ministers are well defined and prescribed in the TEC Standards Guide (one of the contractual documents) which is at the heart of the contractual liability between TECs as private companies and government. The systems which provide central accountability and control to Parliament for the funds voted by them include: the annual funding contract and its sections on management information and reporting; the system of Financial Appraisal and Monitoring; the detailed performance measures of the new three-year licence agreement which comes into effect for those TECs granted a licence from April 1995; contract specification; the audit regimes of Departments, Treasury, National Audit Office, European Commission, private company auditors and the TEC's own internal auditors (which may be a contracted-out provision).

TECs do not suffer any democratic deficit through a lack of auditing of its financial regimes. It could rather be said that the multiple auditing arrangements are excessive in relation to their size of budget. The Annual Funding Contract contains a considerable amount of regulation and accountability in addition to financial matters. The 1997/98 Agreement requires TECs to publish an annual Labour Market Assessment and a summary of Corporate and Business Plans within three months from the beginning of the financial year. The full Corporate Plan has to be made available to the public during normal office hours. The provisions relating to directors, conflicts of interest, public meetings and the publication of the Annual Report are worth reproducing in full as they represent the significant elements of accountability that are currently required of TECs.

Directors

C3   The following requirements apply to members of the TEC Boards:

C3.1   at least two-thirds of the Directors (including the Chairman of the Board) hold the office of chairman or chief executive or top level operational manager at local level of a company or senior partner of a professional partnership within (in each case) the private sector. Exceptionally the Board may appoint one director from the private sector who does not meet these conditions, but whose experience and knowledge is considered appropriate for membership of the Board;

C3.2   the remaining Directors must be senior figures within the local community who support the aims of the TEC. A managing director or chief executive of the TEC is not counted in either category;

C3.3   a Director joins and remains on the Board of Directors as an individual and not as a representative of another company or organisation. A Director ceases to hold office within three months after ceasing to satisfy the eligibility requirements unless the Secretary of State for

Education and Employment and the TEC agree that he may continue in office;

C3.4   the Secretary of State for Education and Employment is notified promptly of all changes is chairmanship, appointments and removal of Directors and of any resignations of any Director. Where possible appointments should be notified well in advance;

C3.5   no Director (except where he holds office as managing director or chief executive of the TEC) may receive any remuneration from the TEC or a subsidiary of the TEC from payments made to the TEC by the Secretaries of State;

C3.6   in the case of its Chairman, the company or partnership referred to in C3 is a company or partnership (as the case may be) of at least three years standing with either an annual turnover exceeding £5 million or 25 or more full time employees and which normally operates in the TEC area.

Conflicts of Interest

C7   The TEC shall take all responsible steps to limit any conflict of interest between its Directors and employees and any other person with whom the TEC has dealings and ensures that:

C7.1   its directors and employees declare any direct or material interest which they have in respect of any contract or other matter in which it is involved;

C7.2   it maintains a register of declared interests which is open to inspection by the Secretaries of State at any reasonable time;

C7.3   if there is any declared conflict of interest, the relevant Director or employee of the TEC shall not be involved in any decision on the matter and;

C7.4   contracts are not made where anyone declares a material interest, without prior approval, duly recorded, of the Board of Directors.

Accountability: To the local community

C8   As well as complying with the TNC Framework for Local Account-ability for TECs in England and Wales the TEC/CCTE must be able to demonstrate its accountability to its local community as a minimum by:

C8.1   allowing members of the public access to a summary of the com-pany's Corporate Plan at the TEC's/CCTE's registered office;

C8.2   publishing at least a summary of its Business Plan within three months of the Business Plan being agreed;

C8.3   announcing and holding a public meeting at least once a year;

C8.4   producing and publishing an Annual Report and audited statement of accounts within nine months of the end of each contract year;

C8.5   the Annual Report must include:

– the amount of financial support claimed from the ESF under its different funding objectives for training delivered by the TEC/CCTE in 1996 using figures to be supplied by the Department for Education and Employment;
– details of the TEC's/CCTE's strategic targets and performance; and
– an account of projects funded in part or in full by Operating Surpluses.

C8.6   requiring training providers to make available such information on trainee success rates as the Secretary of State for Education and Employment may determine from time to time. Where the numbers make this inappropriate the TEC/CCTE must make such information available at an aggregate level.

Accountability: To Parliament

C9.1   The TEC/CCTE must provide to the Secretary of State full statutory accounts within four months of the end of the year. If the TEC/CCTE has subsidiaries, consolidated accounts must be provided to the relevant Secretary of State if consolidation is required by statute or Financial Reporting Standards. The TEC/CCTE must also provide to the relevant Secretary of State full statutory accounts for each company in the group, including the parent.

C9.2   The audited statement of accounts (including consolidated accounts where appropriate) must distinguish between:

(i) reserves attributes to funds derived from payments made by the Secretaries of State; and
(ii) reserves attributable to other sources.

C9.3   The statutory directors report must include a statement of the TEC's/CCTE's uncommitted reserves.

Code of practice on open government

C10   The TEC/CCTE complies with the Government's Code of Practice on access to official information, as a minimum, by:

C10.1   complying with and requires its Providers and their contractors to comply with the Government's Code of Practice on access to official information;

C10.2   agreeing with the Government that information made available under the requirements of any contract with the Government is not deemed confidential unless specifically stated;

C10.3   information deemed confidential is to be released to a third party only with the prior written authority of the party providing that information.

The provisions strongly reinforce the private sector leadership of TECs with the requirement that at least two-thirds of the directors (including the chairman of the board) must be senior-level, private sector people. This is the unique selling point of TECs and the dilemma in drafting any framework of local accountability was to keep this private sector leadership while ensuring TECs are seen to serve and listen to the local community they represent.

As private sector companies limited by guarantee, TECs are subject to the Companies Act. As a precondition for contracting with government, the Memorandum and Articles of Association must meet the approval of the Secretary of State so that he can ensure that acts committed with their jurisdiction confirm with parliamentary authority. The Companies Act also sets statutory obligations for reporting, auditing and the conduct of directors. The Code of Practice on Open Government published by the Cabinet Office in April 1994 also applies to TECs.

It is worth referring in more detail to the introduction of a system of three-year licences for TECs from April 1995 to see if they have strengthened accountability. Paragraph 3 of the Employment Department's document, 'The New Contract Framework', states: 'The new contract arrangements are designed to support, ensure and to demonstrate continuous improvement in TEC's performance, value for money and accountability. This relationship will bring benefits for government, TECs and customers.' It goes on to explain that, 'The new arrangements have similarities with the preferred supplier relationship common in industry. The key features will be the introduction of a three-year licence, supported by individual annual service agreements for the activities for which the government contracts with TECs.'

The key principles upon which the new contract arrangements are based are defined as: 'a strategic partnership based on trust and shared goals; a relationship which focuses on TECs, strategies and their impact on their local economies; a more stable relationship with government; authority for TECs, as separately established local companies, to operate in addressing the needs of their areas; a simpler process for contracting.' The document outlines 12 elements which support the key principles, of which one is the accountability of TECs locally, and to government through their contracts.

The benefits for licensed TECs are few and are said to be guaranteed funding for a proportion of a TEC's core administration costs, greater freedom in spending reserves, simpler contract and audit arrangements, opportunities to bid for additional government funds appropriate to TECs, and a shorter annual contracting round. There are no guarantees about the level of funding of major government programmes over a three-year period which is the prize TECs would most value. It is widely believed that the government hijacked the TECs ideas for a licensing system to convince the Treasury about their efficacy so as to justify their freedom to use public funds and use surpluses built up since their inception.

To qualify for a three-year licence, four criteria relating to the TECs' Corporate Plans, indicators of the TECs' strategic impact, programme performance and capability have been defined on a mixture of objective and subjective indicators. A TEC is assessed against these criteria by the staff of the Department of Employment's Regional Office who make a recommendation to a Regional Panel chaired by the Regional Director and will involve members of the TEC Assessors Committee, the Department's Head Office and the Director, Employment and Training. Each TEC seeking a licence will make a case to the panel. The Assessors Committee advises ministers on the overall performance of individual TECs in England and on regional and national performance (including the degree to which TECs are fulfilling their broader remit to raise the skills base and to stimulate local economic growth) and the eligibility criteria for TEC Directors and the composition and calibre of TEC boards. It is required to take an overview of all the recommendations before they go to the Secretary of State for Employment. There is no system for appeals. The three-year TEC licensing system has been a powerful system for enhancing TECs' accountability, but it is an internal system of assessment that only touches the local community through assessing the role of the TEC board members as part of the criteria against which TECs are judged for a licence.

Under the indicators relating to a TEC's capability, there is one indicator which specifically refers to its role in the community, 'What is the TEC's capability as respects; influencing its constituency?' (C1.5). On a scale of 1–5, the TEC is judged by the following criteria. How much credibility does the TEC have?: match of board to local economy and businesses; representative of ethnic groups and women; directors' own organizations set an example; status and authority of staff; arrangements for communication with key local interests; what the constituency thinks of the TEC; response to corporate plan. What evidence is there that the TEC is effective at influencing: profile in the community; participation in partnerships and joint ventures; organizations upon which the TEC is represented; relations with and track records in influencing key players, for example FE colleges, local authorities and chambers of commerce; track record in putting strategies into action. The process has no provisions for consulting the community in any formal or public way as to whether in their judgement, the TEC warrants the granting of a three-year licence.

So far we have seen that TECs have to operate within a complex system of centrally determined arrangements for accountability particularly geared to meet the needs of governments responsibility to Parliament for the use of public funds; to meet government's requirements for those functions it requires TECs to deliver and to agree its strategic plans. Companies Acts' requirements and accountability to government for public money and the delivery of public programmes complement each other. They are both relevant to local accountability, but do not by themselves guarantee local acceptability. Neither the requirements of parliamentary accountability nor the Companies Acts' prescriptions are sufficient to demonstrate local accountability. As TECs are geographically defined and exist to serve their local communities, they must demonstrably meet their responsibilities to those communities. Which is why the TEC National Council developed a framework of local accountability which encompasses the three principles of openness, integrity and local accountability. This was published in June 1995 and has been adopted by all TECs.

THE TEC FRAMEWORK OF LOCAL ACCOUNTABILITY

TECs see themselves accountable to the community in its area and specifically to employers in businesses of all sizes and in all sectors of the local economy and the self-employed, individual clients and customers, actual or potential, for all TEC-sponsored or supported programmes. They recognize that two other constituencies play an essential part in the delivery of this accountability: partners in local government, the enterprise network, education, community and voluntary organizations, together with those sub-contractors who deliver TEC-supported programmes direct to customers.

The framework is built around five practical principles.

Clarity and Openness in the Selection of Well-qualified and Trained Board Members

TECs primarily draw upon the private sector leadership and business expertise to fulfil their main objectives. Boards may also include local authority chief executives, elected councillors, Directors of Education, head teachers, trade union officials and people drawn from the voluntary sector. Most will make serious attempts to include women and, where appropriate, representatives of the ethnic minority community. A number of TECs have membership schemes either separate from or in conjunction with the local Chamber of Commerce and there are now arrangements for TECs and Chambers of Commerce to merge where this is deemed to be appropriate. This may mean that the members help to determine the board membership at the Annual Meeting. The limitation of these arrangements is that membership will be drawn from a section of the business community and may not include all parts of the wider community served. A wide variety of selection processes exist and this will continue to be the case.

TECs are expected to provide the following evidence in support of this principle:

(i) An established process, clearly and publicly set out and involving the local community, for the identification and selection of new Directors;

(ii) Where there is demand, keeping an open register of individuals interested in appointment;

(iii) Maintaining a Board membership which has the necessary breadth and balance to reflect the priorities of the local community and economy;

(iv) Reporting the remuneration of the Chief Executive, and highlighting the non-remunerated status of the other Directors;

(v) A stated maximum term of appointment, and re-appointment subject to the agreed selection processes;

(vi) ensuring that Directors have the information and training to enable them to perform their duties effectively.

The Board is Seen to Act Effectively in the Best Interests of the Local Community

The principle seeks to ensure that Directors must act as individuals, rather than as representatives of an organization or group, in the best interests of TEC customers and they must not use their position to further private interests. This is sensitive territory and TECs now publish the interests of directors in their annual report and details of when such interests were declared when discussions were taken about awarding contracts. In some TECs the actual value of the contract involved is also published.

The evidence TECs are required to produce to demonstrate they are implementing this principle is as follows:

(i) Extensive consultation about the local marketplace and needs, the plans of the TEC and its partners, and the objectives and priorities of the TEC's Corporate Plan;

(ii) Demonstrating clarity of mission, understanding of local needs and added value at well advertised public meetings;

(iii) Displaying exemplary corporate governance through paying due regard to the Code of Best Practice on the Financial Aspects of Corporate Governance (Cadbury Code);

(iv) Holding regular meetings of the Board and setting minimum standards of attendance by Directors;

(v) Directors acting as individuals in the best interests of all customers, not as representatives of an organisation or group and not using their position to further private or organisational interests;

(vi) An agreed procedure for Directors to seek independent professional advice at the TEC's expense, in the event that they have concerns related to their duties;

(vii) Maintenance of an up to date Register of Interests of Directors and employees, which includes all paid employment, appointments and directorships, equity interests over 10% and other interests (including those of close family) which may be relevant to the business of the TEC;

(viii) A procedure for handling a conflict of interest in the course of day to day business, whether related to a financial or non-financial interest of a Director or employee, whereby it is declared and minuted and Board take a minuted decision on whether the Director or employee should attend, participate in the decision or see relevant papers; (where such business arises from the TEC's contract with Government, Directors are contractually precluded from taking part);

(ix) Where contracts are awarded to Directors or employees, or to businesses in which they have a financial or non-financial interest, these are registered and the availability of the register of such interests is disclosed in the published Annual Report.

TECs are Open about their Performance and their Employment and Financial Policies

It is vital that TECs set performance targets and measurements and communicate them widely. Statements of performance against performance targets should be published at regular intervals on a basis that makes comparison over time possible. Both self-assessment and appraisals by bodies independent of government and TECs should form part of this. Performance on the building of partnerships and on the profile and reputation of the TEC in the community should be included in any performance monitoring.

Information about financial operations has to be made public. Full copies of accounts must be available to the public, including details of the contracts given and received. There will need to be some exceptions for reasons of commercial confidentiality, but these have to be carefully defined. Information on TEC costs, organization, targets and results achieved must be published in the Annual Report and made public in the local community.

The specific evidence required to demonstrate this principle is as follows:

(i) widely communicated performance targets and measurements which meet the interests of the local community and employers, alongside those to which TECs are committed by their contract with Government;

(ii) published statements of performance against targets and measurements, on a basis which makes comparison possible over time;

(iii) presentation of a balanced, fair and understandable assessment of results with full reporting on sources of finance, expenditure on projects and administration, and organisation, in the published Annual Report;

(iv) demonstrating high standards of employment practice, in particular in becoming Investors in People, and providing a role model of good employment;

(v) while maintaining reasonable commercial confidentiality, making available to the public when requested the names of those organisations who receive assistance from or a contract with the TEC.

Dealings with customers will be on a basis of openness and high quality service with a robust complaints procedure.

The key to meeting this principle is a robust complaints procedure with a known point of contact. Complaints should be dealt with within a stated time period. Individuals should be kept informed of progress and granted a full and fair investigation. The confidence of the complainant should be respected and complainants should receive a comprehensive and understandable response and redress where appropriate and for complaints to be reviewed for lessons learnt and improvements to be made. Where the TEC cannot satisfy the complaint, or where the complainant is dissatisfied with the TEC's response, the route of external moderation should be identified to the complainant and it might be possible to have a backstop provision whereby, if requested by a TEC, the TEC National Council would appoint an independent body to consider such complaints and make recommendations. The specific evidence required to demonstrate the application of the principle has to include:

(i) good and clear communication to all interested parties about the TEC organisation, the right routes into the organisation and the responsibilities of personnel dealing directly with customers and other stakeholders;

(ii) giving clear and accurate information and impartial advice to employers and individual customers. Handling applications for support fairly and efficiently, and making payments in accordance with the agreed contract;

(iii) granting the right to be treated equally, regardless of religion, gender or ethnic background and to have any learning difficulties or disabilities taken into account;

(iv) giving a courteous and helpful personal service, based on published standards of customer care. The reasons for administrative and other decisions explained;

(v) establishing a clear, accessible and well published route for addressing any complaints, with a declared point of contact and with complaints dealt with within stated time period. Individuals kept informed of progress, their confidence respected and a full investigation and response given to the complainant;

(vi) where the complainant remains dissatisfied and the TEC is unable to provide remedy, identifying to the complainant a route for external, independent review appropriate to the nature of the complaint;

(vii) undertaking a review of complaints and the complaints procedure for lessons learnt and improvements to be made.

In Dealing with Partners and Suppliers They Will Seek to be Trustworthy, Transparent and Follow Fair Commercial Practice

Many national employers and national training providers who were previously used to contracting with a government body, the Training Agency, have found it difficult to interface with 104 TECs and LECs. Pressure groups such as the Bridge Group of voluntary sector training providers have regularly published reports seeking an improved contractual relationship with TECs. In response to these pressures TECs created a Forum of

National Training Providers which until recently was chaired by the author.

In Calderdale & Kirklees and Leeds TEC three-year framework agreements have been introduced for those suppliers who meet certain demanding performance, audit and viability standards. Such agreements do not guarantee funding over a three-year period, but they do confer a preferred–supplier relationship. Other TECs have introduced similar types of arrangements.

The specific evidence required by the framework is as follows:

(i)   demonstrating commitment to working with appropriate partners in the community in developing strategies and plans, seeking a clear definition of the roles of each partner and monitoring the procedures and progress of the partnership;

(ii)   ensuring that subsidiary companies follow the standards set out in this framework;

(iii) working with suppliers on the basis of a fair and reasonable negotiated contract containing clauses covering at least the setting of performance standards, information gathering, payment and termination;

(iv)   warranting that customers of suppliers under contract to the TEC receive open, honest and fair treatment equivalent to that accorded by the TEC.

TECs have given considerable attention to implementing this Framework of Local Accountability and it was subject to a major review by the second report of the Committee on Standards in Public Life.

IMPACT OF THE NOLAN COMMITTEE ON TEC ACCOUNTABILITY

The Nolan Committee's second report on 'Local Public Spending Bodies' covering higher and further education, grant maintained schools, housing associations and TECs was published in May 1996 and welcomed the steps that have been taken by TECs and LECs to improve their practices on governance, openness and propriety. It went on to conclude:

When the rules that have been developed and promulgated over the last year are fully implemented, these will, to a significant extent, tackle many of the concerns which have been expressed about the organisations and which have featured in those cases that have been given publicity. Nevertheless we are concerned that the local accountability of some TECs remains weak and we believe that the organisations themselves need to do more to improve and explain their policies on local accountability, governance and propriety.

The Report produced 13 recommendations for improving TEC accountability from enhancing the role of the government offices for the regions in this area to ensuring compliance with TEC National Council framework for local accountability through ensuring it is a firm requirement for awarding a TEC licence or contract. None of these recommendations provided any difficulty for TECs and they were primarily concerned with ensuring consistency of approach across all TECs. They have been included in a revised version of the framework for local accountability which is currently subject to consultation with TECs.

The Nolan Committee wrote to TECs on 19 August 1997 launching a comprehensive review of how TECs and LECs had responded to its recommendations. TECs and LECs were asked to complete a questionnaire by the end of September 1997. The Nolan Report introduced the seven principles of public life: selflessness; integrity; objectivity; accountability; openness; honesty and leadership. Lord Nolan was concerned to promote common standards and expectations for all local public spending bodies.

In the introduction to his report, addressed to the Prime Minister, Lord Nolan said:

Many early problems which occurred when these bodies were being set up or restructured have been tackled. These are organisations in which very many voluntary Board members and paid staff work hard, maintain high standards, and achieve good results. We pay tribute to them.

Nothing in this report points to any fundamental malaise in any of the sectors which we have examined. But there is, and will continue to be, a tension between the management driven and output related approach which is central to many recent changes, and the need for organisations providing public services to involve, respond to, and reflect the concerns of the communities which they serve.

TECs have worked hard to develop a new model of accountability that does ensure their work reflects the concerns of the communities which they serve. I have no doubt they are succeeding in their efforts.

15 Balancing the Scales – the Growth, Role and Future of the Regulators
Alan Booker

There can have been few policies which have reshaped the work of government more than the privatization of the former great state monopolies. Some of them such as steel making and coal mining could be privatized with no specific checks over the performance of those companies. Others such as the railway system and the electricity industry required the break-up to a greater or lesser extent of the monolithic state enterprise. In the case of all the utilities there was a need to set up a regime of economic regulation to protect captive customers in the home market from exploitation, both as regards service standards and charges.

The nature of the relationship between government, the regulators and the newly privatized utility companies has evolved considerably over the 15 years since British Telecom was privatized. Since that time the theory, practice, methodology and process of economic regulation have all developed. This chapter concentrates on some of the major issues which continue to dominate debate about economic regulation.

The water industry is used as an illustration of the way in which economic regulation of utilities works, drawing on the author's involvement in the regulation of water services. However, while the general nature of economic regulation of utilities is similar across all sectors, the nature of each of the utility industries – telecommunications, gas, water, electricity and railways – is such that there are significant differences in application in each area.

Broadly, the duties of each sectoral regulator, the Directors General of telecommunications, gas supply, water services, electricity supply and rail, are the same. They are to protect the interests of customers by ensuring that companies carry out their statutory functions and are able to finance them, and to promote economy, efficiency and competition. The exact form of words is different in each case, but the objectives are the same.

In the water sector, the regulatory framework includes the regulation of drinking water quality by the Drinking Water Inspectorate, part of the Department of the Environment, Transport and the Regions and environmental quality by the Environment Agency a non-departmental public body appointed by the Secretary of State for the Environment.

The Directors General are statutory office holders who are required each year to lay before Parliament a report to their sponsor Secretaries of State. Their offices known as Oftel, Ofgas, Ofwat, Offer and ORR are known as non-ministerial government departments. The Directors themselves are not civil servants and are subject to statutory contractual appointments. Their respective offices are staffed by civil servants.

There are two unique features about the British approach to economic regulation. The first is the application of incentive regulation primarily through price caps set on a forward-looking basis – the so-called RPI-X regime. The second unique feature is the customer representation framework. In the case of water and electricity, regional customer service committees are appointed by the respective Director to help in his duty to protect customer interests. The chairmen of these regional committees meet as national committees to deal with customer protection issues at a national level. More will be said of the working of customer service committees later in the chapter.

Six issues will be discussed. They are the institution of regulation, the independence and accountability of regulators, regulatory processes, changing market structures, changing expectations and customer interests. These issues seem to cover all the question marks which have been raised about the growth in economic regulation in the UK over the last 15 years.

The institution of regulation constitutes just one of four contributions to the delivery of public services. The first is 'policy-making' which is the prerogative of government. The second is 'corporate governance' of the operational units set up to deliver services. Corporate governance is an interesting role. In a fully privatized model such as the UK, corporate governance is generally exercised jointly between government, the regulator and the boards of service delivery companies, subject, of course, to the law and the rules of the financial institutions. The third is the delivery of services. This is a task charged to specialist organizations which in a privatized model is done by investor-owned companies. The fourth contribution is 'regulation' of service delivery.

THE INSTITUTION OF REGULATION

The institution of regulation has been and will continue to be a function of the state. There are four roles which can be identified and which need to be accommodated in any comprehensive system of regulation. The first is

the sectoral requirement which needs to be tailored to suit individual sectoral circumstances. Utilities require a different approach from financial
services for example. The second is functional regulation such as health
and safety or quality. This requires the implementation, monitoring and
enforcement of standards. The third and fourth roles are interrelated. They
are the national and international setting of standards. This is often to do
with the establishment of common market conditions, possibly about product quality, the protection of employees and the public and the harmoniza-
tion of markets. The EU is a prime example of the international dimension.
The function of national government is to reflect international standards in
domestic law, to set up institutions to implement, monitor and enforce
them, and to keep under review the working of the regulatory institutions
and reform them as necessary.

Of course, this leads to a redefinition of the role of the state. In the past
this role was to be an active participant in each of the four areas. Private
sector delivery of services demands separation of duties and clarity of
roles. The main premise which underpins this redefinition is that delivery
of services is more efficiently undertaken by the private sector subject to
the incentive of profits. The role of the state is now much more strategic.
It needs to determine the structure for most efficient service delivery and
create an institutional framework within which the behaviour of participants
is supervised.

But nothing stands still for long in this changing world. The dynamic of
change is such that what is yesterday's objective and today's achievement
is no longer acceptable tomorrow. Change is now endemic and continuous.
Regulators need to adapt continuously to changing needs. Regulatory
regimes need to develop as new circumstances create new problems to be
solved. The framework of regulation as well as the performance of the regulators needs review from time to time to determine whether structural or
personnel changes are needed.

THE INDEPENDENCE AND ACCOUNTABILITY OF
REGULATORS

An important consideration is the independence and accountability of regulators. Much has been said and written on this topic over the last few
years. Independence is a myth. Regulators are subject to pressures from
many directions. Governments generally retain some formal mechanism
for influencing the performance of regulators. This is normally incorporated in the law which creates the institution and defines its duties.

In the UK the sectoral utility regulators are subject to scrutiny by parliamentary committees. In particular, the Trade and Industry, Environment and the Public Accounts Committee conduct regular reviews of the different aspects of the work of the regulators. Appearances before select committees are high-profile events for which the regulators need to be well prepared. Although most MPs are not knowledgable about regulation, those who play an active part in the work of the All Party Groups, such as the All Party Parliamentary Water Group, certainly develop a good understanding over time.

Regulator's determinations are subject to appeal mechanisms. For instance, the Monopolies and Mergers Commission has been given a powerful role as an appeal body. The handling of customer complaints by the [regulator] is subject to scrutiny by the parliamentary Ombudsman. As statutory office-holders, regulators are subject to judicial accountability if there is sufficient concern that they are not carrying out their statutory duties. This is a rare occurrence. Ofwat has not as yet been subject to a judicial review. But there is a case pending relating to the use of budget payment units for the recovery of water charges. The mere existence of this channel of challenge to regulatory decisions means that all regulatory policy has to be developed with an eye to scrutiny by the courts. It places a premium on due process and the principle of natural justice.

In practice, regulators need to operate in an open and transparent way in order to avoid undue influence from whichever quarter. There has been a much discussed concept of regulatory capture by the regulated companies. Regulators go to substantial lengths to avoid capture and to dispel those concerns. Regulatory capture is much more likely to be attempted by pressure groups or indeed by government departments. This is why sectoral regulators need to be strong individuals capable of resisting substantial pressures to take particular courses of action. This historic example of government pressure on the boards of the former state industries is salutary and must not be repeated.

So far the UK sectoral regulators have been very successful in avoiding capture by specific interest groups. The UK is envied around the world for having such people with integrity, wisdom, strength of mind and purpose, yet capable of seeing the long game as well as the short one. Attacks on their independence have never as yet been substantiated. Their accountability to a wide range of formal and informal stakeholders needs to be sustained by regulatory processes embodying openness and transparency. The willingness of regulators and regulation to 'go public' on issues which might compromise their independence and to maintain a high public profile means that their independence should be assured. This is discussed shortly.

There are, of course, different institutional models available. Regulatory commissions are often thought of as the answer to the issue of accountability. In the UK the Monopolies and Mergers Commission follows this model. In Australia, the tradition of cross-sectoral regulatory tribunals is achieving credibility. Where individual sectoral regulators have been appointed, there is something to be said for building a formal collegiate approach. Each regulator would be separately responsible in his own domain, but could be given a statutory duty to consult other specified regulators. A formal college of regulators could be an effective mechanism for transferring good processes and good methodology between the regulatory offices. At present in the UK there are informal arrangements set up by the utility regulators where contact is established at various levels between regulatory offices to exchange views and to consider common issues.

Some interdependence between regulatory offices might be expected of organizations doing work of a similar nature. For instance, close co-operation between Ofwat and Offer is necessary on regulating the multi-utilities. The college might, for instance, be extended, to embrace learning from the appeal mechanisms. In each of these former state monopoly enterprises providing public services there will always be a need for government to perform a role in relation to social policies. Such policy is at the heart of government activity in a wide range of ways. Regulators can be expected to work within a given set of rules, but balancing for instance, affordability against the pace and scale of quality improvements in the environment, is not an issue which regulators can be fairly expected to handle.

REGULATORY PROCESS

Openness and transparency have already been mentioned several times in this chapter. Freedom of information is a highly political issue, and the new Labour government is now committed to a Freedom of Information Act. But in many ways regulators have led the way on freedom of information. When these enterprises were run by the state little information was published. Now a great deal of information is collected and published by the regulators about the performance of the privatized companies. Regulators generally have very wide powers for requiring the provision of information from regulated companies. Commercial confidentiality must, of course, be respected, but often it is difficult to determine whether there is a true case of commercial confidence which should be maintained, or whether the claim is a smoke-screen to avoid publication of what might be embarrassing information.

Most regulators now take the view that the information they collect should be published unless individual companies can prove that commercial confidentiality would be compromised by publication. The onus of proof is placed on the company and not the regulator. But there is a dilemma as to where the line should be drawn between privacy and publication. Most published information is challenged and analysed. As well as serious issues of commercial confidentiality, unnecessary resources can be devoted to answering challenges of a trivial nature.

An example of how this might work in practice is the 1999 review of water price limits. The Director in his consultation paper on the review process, issued in July 1997, accepts that some information submitted by companies should be treated in confidence. The companies justification will be made public. Regulatory processes are developing continuously. Each time one of the sectoral regulators moves through a determination process such as setting price caps the game moves on. Much of what regulators do is now subject to the close examination of analysts, researchers and commentators, requiring the regulator to take into account many more challenges to his decisions than just a few years ago.

There are two main aspects to consider. The first is the legal 'due process' which will allow the company on the receiving end of a determination a proper opportunity to challenge the regulator and to point out where they think he is wrong. Generally this means that the regulator will go through a process of collecting information then telling the regulated company what he is minded to determine and then giving them a formal opportunity to tell him what they think in advance of the regulator formally concluding and publishing his determination. This natural justice approach to important regulatory decisions is fundamental to a satisfactory legal process.

The wider aspect of process, particularly important in public services, concerns the business planning process and the necessary consultation arrangements which need to be put in place as part of it. The process required here is to collect information about outputs and costs and publish it. That information may then be subject to challenge and comment and possibly to formal consultation. In addition, there may be more formalized statutory or non-statutory arrangements which might be put in place for special circumstances. For instance, in the 1994 Periodic Review of water prices the regulator established the quadripartite process, comprising the Department of the Environment, the water companies, the quality regulators and the economic regulator, all under the aegis of the Department of the Environment. This mechanism was instituted with the specific intention of advising the Secretary of State for the Environment in a public way as to the costs of new environmental obligations. The results of the quadri-partite process were able to be used by the Secretary of State, in determining the pace and scale of environmental improvements, within the limits of affordability of low income customers, in some environmentally sensitive parts of the country. Again, his decisions were published as guidance to the regulator.

The scope for legal challenge to regulatory process is not particularly clear. But there are rules about natural justice which regulators do need to heed if they are to avoid legal challenge to the way in which they do their work.

REGULATION IN A CHANGING ENVIRONMENT

Of course, much of what regulators do is subject to a constant change. The remainder of this chapter covers some of the more important changes which regulators have had to respond to.

CHANGING UTILITY MARKETS

The structure of the utility markets has changed significantly over 15 years. In telecommunications the break-up of the BT monopoly has opened the way to liberalization. In gas and electricity the development of direct competition for customers through common carriage in the marketplace has created new issues for regulators. In water the development of quasi-markets, such as the result of comparative competition, places a premium on the reliability of information from companies, and dependence on a robust system of 'independent' engineering and financial reporting. In railways the vertical separation of railtrack from operations has created a completely new look to the system.

The recent phenomenon of multi-utilities covering water, gas, electricity and telecommunications also poses problems for comparative competition. For instance, should these large new groupings be expected to reduce costs more quickly and further than single-utility companies? If they can, should their lower costs create the new efficiency frontier for single-utility companies? If that is the case, will the market for utility services move towards the creation of more multi-utilities?

Stakeholders have considerable influence in normal market structures. Unscrambling the public interest from customer sovereignty is not an easy task and in any case should it be a task for the regulator or for the government? Competition both for and in the market creates problems of cost allocation for regulators, while there are substantial regulated costs for operating the common network. Alternative networks such as those developing in telecommunications allow the regulator some scope in disregarding cost allocation. But this itself does raise other issues such as the nature of regulating telecommunications. The issue in this sector is whether the task is more closely associated with a more general competition regulatory body or a specialist body covering convergent communications' networks. Regulators struggle to keep up with these changes and while ultimately legislation will undoubtedly catch up with developments, regulators have to live with the reality of the situation they are in. That situation is a fast-moving one for utility regulators.

At the other end of the regulatory spectrum from a competitive market where the regulator is intent on emulating competition as best he can it is often forgotten by those not involved in the task of regulation that the main response in keeping up with change is to change the contract or licence of appointment. Regulators can achieve quite a lot by changing the licence by agreement. The introduction of a new condition into the water licence to compensate customers where supply is interrupted under a drought order is a recent example. They can also be opportunistic about licence changes such as in the event of mergers. However, significant changes in any contract are hard to achieve without some bloodshed. There is an appeal mechanism for the regulated companies to the Monopolies Commission. But the process which the Commission applies in achieving a licence change is cumbersome and out of tune with current thinking on openness and transparency.

The general movement of economic regulation has been significantly towards more intrusive supervision of the behaviour of regulated companies. The essential nature of incentive regulation, the provision of both sticks and carrots to improve performance might be in danger of being lost in a more confrontational, US-style of regulation, set firmly into a judicial process. It would be a great pity if this were to happen. It would herald the demise of incentive regulation and the establishment of a cost-of-service approach to regulation. The economic breakthrough undoubtedly achieved through privatization may then stagnate in the heavy costs associated with that process and the lack of incentives to improvement.

CHANGING CUSTOMER EXPECTATIONS

Of course, change is not confined to changes in the marketplace. Customer expectations of privatized utilities have increased dramatically over recent years. Customers cannot have it both ways. They want the certainty of improved performance and lower costs, but are rarely prepared to see the risks taken by private companies reflected in high salaries and high profits. Hence the 'fat cats' debate, which runs and runs.

Then there is the changing face of what constitutes the public interest and how that is politically reconciled with customer sovereignty. In a democratic system the public interest is ultimately reflected through the ballot box. Customer sovereignty is expressed in terms of willingness to pay and the exercise of choice. However, the classic clash between the rights of individuals and the rights of the public can, by definition, only be resolved through a political process. What might be needed is a redefinition of public services which would mainly reflect the element of choice that customers have in the purchase of those services. That in turn might be to do with the existence of alternative networks and the degree to which suppliers depend on a single network. For instance, all retail groups need to use public highways for distribution of their goods. But no one would suggest that Marks & Spencer or Tesco are delivering a public service. Presumably the cost of using public facilities is a negligible part of the cost of the purchased goods.

It is in this area of public policy that the relationship between regulators, ministers and their officials is at its most interesting. While regulators have a defined statutory independence from government, they can only exist within a consensual relationship with government. This requires regular contact between regulators and ministers and between departments and regulatory offices, for example Ofwat and the Environment Agency. Like all relationships the productivity depends on understanding clarity and consent. When the parties to a relationship change there is a period of adjustment to re-establish understanding clarity and consent. The new government is conducting a review of utility regulation which will reaffirm the general direction of regulation or establish a new direction for regulation, either within the existing law or by changes in the law.

Formal links should be defined in the law, or be subject to openness and transparency such as existed to facilitate decisions on the cost of quality at the 1994 review of water price limits. In addition informal contact is needed at various levels between government departments and regulatory offices. Contact about incidents or events could be at an appropriate level, dependent on the importance of the incident. The keys to establishing understanding, clarity and consent are communication and publication. But 'megaphone diplomacy' is rarely satisfactory or successful.

There are also issues about how the expectations of vulnerable groups have changed and whether the same degree of protection of these groups is now required. For instance, there is an issue as to how far such groups should be cross-subsidized by less vulnerable groups. In water this issue crystallizes in the metering debate. Generally people who oppose metering would lose out on the introduction of meters, but that implicitly means that they are currently being subsidized by other customers.

In a service such as water and sewerage provision there are also significant issues about universal service and community service obligations. For instance, should services be universally available to new customers at average or long-run marginal cost? How should community service obligations be financed? There is, for example, general agreement that water for fire-fighting services should be paid for by everyone. But it is costly to give the same degree of mains water protection to rural properties as to urban properties. In consequence risks vary and are reflected in fire insurance premiums. This is probably a trivial example, but such issues as this are rarely the subject of informed debate. Proper understanding of the detailed cost structure of service provision is fundamental to determining an acceptable level of cross-subsidization and in tempering some unrealistic expectations of customers.

PROTECTING THE INTERESTS OF CUSTOMERS

The final subject for discussion is the issue of customer interests. How, for instance, should the interests of affordability be weighed against the interests of customers who want to see ever higher environmental standards? How in general might value for money be expressed in a way which is helpful to the delivery of services to subsets of customers?

At the present time the utility companies, particularly the water and sewerage companies, make little attempt to differentiate between the different customer subsets. There is a movement towards cost-reflective tariff structures with costs determined on a long-run marginal cost basis. But that economic concept can sit uneasily with social tariffs. Who should decide where lines are drawn. In recent times customers have been led to believe that leakage from water mains is a bad thing. But if water is plentiful it may well be cheaper to allow higher levels of leakage than where water is scarce. However, if the scarcity or abundance of water is largely due to accidents of history or the distribution of rainfall, where should the line be drawn between social acceptability and economics? To what extent can incentives to efficient outputs be squared with social obligations?

There are clearly plenty of regulatory issues for both regulators and legislators to grapple with. This highlights a major issue as to how far regulatory policy needs to be reflected in the law, which can only be done by Parliament, and how far regulatory policy objectives can be attained through changes in the contract or the licence, which can be achieved by regulatory action. It would be relatively easy to set out a shopping list for a law reform agenda. But the shopping list would be a moving target and much of it could be achieved by a smart regulator working with the grain of government through coercion, persuasion or licence amendments. But how desirable is that in a democracy? In practice, in an open process, subject to public consultation and a good working relationship between regulator and minister, the outcome should be at least as good as an outcome derived from parliamentary debate.

It is worth reminding ourselves at this point that customer committees specifically exist to help regulators in their duty to protect customers. There is an issue as to the most effective model for customer committees as to whether independence or integration is better. But in either case informed customer representatives bring practical experience to the decision making process. The non-statutory Ofwat National Customer Committee is an example of an integrated arrangement which has had and continues to have a positive and beneficial influence on the economic regulation of water companies.

Customer committees have their own statutory duties and their chairmen are strong individuals with their own style and approach. There have been clashes in the course of their public meetings with water companies which have been well reported. Such clashes are infrequent and the director is entitled to expect chairmen to have effective and efficient working relationships with companies overtime. But too cosy relationships do not breed healthy regulation.

It is probably quite impossible to codify the process issues such as business plans consultation, due process, methodology, independence and accountability within a statutory framework. Surely it is far better to develop these things in an organic way by learning and adapting from experience. From time to time there may well be the need for statutory changes but it has to be said that the legislation which created the regulatory structure and institutions has largely stood the test of time. The regulators have managed to survive their scares for 15 years and the various regulatory regimes have developed with very little change to the basic legal framework.

Incentive regulation is working. It is providing increasing value for money for customers and making a positive and substantial contribution to economic prosperity in the UK. The performance of the companies is improving all the time. It is difficult to see that significant change is needed. The old adage applies: If it ain't broke, don't fix it.

16 Reforming the
Patronage State
Tony Wright

Patronage lubricates the machinery of British politics; it always has done (Richards, 1963). From ministers to magistrates, peers to judges, honours to quangos, government by appointment rules. It is a myth that elected government has replaced appointed government. It is more accurate to say that elected politicians have inherited the resources of the patronage state. The cruder excesses of Old Patronage may have been reined in (the civil service reforms of the nineteenth century, the sanitary checks on the sale of honours in the twentieth century), but New Patronage is alive and well. If a reminder of this was needed, quangos have supplied it in abundance.

When politicians turned to quangos to advance their purposes, extending the territory of appointed government and narrowing the territory of elected government in the process, they had all the resources of the patronage state at their disposal. In short, they could appoint whom they liked, to what they liked, and how they liked. The doctrine of ministerial responsibility provided, as ever, the legitimizing constitutional ideology. Such unchecked patronage power had, at least in the recent past, been constrained in its usage only by the force of convention against partisan excesses. What was new in the 1980s was the arrival of a kind of politics (and politician) that explicitly repudiated consensus and was not to be detained by conventional restraints, buttressed by a governing arrogance that derived from a long and uninterrupted tenure of office. It is interesting to note that, in the standard academic study of the patronage state published a generation earlier, these were the only circumstances in which it was envisaged that patronage might again come to be contentious: 'At present the abuses are not grave due to adequate ethical standards in the conduct of public business. Perhaps the greatest danger for the future is the possibility that one party will exercise uninterrupted power for too long a period. Temptations would grow as security bred carelessness' (Richards, 1963: 257).

And so it has proved. The quango-stuffing of the long Conservative years after 1979 eventually produced its reaction with a leading place for patronage (though the term was usually avoided as too indelicate) on the Nolan agenda. The importance of Nolan, on this front and others,

191

can scarcely be overstated. When a beleaguered John Major conjured up a Committee on Standards in Public Life on a standing basis in October 1994 the immediate intention may have been to dig his government out of an enveloping mire of sleaze but the enduring effect was to open the floodgates of scrutiny and reform in areas where this had been studiously avoided in the past. It is not surprising that many in his party were unforgiving. In the absence of a full-blown Constitutional Commission, which is what is really needed, Lord Nolan's Committee has proved to be a remarkably effective substitute.

In looking at appointive government the Committee had to consider whether there were sufficient safeguards in the system to prevent partisan excess of the kind that was being widely alleged. Departments made their own appointments with a servicing role only performed by the Public Appointments Unit in the Office of Public Service and Science in the Cabinet Office. Anticipating Nolan and in response to mounting political pressure the Conservative government produced a review of the public appointments system offering its recommendations (on more coherence, transparency and openness in the procedures) as its evidence to Nolan. It also offered its new guidance on NHS appointments which had become an area of particular controversy. In its first report, in May 1995, the Nolan Committee welcomed the government's proposals, but also judged them inadequate in important respects and made further recommendations of its own.

On the matter of political bias in appointments the Conservative government claimed that the Committee's report vindicated its assertion that no such bias existed. In fact, the report concluded that the closed nature of the appointments process, with its lack of independent checks and balances, meant that 'suspicions of bias remain nearly impossible to prove or disprove' and that this 'does not provide solid ground on which to build public confidence in the system' (Nolan, 1995, para. 25). The fact was that ministers appointed up to 10,000 people each year to a plethora of posts, including over 2000 appointments to executive quangos and NHS bodies, and it was clearly important that such 'considerable powers of patronage' were properly scrutinized and checked.

One way in which this could be done would be to remove the power of appointment from ministers and give it to an independent body. I have argued the case for an independent Public Appointments Commission (Wright, 1995) and put this case in evidence to Nolan. If it had been thought desirable in the past to take civil service appointments away from politicians there was surely a strong argument now for treating a range of other public appointments in the same way. Yet the principle of ministerial appointment had always been treated as sacrosanct in reviews of the public appointments system. In the event, Nolan also endorsed it, though the endorsement is weakly argued. The report finds the arguments for an independent commission 'persuasive', but suggests that there are 'practical difficulties', then settles for 'accountability to Parliament' as a key constitutional principle that should not be weakened. The report is not at its strongest on this point – seemingly uncertain whether the issues were practical or constitutional – and, as we shall see, Lord Nolan himself was later to revisit the principle of ministerial responsibility in a more radical and interesting way.

Unpersuaded of the case for an independent public appointments commission, the Nolan Report nevertheless recommended the creation of a Public Appointments Commissioner. This person would scrutinize, regulate and audit the way in which Departments made appointments, promulgate a new code of practice and ensure that the other Nolan recommendations – on an independent element in appointments, disclosure of political activity by appointees on a register of interests, annual reporting of appointments by Departments – were implemented. The government hastened to embrace the Nolan package claiming that it merely extended the approach already being adopted, and Sir Len Peach was appointed as the first Public Appointments Commissioner in December 1995. The new Commissioner published a Code of Practice in April 1996 which came into operation on 1 July of that year, incorporating the government's reviews and adding the strengthening elements from Nolan. When, in its final days, the Conservative government produced its White Paper on *The Governance of Public Bodies: A Progress Report* (February 1997, Cm 3557), it could cite the appointment of a Commissioner for Public Appointments as one of its achievements.

In fact, the government had rejected the need for an external monitor of the patronage system; accepting it only when Nolan proposed it. Even then, it was only to be regulation with the lightest of touches. The Public Appointments Commissioner was part-time and without a statutory basis, while the Nolan proposal that the Public Appointments Unit should be transferred from the Cabinet Office to become the executive arm of the new Commissioner was not accepted. It was a very British way of proceeding. At a moment when codes and commissioners were sprouting on all sides, the politicians tried desperately to subdue the waves that Nolan had sent crashing down on them.

The first real evidence of the Commissioner's work came in his second annual report, published in July 1997, and covering the nine-month period from July 1996 to March 1997 during which the Code of Practice for

Public Appointments Procedures had been in operation. The statistics from the audit of the 1753 appointments (including reappointments) made by Departments during this period revealed that:

- 99.1 per cent were part-time posts;
- 83 per cent were paid posts (the February 1997 White Paper had put this figure at only 71 per cent);
- most appointees received less than £10,000 per annum;
- 66 per cent of appointees were male and 34 per cent female (for chairs the ratio was 80:20);
- 4.7 per cent of appointees were from an ethnic minority (none as chairs);
- 10.3 per cent of appointees declared political activity during the previous five years (17.1 per cent of those appointed of chairs) of which:

  * 5.9 per cent were Conservatives (13.9 per cent of chairs)
  * 3.3 per cent as Labour (only 2.3 per cent of chairs);

- 8.3 per cent of appointees held one or more posts in addition to their new appointment;
- 53.9 per cent were reappointments;
- the overall age range for board members was 44–68 (48–70 for chairs).

The report issues a caution about these figures (covering only a nine-month pre-election period and produced for the first time), but they are based on the records collected by Departments and are broadly in line with the data published annually in *Public Bodies*. They are most interesting in those areas – notably political activity – hitherto unrecorded. These statistics are supplemented in the Commissioner's report by an audit of all appointing departments carried out by Ernst & Young, which involved a look at 243 appointments and reappointments made during the reporting period.

The picture that emerges from both the statistics and the audit is not altogether clear. Departments were found to be trying to implement the Code of Practice, although there was variable performance both between and within Departments. An interesting finding from the audit was that at least one in three new appointments were made from among candidates who had responded to an advertisement suggesting that it was possible by this innovation substantially to enlarge the pool of candidates. General compliance with the Code was judged to be high, but there also remained much room for improvement (especially on reappointment procedures). There was wide variation in the methods used to recruit and involve independent panel members, while some of the approaches to interviewing candidates breached the spirit of the Code. The Commissioner concluded that it would be necessary to regard the first years of the new appointing arrangements as a 'learning period'.

On the whole, the statistical picture confirmed much that was already known. The gender imbalance (especially for the Chair) and age spectrum of appointees (with young people almost entirely absent) are particularly striking. On those matters where information had been collected for the first time and where there had been controversy – multiple appointments and political activity – the Commissioner's report is presented in a tone of public reassurance. Yet it is not clear that this is justified. A considerable number of appointees do turn out to hold more than one appointment (and the figure is higher for chairs than board members), while the evidence on political activity surely does reveal a marked partisan bias in those appointments where past political activity is identified and especially in the case of chairs. It may not confirm the caricature of every quango stuffed with partisan appointees but it does confirm the fact that a substantial number of key quango appointments during the period of the last government were held by people with a history of political activity on behalf of the Conservative Party. Moreover, the majority of appointments in the period covered by the Commissioner's report were reappointments and (on his own evidence) these received scant attention under the new Code. Consequently, many adherents of the previous regime were securely in place when the new government came to office.

I want now briefly to raise a number of issues concerning government by appointment against the background of this emerging picture, a picture which will be filled out in the future reports of the Commissioner and in the annual reports on appointments that Departments are now required to make. These are likely to be continuing issues, on some of which the Labour government has announced its intention to act, and on which it is possible and proper for there to be different approaches. What is offered here is simply a brief view on a few of these issues.

First, there is the vexed question of the political affiliation and record of appointees. Ministers will properly want to ensure that public bodies are headed by people who are broadly sympathetic to their purposes, or at least not positively unsympathetic, and this is perfectly consistent with the Code requirements of appointment on merit and procedural integrity. What is not acceptable is crude partisanship that offends the principles of balance and merit, the issues provoking the attention of Nolan. Judgement can only be made on such matters if we have information on the politics of appointees. The post-Nolan requirement was that political activity to be recorded covered office-holding in a political party over the previous five years or expressed public support or candidature for a party. This is surely not an adequate requirement in terms of information. Far simpler and more useful would be a declaration about current and past party membership, coupled with further relevant information about political activity and donations. There is no case for coyness on this front in a mature democracy.

Yet this information requirement, on grounds of openness and transparency, should not mean either that such political affiliation is seen as an obstacle to public service or that public body membership should be dominated by the search for party political balance. In my view both these consequences would be disastrous. Party membership and activity should be seen as a natural constituent of active citizenship, not as a dark and disabling secret as far as the rest of public life is concerned. At the same time the overwhelming majority of citizens are not and will not be members or activists of a political party. It would therefore be ludicrous if a search for party balance or proportionality in public body membership served to exclude most citizens from participation. Examples to avoid might include the magistracy, where party imbalance is usually seen as a contentious issue rather than whether it is sensible to make party a factor at all; and school government, where it might be thought more sensible for local authority appointees to have an engagement with education rather than an engagement with party. So information about party membership and activity should be neither an unwarranted obstacle to public appointment nor an easy access to it.

A further issue concerns the range and remit of the Commissioner for Public Appointments, as the guardian of the Code and its associated guidance. Labour came to office with a commitment to extend the jurisdiction of the Commissioner and of the Nolan principles across the whole range of public bodies. This is clearly necessary, as the original remit was unduly restrictive in being confined to the executive quangos and NHS bodies (230 executive quangos and 654 NHS bodies), which between them account for around 8300 public appointments with something over 2000 appointments and reappointments each year. Yet there are over 40,000 appointments made by ministers, of which around 10,000 are made or renewed each year. These include advisory bodies, tribunals, boards of visitors, public industries and the extensive range of patronage appointments by the Prime Minister. It is clearly right that the Nolan principles and the oversight of the Commissioner should apply to this wider world too, where appointments range from the most routine to the most significant.

Indeed the scrutiny could and should go further still. Although rejected in the second Nolan Report on *Local Public Spending Bodies* (May 1996), there is a good case for bringing these local bodies – such as the Training and Enterprise Councils, which perform public functions and spend large amounts of public money – within the monitoring and regulatory framework of the Commissioner for Public Appointments. The fact that they mostly appoint, and reappoint, themselves is not a reason for excluding them but for ensuring by their inclusion that they adhere to good practice. Similarly, the third Nolan Report on *Local Government* (July 1997) is silent on the appointive role of local councils, but this too needs to be brought within the net. There is also the need to have a register of all appointees which is regularly updated and contains all relevant information about them and for this to be produced either by the Commissioner or under his supervision. If the Nolan recommendation for the Public Appointments Unit to be transferred to the Commissioner was implemented, it would provide the machinery through which this could be done.

A final, but fundamental, issue concerns the responsibility for making and approving appointments. From this all else flows. As mentioned above, the Nolan Report concluded that the principle of ministerial responsibility meant that the power of appointment had to remain with ministers. Not for the first time, the doctrine of ministerial responsibility had been mobilized to block reform. In the name of formal responsibility it has proved perennially difficult to make changes that would strengthen real accountability. On a range of issues (such as parliamentary reform, freedom of information, scrutiny of executive agencies) constitutional orthodoxy about the responsibility of ministers to Parliament has prevented the development of effective mechanisms for enforcing responsibility. In recent years, both Sir Richard Scott and Lord Nolan in their separate inquiries have been confronted by this paradox and been required to think their way through it.

In the matter of patronage, the orthodoxy that prevailed in Lord Nolan's first report looks much less secure in the light of his own subsequent reflections. Delivering the Radcliffe Lectures at the University of Warwick at the end of 1996, he identified the disabilities of a doctrine that sought to compress responsibility into a single channel: 'Ministerial accountability is now in danger of being used to slow down the growth in accountability of public servants ... That cannot be achieved by a chain of accountability that runs upwards from literally thousands of independent or quasi-independent bodies, of varying size, structure and legal status, to a handful of ministers, laden with half a dozen or more red boxes of paperwork to take home each weekend' (Nolan, 1996). Once a unique channel of responsibility is converted into a broader multi-channel accountability, a range of possibilities is opened up. Far from weakening responsibility this serves to strengthen it. In relation to patronage, even though Lord Nolan himself has not revisited his original position in the light of this richer analysis, there are some interesting implications.

For example, it is not clear that all appointments have to be treated in the same way or rolled up into the demands of a single doctrine. Even if the power of ministers to make appointments is retained for a range of posts, it would be quite possible for a range of other appointments to be made by an independent commission. If such a commission was answerable to Parliament for its work, it is difficult to see that this would diminish accountability. It would certainly enhance legitimacy. Furthermore, even for appointments made by ministers there remain other devices (beyond the post-Nolan safeguards inserted into the system) whereby the process could be improved. For example, a number of major appointments to key public bodies could be subject to an 'approval hearing' by a relevant House of Commons committee. This is not without its difficulties (and would require a reformed Commons not to play party games with the process) but it is one obvious development with good precedents from elsewhere. Again, it could scarcely be claimed that an innovation of this kind would undermine responsibility.

In thinking about these issues, it should be remembered that appointive government is here to stay. Government by appointment is a fixture whatever modifications are made to the quango landscape. The real issue is how it operates. This involves thinking critically and imaginatively about the relationship between appointive government and elective government, and in ways that enhance the democratic effectiveness of both. In positive terms, government by appointment is the means whereby large numbers of citizens can make their contribution to public service and public life. That is why it is worth making sure that the system works well.

REFERENCES

Cm 2850 (1995) *First Report of the Committee on Standards in Public Life*, May.
Lord Nolan (1996) Second Radcliffe Lecture, University of Warwick, 21 November.
Richards, P. (1963) *Patronage in British Government* (London: Allen & Unwin).
Wright, T. (1995) *Beyond the Patronage State* (London: Fabian Society).

Conclusion

17 Realizing the Democratic Potential of Quangos

Mathew V. Flinders and Martin J. Smith

The platform that won Labour the general election in May 1997 reflected a mixture of economic caution, political morality and constitutional radicalism. Plans for devolution, decentralization, openness and the dispersal of power permeated Labour's manifesto. A new social contract was to be drawn up between the governors and the governed. Given the anti-quango rhetoric of the pre-election build-up it was widely assumed that a central strand of the reform package would be an attack on the 'quango-state'. Yet one of the first decisions of the new government was to pass over control of interest rates from an elected and parliamentary accountable minister to the unelected Bank of England. This paradox – the election of a government committed to democratization and the immediate transfer by that government of a crucial instrument of macroeconomic management to a quango – is that the move received virtually universal approval.

This reform reflects the complexity of the issue we are trying to explore. Before we go on, three simple and interrelated ground rules need to be clarified. First, quangos are a permanent feature British politics. They have been created by parties of the Left and the Right for a variety of reasons and it is doubtful whether the quango cull promised by parties while in opposition will ever happen. Second, the quango debate has been restricted by commentators looking back to the past to a nostalgic and often rosy perspective of the classic 'Westminster model', which in itself was beset with problems. Local government was often inefficient and controlled by strong personalities or party groupings who dominated proceedings with a minimal local vote. At the central level, government departments were overloaded and generalists dominated. Moreover, lines of responsibility were non-existent and the convention of ministerial responsibility a façade in the face of an executive-dominated legislature. Finally, the word 'quango' is surrounded by negativity, and this suffocates meaningful debate. Let us dare to suggest that quangos are not bad; that they have the potential to save us from the apathy and distrust which currently surrounds British politics. The quango debate has up to this point been bi-dimensional in that it was thought there were only two clear choices: maintain the status quo, or abolish quangos and return the functions to either central or local government. But the latter option forgets that the public distrusts politicians. Public concern over recent miscarriages in the criminal justice system would not be allayed by closer ministerial involvement. On the contrary, distance from party politics was seen as a positive rather than a negative.

We need to be more innovative. There is another, as yet unexplored option which moves us beyond the simple abolish/maintain dichotomy. We need to go down the third road. The third road builds upon the democratic potential which quangos offer a political system, which is haunted by public disillusionment. Quangos can be used as a tool to rebuild civic society. Quangos as they exist today should not be confused with quangos as they might and ought to be. A pure system of Athenian direct democracy is not possible in today's modern society but quangos have an untapped ability to strengthen not weaken public involvement, diffuse power, extend participation and offer more active and direct forms of citizenship. This will never be achieved until a ruling elite stops using quangos in its own interests and instead uses them in the interest of society as a whole. Quangos have been linked to corruption, patronage and sleaze, not because these factors are inherent in quangos but because this is how successive governments have chosen to use them. Given the diversity of bodies labelled as quangos it would be impossible to provide a clear, step-by-step plan to solve the quango problem and reinvigorate democracy. But there are wider and more general reforms which could be instituted.

The traditional 'Westminster model' of democracy has never encouraged participation but the traditional deference which supported this system has now crumbled. Deference has been replaced by questioning, acceptance by challenge and contentment by apathy. The Westminster model is unable to offer avenues to participation; new channels need to be found. A reformed quango state has the potential to offer a myriad of channels of participation but before we plot this third road let us look back on what this book has contributed to the debate.

Although quangos have been used by government since at least the eighteenth century, are present in many policy areas and exist in a range of countries, there is still little agreement about what a quango is and what processes of accountability are most appropriate. However, there is a consensus that changing forms of governance have placed quangos in an increasingly central role in the policy-making and implementation process. Therefore, as their role and importance grows there is an ever-increasing need for rules concerning their operation. In Britain the changing role of quangos seems to have been cyclical. As the government began to intervene in society the state used quango-like organizations rather than intervene directly. Increasingly in the late nineteenth and early twentieth centuries local authorities took over their functions. Preceding and following the Second World War policy was nationalized and increasingly controlled directly by the state. However, as a response to problems of overload, attempts to reduce public expenditure and New Right ideology functions shifted back to a range of bodies not controlled directly by the state. Local authorities increasingly lost control of their remaining functions to quangos while even at the national level privatization, contracting out and the creation of Next Steps agencies saw economic, welfare and implementation functions move from the central state. At the same time an increasing number of social and economic responsibilities shifted upwards to international bodies such as the European Union, the World Trade Organization, the World Bank and the International Monetary Fund.

This proliferation of bodies with varying degrees of autonomy from the national government has created diverse perceptions concerning what quangos do and what their relationship is to the national and local state, the voter and taxpayer. These conflicting perceptions derive from two factors. First, there is no agreement over what quangos are or what forms of accountability they should be subject to. The term 'quango' effectively covers all bodies with some degree of independence from the national state. Some therefore undertake very routine and mundane functions with minimal interest to most people. Others spend billions of pounds and can have very dramatic and central effects on people's lives. Unless some attempt is made to decide what tasks should go to which particular bodies, it is very difficult to decide what forms of accountability should apply. Therefore, there is a need for the government to be much more explicit about the nature of the range of bodies that deliver public services and why certain functions go to agencies, local authorities, established or new quasi-independent bodies, or private contractors. There should be a clear statement of the forms of non-governmental bodies, which tasks should go to which type of bodies, and what form of accountability is used with each body.

Second, quangos are about power. They have the ability to make decisions over the distribution of resources to different people. Therefore the fight over what they do and who they are accountable to is a fight over who is in control. This power conflict is most apparent between local authorities and quangos. Local authorities see their functions being usurped by unaccountable bodies. However, the chapters in the book written by chief executives of quangos imply that they face multiple levels of accountability and they would suggest that they are indeed more accountable than local authorities. These different perceptions derive from the different locations of the actors.

What is needed is to bring quangos and local authorities together. If quangos are a better way of delivering services, then local authorities should recognize their own limitations. However, local government and the representative role that councillors play should be brought into the accountability process. Formal institutional relationships have to be developed between local quangos and local authorities. Local authorities, if they are not delivering services, should have a regulatory role.

Similar conflicts also occur between national government and quangos. Brian Landers reveals that there were very different perceptions between the agency and the department over the role of the prisons agency. They disagreed on the degree of independence that existed and on what was policy. As a consequence there were arguments over the respective spheres of responsibility between department and agency. The political difficulties arose because of a different interpretation of roles. The relationships between agencies and government departments need to be clearly stated. In the early stages of the Next Steps reforms there was clarification, with considerable attention being paid to the design of framework documents. With the profusion of agencies in the 1990s there has been a tendency for departments to set them up without fully thinking through the implications bureaucratically, constitutionally and politically.

Quangos create significant problems for national government. On the one side quangos are useful because they mean that difficult decisions can be hived off to non-governmental bodies. On the other, the rapidity with which unpredictable issues can become salient means that governments often wish to reimpose control at times of political controversy. There is a strong incentive for government to retain a flexible relationship with quangos. Consequently, central government has an interest in not according quangos too much legitimacy. If they are seen as accountable and legitimate it is more difficult for government to interfere in their work, override their decisions or abolish them. This is illustrated well by the Committee on Standards in Public Life, a quango that because of its legitimacy is effectively in a position of being able to tell government what to do. Government wants to ensure that quangos remain 'quasi' and so are dependent on government rather than independent and dependent more on their own constituencies with their own sources of authority.

These problems are exacerbated by three elements of the British political system. First is the unwritten nature of the constitution and the extent of authority this gives to Parliament and effectively the executive. The executive can decide what bodies exist, what their powers are, who they are accountable to and how long they exist. Second, as Hennessy has said, secrecy is the calcium in the bones of the British constitution and therefore there is a degree of legitimacy in sanctioning secretive procedures and appointments because we know the British political system is run by 'good chaps' who can be trusted to make decisions in the public interest. Much of the quango regime has been operated on the good chaps system of government and, as Tony Wright argues, the patronage system must be brought to an end. Third, ministerial accountability is still the fundamental legitimizing principle that runs through the British political system. Therefore it is very difficult to set up systems of accountability and responsibility that do not ultimately return to the minister. A tension is created when bodies have independence because alternative processes of political accountability have not been established. The problem is that new forms of governance have developed which need new rules of accountability, but the old constitutional precepts remain in place. The argument for an unwritten constitution is that it is flexible. The new forms of governance of recent years have demonstrated that the British constitution cannot adapt to the changes that have occurred in the way that we are governed.

Indeed, almost no consideration has been given to the accountability of bodies that exist at the international level. Many European quangos and international quangos have a very direct impact on our everyday lives but the only source of influence for most citizens is through the chimera of ministerial responsibility. British ministers or, usually, officials, or even, in the case of the World Trade Organization, EU officials, present Britain's case and they are answerable to MPs for the decisions made in these fora. However, the chain of accountability has become so long as to make any notion democratic control laughable. British ministers can now have very little impact on the ruling of the World Trade Organization to the extent that even though Britain decided to ban hormone-implanted beef, the WTO ruled that Britain cannot prevent the import of US hormone-fed beef because it is a restraint of trade.

What has this book told us about what needs to be done? The first step must be to define explicitly the range of bodies that are used to deliver public goods. Indeed the consultation paper released by the Cabinet Office on quangos in November 1997 suggests some recognition of this issue. The paper points out that the bodies referred to as quangos are much wider than the traditional government position of NDPB and therefore suggests:

> that the public should have ready access to important summary information on all these bodies (i.e. on numbers, appointments, expenditure, etc.). There should be clear definitions of various groupings, so that published information is helpful to readers. In particular, local bodies should remain locally accountable; their reports should be available locally; and information on appointments should be available locally. (Cabinet Office, 1997: 5)

Moreover the paper recognizes a 'route map' is required for bodies that do not fall under the remit of NDPB such as TECs, LECs, grant maintained schools, housing associations and higher and further education bodies. 'It therefore proposes that *Public Bodies* should in future provide appendices with basic information about these bodies, together with a list of published source material where more detailed information about these bodies can be obtained' (Cabinet Office, 1997: 14–15). This would be an important step forward. The quango topography needs to be mapped out employing a maximalist rather than the usually restricted government approach.

Building on earlier independent research, there needs to be one clear, accessible and comprehensive database which highlights the full range of quangos (executive and advisory). This database would provide a range of information including: the chief executive's name, executive and non-executive board members, other positions held by these individuals, remuneration details, addresses, contact phone numbers, annual reports, business plans, accountability processes, funding sources and amounts, etc. Such a database would be a significant and vital resource in opening up the quango state. Once created, the database should be placed on the internet for full public access. Regularly updated, its potential is significant as various quango documents (even minutes of meetings) could be placed on the internet, as could information about vacancies and how members of the public can apply.

The information technology revolution does provide a new and dynamic potential. As a two-way channel of information, a comprehensive quango website could provide email links to all quangos as a way of allowing the public simple access. Old-school quangocrats may claim that the information the database would provide is already available but the important point is that very often literature is hard to obtain and the information is not clear to the layman. Pulling together all this information would also map out the complex world of individuals who sit on the boards of several quangos, charities and private companies. Potential conflicts of interest would be much easier to see and regulate. Whether such a database should be built and maintained by the government is a moot point. We would prefer that the government funded the project but delegated the work to an independent research centre (dare we say quango?).

Openness with regard to the bodies which exist needs to be combined with a clarity of the role the bodies are expected to perform. As Britain does not have the public law that exists on the continent it is essential that the role and relationships of the range of bodies is clearly defined. It is important to have criteria to judge when quangos are carrying out the wrong task, when the lines of accountability have gone astray and when it is acting beyond its remit. In effect each quango should have its own constitution, similar to the framework documents of agencies, which clearly outlines their role and their stakeholders and highlights how the stakeholders are to be included in the decision making processes and in holding the quango to account. The stakeholders could be ministers, councillors or members of the public but they should be clearly identified. Many people may not want to get involved, but what is important is that the structure is open and responsive enough to allow the aggrieved to become involved when they so desire. Instead we see ministers increasingly being drawn in to local affairs, such as over school standards.

All quangos, be they local, regional, national, executive or advisory, should have to produce an extensive annual report. The jurisdiction of the regulatory quangos, such as the National Audit Office, Audit Commission, Parliamentary Commissioner for Administration, etc., should be extended to cover all quangos. The Nolan principles should also be extended to cover all bodies and not just executive NDPBs. It is also crucial that these regulatory quangos enjoy sufficiently strong powers and resources to operate effectively. The Prisons Ombudsman is neither an ombudsman nor a quango. But in this area there is a need for quangoization. Given the recent troubles in prisons and the increasing encroachment of the private sector into prison management it is vital that this office holder enjoys a wide remit and sufficient powers. The Prisons Ombudsman should have his recently limited powers extended and should be accountable to Parliament, preferably to the Home Affairs select committee, rather than to the Home Secretary.

We have mentioned the need to forge a new relationship between local government and quasi-government, one based on co-operation rather than friction. A relationship that combines the efficiency and specialism of quangos with the democratic legitimacy and local knowledge of elected councillors. Local government is vital to democracy but in recent years its role has changed from direct service provision to oversight and regulation. This can take many forms and can be formal and informal. Andrew Peet highlighted the role of 'Quango Watch' in his local authority. The creation of small teams of councillors to monitor and oversee the work of local quangos has proved valuable and is increasingly being adopted by a number of authorities. The information collected by these teams is not only of interest to the council but is utilized by a wide range of local interest groups. It also creates a chain of accountability for the citizen via councillors.

'Advice and consent' procedures could be built into the framework documents of quangos by central government. These would mean that any senior appointments within local quangos would have to be approved by the respective local authority. In the vast majority of cases the appointments would be approved without question but the procedures would provide a role for local government and confer a degree of legitimacy on the appointee. Appointments themselves need to be publicized much more vigorously in a wider range of publications with particular thought being given to how to attract more women and individuals from ethnic backgrounds.

Another way of engaging local authorities with quangos might be Ted Cantle's proposal for a 'duty of partnership'. Local quangos would be required to consult local authorities before producing their annual plan and to demonstrate that their objectives complimented those laid out in any plan for the area published by the local authority. Reforms could also provide local councillors with places on the boards of various quangos as used to happen in health authorities. Their voting powers could be restricted, but this would still allow councillors to contribute their views, and the views of their constituents, to the decision making process. The councillors would also gain a deeper understanding of the thought processes behind a decision and report this insight back to the full council.

But accountability need not be upward to councillors or ministers. It can also be horizontal to local user groups and interest groups and downward to members of the public. There are a wide range of innovative mechanisms through which the views of the public can be heard and taken in to account. Citizens juries, user surveys, local referendums, open meetings, public debates and forums can all be utilized, and increasingly are, by quangos to build the views of the public into their decision making processes and in doing so taking the views of the public into account. Open meetings and debates should be advertised in the local media in advance to allow members of the public to canvas opinion, submit documents and prepare questions. They should also be held out of traditional working hours. These downward forms of accountability represent a way in which local quangos can rebuild their legitimacy and forge links with their local communities which have previously been absent. Problems exist. These mechanisms of local involvement risk being used as cosmetic public relations exercises, they are also expensive. But they do bring new possibilities and avenues for public involvement and participation which could be built upon. It would not be unrealistic to force most quangos to hold their board meetings in public, or at least hold one public annual meeting at which the plans for the next year could be outlined and debated in public.

At the central level the answers lie with Parliament generally and with the select committees specifically. Each select committee should take charge of overseeing the major quangos operating within its respective policy sphere. Although some bodies might cross committee boundaries it would not prove impossible to draw up thematic categories and ensure that all bodies came under the overview of a select committee. The select committees would then be free to discuss and debate framework documents, annual reports, budgets and other supporting literature. Senior executives could be called before the committee and questioned on salient issues. 'Advice and consent' procedures could be introduced so that the relevant select committees had to approve senior appointments in the larger quangos (including Next Steps agencies). Fulfilling such a role may well require additional resources in terms of finance and personnel for the committees, thus allowing the committee members to be well briefed and raise the overall standard of questioning and analysis. If the individual select committees felt unable or were unwilling to extend both their remit and workload, an alternative reform might be the creation of a new select committee specifically dedicated to overseeing the quango state.

But what Parliament desperately needs if accountability is ever to be secured is not only more resources but, more importantly, an influx of independent members. It does not need more powers, just the ability to assert the powers it already has. Party discipline, the whips and the fact that every backbencher is an 'embryonic frontbencher' ensures that very few MPs exert anything like the independence of traditional parliamentarians. The introduction of substantially higher wages for select committee chairmen, while probably unpopular with the public, would deliver a number of positive benefits not least increasing the legitimacy of the committees and creating an alternative career structure to the ministerial ladder.

The processes of governance have changed. The idea of the executive answerable to a sovereign Parliament and implementing decisions through a hierarchical bureaucracy, to the extent this model ever existed, is now a thing of the past. The boundaries of the public and private are increasingly blurred and governments are using a range of different mechanisms for delivering services. There is, as Greve points out, an increasing grey zone and the task that faces us is not how we dismantle the grey zone but how we ensure that it is more open and accountable. As we have suggested, this is possible through making the whole process more transparent and by formalizing the processes of accountability particularly where Parliament is concerned.

It is crucial to remember that quangos are not objective independent organizations. They exist in time and in particular political relationships which are dynamic. Different governments want quangos for different reasons and this dictates the form they take and the mechanisms for control that exist. In the 1970s quangos were a way of opting out of difficult political problems, in the 1980s they were seen as a way of reducing the power of local authorities and of making government more effective and thereby less expensive. Labour in the 1990s seems to want to make them more democratic and open, but we have to examine what the Labour government sees as the purpose of quangos. If the goal is taking government closer to the people, then issues of accountability will be central. But if they exist to divert political flak from government, issues of democracy and openness will fade into the background.

The new Labour government has certainly 'hit the floor running', but in the area of quangos it still has a lot of running to do. The recent consultation paper represents a positive, if rather timid, step in the right direction. In many ways the reforms and developments we propose are not radical. They are based in our commitment to openness, consultation, inclusion and accountability – principles that the government has also commited itself to. Quangos have an, as yet, untapped democratic potential. They can be used as tools to reinvigorate politics by offering more opportunities for involvement and participation. Embrace them, don't destroy them.

Index

ACAS, 32
Access
  to government information, code on, 21
Accountability, 4, 9, 21–4, 35, **45**, 159,
    111–19, 205
  definition of, 49, 112
  in Denmark, 102–4
  external, 112–15
  in Germany, 61
  improving, 49–50, 118–19
  Index, 166
  internal, 115–17
  local, 47, 169–70, 178
  of local government, 40, 49–52, 137, 150
  ministerial, 14, 18, 23, 137, 197
  multi-layered concept of, 49, 203
  in the Netherlands, 78–82, **80**
  in New Zealand, 84, 88–91
  and Parliament, 14, 118, 157, 167, 170,
    207, 209
  and quangos, 10, 11, 12, 14, 17, 18
  and the regulators, 181, 182–3
  of TECS, 162–79
Advertising Standards Authority, 20
Advisory bodies, 4, 5, 18
  in the Netherlands, 76
  in New Zealand, 87
Ambrose, Peter, 140
Appointments, **42**, 193–5
  to civil service, 192
  to quangos, 33, 37, 43, 44, **45**, 52, 146–7,
    173–4
  Code of Practice for Public, 193–4
  Commissioner for Public, 193, 195, 197
Arthur Andersen & Co., 81
Arts
  Council, 20, 21, 28
  Council for the Encouragement of, 17, 28
  in Germany, 60, 61
  in New Zealand, 86
Association of Metropolitan Authorities,
    132
Attlee, Clement, 135
Auditors, 115, 208
  see also National Audit Office

Bank of England, 21, 201
Barker, Anthony, 4, 15, 33, 93

Basic Law (in Germany), 58, 62
Bazeman, Barry, 93, 97
Beck, Jørgensen, T., 98
Beck, Ulrich, 30
Beckett, Margaret, 150
Besant, Annie, 134
Beveridge Report (1942), 153
Blair Revolution, The, 142
Blair, Tony, 150
Blunkett, David, 164
Board of Trade, 27
British National Oil Corporation, 36
British Telecom, 180
Bundesländer
  administrative structure of, 58–59, 65
Bureaucracy, 4, 8, 120
  growth of, 29–30, 33
  in the Netherlands, 73–**4**
  in the NHS, 154
  reform of, 27

Camelot, 35
  see also National Lottery
Cantel, Ted, 205
Castle, Barbara, 31
Central government, 113, 204, 207
  and local government, 42, 43
  size of, 73
  and TECs, 163
Chadwick, Sir Edward, 134, 152
Chamber of Commerce, 52
  and TECs, 174
Chambers of Professions (in Germany), 60
Charter 88, 133
Christensen, Jan, 99
Citizen's Charter, 159
Citizens juries, 48, 208
Citizenship, 202
Citizens' rights
  in Germany, 70
City Challenge, 41
Civil Aviation Authority (CAA), 28
Civil law bodies
  in Germany, 64
Civil service, 126–7
  in Germany, 62, 66, 67–8
Clark, David, 10
Clarke, Kenneth, 121

Code of Practice on Open Government, 170–1
Colonial Empire Marketing Board, 28
Community Charge, 133, 136
Companies Act, 167, 171, 173
Conservative government, 4, 5, 8, 40, 136, 163
  rejection of, 133
Conservative Party, 195
  and local government, 133
Constitution
  in Britain, 8, 12, 18, 204
  German, 27, 59, 66: *see also* Basic Law
Contracting out, 4
  in Denmark, 96, 97–9
Contrat de ville, 47
Councillors, 31, 133, 137, 207, 208
Criminal Cases Review Commission, 9
Crown Entities
  in New Zealand, 85–90

Davies, Ron, 13
Decentralisation, 22, 32
  in New Zealand, 91
Democracy
  institutional change in Denmark, 96
  local, 140
  and quangos, 11, 201–10
  'Westminster model' of, 201, 202
Democratic
  Audit, 37
  control in Germany, 70
  control and the NHS, 154
  deficit, 168
  innovation, 48
Devolution, 12, 139, 142
  Scottish, 13–14
  Welsh, 12
Doig, A., 8

Eastern Europe, 57
Economic Development Agency, 13
Education, 17, 18, 20, 21, 34, **42**, 50
  City Technology Colleges (CTCs), 41, **42**, 50
  Funding Agency for Schools, 137, 150
  in Germany, 60
  grant maintained schools, 7, 41, **42**, 50, 206
  Higher Education Corporations, **42**, 51
  National Curriculum Council, 22
  in the Netherlands, 77
  in New Zealand, 86, 87, 89
  see also TECs

Elected mayor, 48, 140
Environment
  Agency, 5
  in New Zealand, 87, 90
  Select Committee for, 114
Equal Opportunities Commission, 17, 28
ESRC
  Whitehall programme, 49
European Monetary Institute, 26
European Structural Funds, 163
Extra governmental organizations (EGOs), 21

Fabian Society, 134
Flinders, Matthew, 11, 21
Food Safety Council, 9, 38
Forsyth, Michael, 125
Fowler, Sir Norman, 158
Freedom of Information Act, 12, 36, 184
Fulton Report, 34

Gaebler, Ted, 98
General Civil Law
  in New Zealand, 79
German Unification, 57
Globalization, 3
Greve, Carsten, 11, 209
Grey Zone, 93, 96, 100, 103, 209
Griffith, Sir Roy, 155, 156
Grøndahl, Øyvind, 97
Grønlie, Tore, 97
Governance
  community, 47–8
  corporate, 43, 181
  new forms of, 205
  of Public Bodies, 193
Government
  departments, 111, 112, 154, 157, 159, 163, 165, 166, 171, 181, 185, 195
  role and function of, 30–2
Guilleband Committee (1953–6), 155

Hall, Wendy, 7, 21, 33, 93
Hansen, Claus, A., 98
Harden, Ian, 102
Health
  authorities, 5, 41, **42**
  DHSS, 52
  in Germany, 61
  National Health Act (1946), 135, 153
  in New Zealand, 86, 87
  and Safety Commission, 28, 32
  see also National Health Service (NHS)
Heath, Edward, 31, 34

Hennessy, Peter, 24, 204
Heseltine, Michael, 28, 37
Hidden Agendas, 121, 122
Hirst, P., 51
Hogwood, B., 5, 49
Holtby, Winifred, 135
Hood, Christopher, 33, 34, 36, 93, 102
Housing
　Act (1996), 111
　associations, 7, 21, 41, **42**, 50
　Housing Action Trusts (HATs), 26, 29,
　　41, **42**, 50, 51, 133
　in the Netherlands, 77–8
　in New Zealand, 86
　regional associations, 26, 29
　registered social landlords (RSL), 111, 117
Housing Corporations, 17, 111–19
　accountability of, 112
　appointment to board of, 111, 115
　Chief Executive of, 111–12
　role and function of, 111
Howard, Michael, 120, 121, 122, 125
Human Fertilization and Embryology
　Authority, 9, 20

Industrial relations, 31–2
　Act (1971), 31
Internet, 206

Jones, M., 52
Judicial
　role of quangos, 76
　Review, 114, 183

Kalms, Anthony, 146
Keith-Lucas, B., 134, 135
King, Anthony, 146
King, D., 143
Klausen, Kurt, 99

Labour government, 8, 9, 12, 15, 36–7, 69,
　142
　in New Zealand, 84
　and TECs, 164, 196, 201, 210
Labour Party
　and local government, 48, 133
　and quango reform, 51–2, 139
Landers, Brian, 204
Laski, Harold, 125
Lean management, 57
Lewis, Derek, 120, 121, 122, 123, 125, 126,
　129, 130
Liddle, Roger, 142

Local democracy
　Commission for, 52
　and government, 40–52
Local Enterprise Companies (LECs), 20,
　42, 163, 167, 177, 179, 206
Local government, 21–3, 40–2, 132–43,
　207
　accountability of, 49–52
　Act (1929), 135
　in Denmark, 99
　funding of, 136, 137
　history of, 134–6
　hollowing out of, 31
　and the Labour Party, 48
　loss of power of, 22, 133, 136, 138
　in New Zealand, 87, 91
　and quangos, 144–51
　reforms of, 23, 141, 142
　role and function of 139–41
　Royal Commission on (1966–9), 155
　in Scotland, 40
　and Thatcher, Margaret, 32, 136
　transformations of, 40
Local self-government
　Council of Europe Charter of, 142
　in Germany, 58
London
　County Council, 134
　Docklands, 18, 137–8, 140
　Greater London Authority, 139
　Greater London Council, 133

Major, John, 160, 192
Management
　new techniques of, 10, 33
　in the prison service, 127–8
　techniques in private sector, 20
　see also New Public Management
　　(NPM)
Mandarins
　and the prison service, 122–3
Mandelson, Peter, 142
Manpower Services Commission, 32
Marcusson, Lena, 106
McSmith, Andy, 142
Medicines
　Committee on the Safety of, 9, 20
Metropolitan Authorities
　Association of (AMA), 50
Millennium Commission, 28, 34
Milward, H. Brinton, 102
Ministers, 18, 31, 72, 112, 115–16, 117
　and the Prison Service, 121–2
　and local government, 136

Modeen, Tore, 93
Molin, Jan, 99
Monopolies and Mergers Commission, 183, 184, 187
Municipal Corporations Act (1834), 134
Murdoch, Rupert, 10

National Assistance Act (1948), 135
National Audit Office, 35, 113, 118
  in Denmark, 102–3
National Breastfeeding Working Group, 5
National Enterprise Board, 36
National Health Reorganization Act (1973), 136
National Health Service (NHS), 152–61, 192, 196
  establishment of, 153–5
  and poll tax, 155
  trusts, 5, 7, 29, 51
National Lottery, 10
Netherlands Court of Audit (NCA), 72, 73, 76, 78, 82
New Deal, 165
New Public Management (NPM), 11, 20, 33–4, 35
New Statesman and Society, 141–2
Next Step Agencies, 4, 5, 8, 17, 18, 20, 27, 29, 30, 34, 209
New Towns Act (1946), 135
Nolan, Lord, 179, 197–8
Nolan Committee for Standards in Public Life, 35, 139, 148, 151, 167, 178–9, 191–3, 195–8, 204
  principles of, **45–6**, 196, 207
Nolan Report, **42,** 145, 147
  recommendations of, 44–6, 146, 178–9
  on Local Spending Bodies, 196
  on Local Government, 197
Non-Departmental Public Bodies (NDPB), 4, **6**, 7–8, 10, 17, 205–6, 207
  and legal aid, 5
Non-Governmental Organizations (NGOs)
  in Germany, 62–3
  growth of, 26

Official Information Act
  in New Zealand (1982), 91
Ombudsman, 115, 118, 166, 183
  in the Netherlands, 79
  in New Zealand, 79
  pensions, 5
  prisons, 124, 131, 207
Open forums, 48

Openness, **45**, 116, 206
  in the Netherlands, 78–9
  of quangos, 43, 44, **45**
  and TECs, 170–1, 173, 175–7
Osborne, D., 98

Parliament, 10, 21, 117, 118, 121, 128–30, 137, 155, 167–8, 170, 198, 204, 208–9
  members of, 114, 205, 209
Parliamentary
  Committees, 129
  Questions, 129, 130
  sovereignty, 20
Partnership, 48, 166, 171, 208
  between public and private, 18
Party
  politics, 20, 21
  membership, 196
Patronage, 36, 37, 191–8, 202, 205
  and Conservative government, 191–2
Peach, Sir Len, 37, 193
Petterson, Oluf, 93
Pliatsky, L., 18, 98
  Report, 14, 28–9
Polar Medal Group, 5
Police
  authorities, 7, 41, 133
  complaints authority, 86
Policy
  areas in the Netherlands, 77–8
  Home Office, 123–7
  making, 9, 181
  in the Prison Service, 123–7
Political Economy Research Centre (PERC), 37
Politicians
  distrust of, 17, 21, 30
Politics
  British tradition of, 22
  and public apathy, 30, 140, 201, 202
  public distrust of, 17, 30, 36, 201
Porritt Report (1964), 155
Press Complaints Commission, 20
Price Commission (1972), 36
Prison
  in Germany, 61
  Service, 23, 120–31
Privacy Act
  in New Zealand (1993), 91
Private Finance Initiative, 69
Private law
  structures in Germany, 61–4, 65
  in the Netherlands, 75, 78

Private sector, 3, 182
    management techniques in, 20
Privatization
    in Denmark, 97
    in the German Democratic Republic
        (GDR), 64
    in the Netherlands, 72
    in Britain, 4, 180
Provan, Keith, 102
Public Accounts Committee (PAC), 113–14,
    115, 118, 129–30, 183
Public Appointments Commission, 193, 196
Public Finance Acts
    in New Zealand, 86, 88, 89
Public law
    in the Netherlands, 78
    structures in Germany, 59–61
Public/private dichotomy, 3, 26, 34, 65
    in Denmark, 95
Public sector, 3
    in Denmark, 97
    in New Zealand, 84
Pyper, Robert, 21

'Quangocide', 29
Quango Debate, The, 167, 201–2
Quangos
    abolition of, 5, 13, 28, 73
    advantages of, 42–3
    amalgamation of, 28
    awareness of, 144–5
    Code of Conduct of, 44, **46**
    continuum, 4, 8, 17, 19
    creation of, 3, 27, 29–33, 37, 42, 72, **73**,
        75, 78
    definitions of, 4, 5, 7, 8, 17–21, 72,
        145–6, 203
    disadvantages of, 43–4
    drift, 8, 17, 21, 33, 37, 43, 44
    and economics, 31–3
    effectiveness of, 22
    efficiency of, 10
    election to boards of, 23, 111, 115, 116
    at EU level, 18, 26, 182, 203, 205
    expertise in, 10
    flexibility of, 9
    funding of, 5, 76–7, 135
    future trends of, 12, 15, 35–8, 97–100,
        201–10
    history of, 26–9, 95–6, 135
    image of, 10
    independence of, 17
    legal basis of, 74–5, 93
    at local level, 18, 26, 40–52

    and political patronage, 43, 191–8
    public involvement in, 22
    regulation of, 8, 180–90
    role and function of, 29–33, **75**, 76, **94**,
        202, 203, 209–10
    and specialists, 30
    standards of, 43
    Welsh reform of, 13

Quasi-Autonomous Non-Governmental
    Organizations, *see* Quangos

Race relations
    Commission for Racial Equality, 9, 20,
        28, 30
    Conciliator in New Zealand, 86
Rasmussen, Nyrup, 98
Reform
    of central government, 23
    constitutional, 133
    of local government, 23
    of quangos, 36, 51–2, 104, 151, 201–10
    procedural, 44–7
    of public sector in New Zealand, 84
Regional assemblies, 14
    English, 12
    Yorkshire and Humberside, 14
Regional Development Agencies (RDAs),
    14–25, 116, 167
Regionalism, 116
Regulators, 10, 20, 180–90
    in New Zealand, 76
    offer, 184
    Ofgas, 181
    ORR, 181
    Oftel, 10, 181
    Ofwat, 183, 184
    role and function of, 181–2
Research
    in Germany, 61
    market, 48
    in the Netherlands, 76
    in New Zealand, 86, 90
Responsibility
    ministerial, 23
Richards, P., 134, 135, 191
Ridley, F., 167
Rosas, Allan, 93

Salisbury, Lord, 134
Savas, E., 98
Scandal, 9

Schuppert, Gunnar Folke, 93
Scotland
  local government in, 40, 139
  see also devolution, LECs, Scottish
Scott, Sir Richard, 197
Scottish
  Development Agency, 36
  parliament, 12, 13
  Prison Service, 123
  Salmon Task Force, 5
Scrutiny Committees, 48
Selle, Per, 99
Sheldon, Chris, 166
Service delivery, 181
Social insurance
  in Germany, 60
  in the Netherlands, 76
Sørensen, Eva, 103
South Riding, 135
Sports Council, 28
State Owned Enterprises (in New Zealand), 85, 91
Stewart, John, 50, 134, 166
Stoker, Gerry, 143
Student Loan Company, 20

Take-Overs and Mergers
  in New Zealand, 86
  panel on, 20
  of quangos, 13
Thatcher, Margaret, 10, 28, 32, 34, 149, 155, 160
Trade unions, 31–2
  in Denmark, 101
  and the prison service, 128
  and TECs, 174
Training and Enterprise Councils (TECs), 4, 7, 8, 14, 17, 18, 21, 22, 34, 41, **42**, 50, 51, 52, 162–79, 206
  directors of, 168–9
  licence, 171–2
  and local community, 174–5
  and local government, 133
  in Scotland *see* LECs
  in Wales, 12, 13
Transfer of power, 117–18
  from central government, 73, 162

Transport
  in New Zealand, 86
  Office for Rail Regulation, 10
Tribunals, 5, 18

Unemployment Assistance Board, 135
Urban Development Corporations (UDCs), 29, 41, **42**, 50, 51
Utility
  markets, 186–7
  privatized, 17, 19, 187–90
  public, in Germany, 60

Value for Money (VFM), 9, 112
Vehicle inspection
  MOT, 20
  TÜV in Germany, 61
Voluntary sector
  in Denmark, 96, 99–100
  in New Zealand, 87
  and TECs, 174

Waldegrave, William, 22
Wales, 12–13, 40
  Cardiff Bay Development Corporation, 12
  development board for rural Wales, 13, 28
  economic development plan, 28
  land authority for, 28
  and local government, 139
  unitary councils in, 13
  A Voice For Wales White Paper, 12, 13
  see also devolution, Welsh
Water
  Act (1973), 136
  authorities, 40–1
Welsh
  Development Agency, 13
  Assembly, 12, 13
'Whistleblowing', **46**, 139
Whitehall, 8, 124, 125, 139
White, Jerry, 134
Widdecombe, Anne, 122
Widgery, David, 137–8
Wier, Stuart, 7, 21, 33, 93
Williamson, Alan, 130
Wilson, David, 167
Women, 195, 208
Wright, Tony, 23, 192, 205